CINEMATIC CRYPTONYMIES

Contemporary Approaches to Film and Media Series

A complete listing of the books in this series can be found online at wsupress.wayne.edu.

General Editor

Barry Keith Grant
Brock University

Advisory Editors

Robert J. Burgoyne
University of St. Andrews

Caren J. Deming
University of Arizona

Patricia B. Erens
School of the Art Institute of Chicago

Peter X. Feng
University of Delaware

Lucy Fischer
University of Pittsburgh

Frances Gateward
California State University, Northridge

Tom Gunning
University of Chicago

Thomas Leitch
University of Delaware

Walter Metz
Southern Illinois University

CINEMATIC CRYPTONYMIES

THE ABSENT BODY IN POSTWAR FILM

OFER ELIAZ

Wayne State University Press
Detroit

© 2018 by Wayne State University Press, Detroit, Michigan 48201. All rights reserved. No part of this book may be reproduced without formal permission.

Library of Cataloging Control Number: 2018943984

ISBN 978-0-8143-4562-7 (paperback)
ISBN 978-0-8143-4561-0 (hardcover)
ISBN 978-0-8143-4563-4 (ebook)

Wayne State University Press
Leonard N. Simons Building
4809 Woodward Avenue
Detroit, Michigan 48201-1309

Visit us online at wsupress.wayne.edu

Contents

Introduction: A Cryptic History of the Cinema   1

1. The Crypt-Image and the Taboo Body in the Films of Georges Franju   27

2. Mario Bava, the Phantom-Image, and Transgenerational Debt   61

3. Anasemic Montage and the Cinematic Interval in Jean-Luc Godard's Late Cinema   95

4. Re-Visions: Naomi Uman and Cinematic Decryption   135

Conclusion: The Body under Erasure   175

Notes   181

Bibliography   211

Index   221

Introduction

A Cryptic History of the Cinema

> The translator is twice over a traitor: He betrays the other and himself. . . . May our "betrayal" have been close enough to our text!
> —Abraham and Torok, *The Wolf Man's Magic Word*

The Missing Image and the Absent Body

Following World War II and the economic, spatial, and social transformations that arrived in its wake, European cinemas confronted a crisis of representation that, while not entirely new, was more urgent than ever: how to represent the missing bodies that now haunted the continent. These missing and vanished bodies included not only the countless unnamed victims of the war but also the populations of displaced, forgotten, and impoverished peoples who slipped into social invisibility as Western Europe was rebuilt in the spectacular image of global capital. As Gilles Deleuze argues in his influential periodization, World War II ruptured the regime of cinematic representation because it forced the cinema to account for spaces that eluded clear description and for characters who were unable to act.[1] For Deleuze, this new situation motivated a shift from the action image, based on a clear succession of action and reaction within a defined space, to the time image that foregrounded the displacement of characters within their environment and emphasized the recursive activities of seeing and thinking. The new cinema thus privileged ruptures and intervals over smooth linkages, created false continuities in the place of narrative order, and foregrounded passive and receptive bodies over active and expressive ones. This condition revealed the fracturing and alienation of subjectivities within the nonspaces of a world rebuilt according to the needs of global circulation. The bodies that had vanished in the war and its aftermath, however, were neither the actors of the classical cinema nor the seers of the modern film. Having had no proper burial, they were fated to return as specters of their absence. These are bodies defined by their condition as nonimages, gaps incorporated between the look and the seen. Although largely forgotten, even or especially when they were memorialized as the anonymous dead of the past, a certain, sometimes underground, cinematic tradition registered the haunting affect created by the silences and gaps in which these bodies were buried alive. To account for the presence of these absences, these films invented strategies of in-visibility, the incorporation of the nonvisible within the frame of the image.

While the trauma of the war thus confronted cinema anew with the problem of the unseen within the image, a second aspect of the postwar period was, paradoxically, the feverish proliferation of images. This proliferation is not only qualitative, not merely a consequence of an exposure to an ever-growing flood of audio-visual material brought about by cinema and (eventually) video's increased technical ability to record, store, and circulate images. What I want to emphasize, along with Guy Debord, is that this proliferation is both a product of and helps to usher in a new form of the imaginary: the image as spectacle able to define and, in some senses, replace an ever-expanding territory of the real.

> The spectacle cannot be set in abstract opposition to concrete social activity, for the dichotomy between reality and image will survive on either side of any such distinction. Thus the spectacle, though it turns reality on its head, is itself a product of real activity. Likewise, lived reality suffers the material assaults of the spectacle's mechanisms of contemplation, incorporating the spectacular order and lending that order positive support. Each side therefore has its share of objective reality. And every concept, as it takes its place on one side or the other, has no foundation apart from its transformations into its opposite: reality erupts within the spectacle, and the spectacle is real.[2]

Was the rise of the spectacle partially the consequence of a desire to cover up the gaps in the real? In any case, within this spectacular ascendancy of the image, the absence and failure to record takes on a markedly new quality—namely, that of a real exclusion in the visual and social field. If the image is no longer a representation of an external reality but fully incorporates the territory of the real, then the absence of the image is likewise an expression of a concrete social fact. The unseen image loses its innocence and becomes the memorial trace of an act of occlusion, nonseeing, or withdrawal of the visual. The absent image is thus an inscription, a cryptic sign inserted within the operations of the imaginary.

This sign, as it appears in the films that I analyze, poses a challenge to the dominance of spectacular images, both within and outside the cinema, aimed at rationalizing the emerging postwar order of the hypervisible. Mark Fisher has suggested the term *capitalist realism* to describe the ways in which the postwar global order realizes itself through images and sounds, be they cartographic, cinematic, televisual, advertising, and so forth. These representations aim not at producing an image of the world, but at closing off the limits of the imaginary by naturalizing the social production of capital within the lived environment of modern space: cities, zones of transit, places of visible and invisible labor. Charged with representing the limit of representation, capitalist realism incorporates the very condition of the outside that it makes unthinkable.[3] Treated as the closure of the real, capitalist realism is the production of a false testimony of the world viewed. It is against and as a counterhistory to this horizon of the total image of a false realism that the history of the absent image is written.

This book is a partial history of the cryptic inscription of missing images within the global spaces of postwar capital. It is the history of a figure, that of the human body under erasure, as this figure gets taken up in a variety of institutional, historical, and aesthetic contexts. Thus, whereas traditional film histories remain within the boundaries of national cinemas, institutional practices, or even genres, this book will chart a transversal line, tracking the recurrence of the erased body across these boundaries. The films I analyze do not exhaust this ongoing story. They have been selected because they demonstrate a range of strategies by which filmmakers have tried to figure the invisibility haunting the real. In each case, the cinematographic method is determined by the particular social reality under consideration. For, while the war created a new population of vanished bodies and is thus a concern in a number of the films, each of the filmmakers in the book was equally attuned to a present reality in which the number of missing continued to grow. As we will see, one of the contributions of this history is in uncovering the mechanism by which gaps in the past not only return but also produce new absences in the present. After the war, Europe underwent vast projects of modernization that transformed its social geography, the institutions of family and labor, and the relations between the interiority of the state or home and the exteriority of its other. Each of these rezoned the cultural psyche around an ever-proliferating series of enclaves where bodies were made to vanish from sight.

Georges Franju offers an early and prescient exploration of this new situation in France, as both his documentary and fiction films investigate institutional and national topographies that encircle an internal space variously figured as a family crypt, a national tomb, or an institution of slaughter. In Mario Bava's early horror films, a tension between the return of a lost past and the derealization of contemporary social spaces reveals an Italy paralyzed by the transgenerational legacy of women's erasure. Godard, refusing the melancholia of historical loss, invents a new form of montage aimed at the disarticulation of meaning and the new importance given to the interval as the site of occluded figuration. An analysis of this montage practice in a number of films of his "late period" will dramatize the experience of European identity as the fractured incorporation of the unmourned of history within a national subjectivity and the concomitant projection of violence and loss across the borders of self and state. Finally, Naomi Uman's work stands out, initially, due to her difference from the other filmmakers in the book: where the others are European, Uman is an itinerant filmmaker who has worked in the United States, Mexico, and the Ukraine; where the others maintain various and often conflicted relations with commercial filmmaking, she makes experimental, artisanal films; and whereas Franju, Bava, and Godard all focus primarily on white, European bodies, much of Uman's work addresses the absences of racially othered bodies. Because of these differences, her films are a necessary part of the story I am telling, as she invents a truly critical countercinema that figures the place of the missing image within and across the borders of the global circulation of capital and spectacle.

The advantage of the type of history recounted in this book, the history of a mode of inscription that takes a variety of material forms, is that it reveals connections among films, filmmakers, and practices that are too often isolated within the disciplinary boundaries of film studies. While the specificity of art cinema, genre filmmaking, and experimental films (not to mention the conditions of France, Europe, and the Americas) undoubtedly shape the work created by their practitioners, this specificity threatens to obscure shared concerns born of the antagonisms within a world system or states of crisis. In this case, we can isolate a singular task within the diversity of practices and modes of production—namely, to produce a cinematic counterhistory told through the eyes of the occluded, erased, and vanished body. The central task that the films take on, and that I will also attempt in my own way, is to capture these bodies in their modes of erasure within the particular dynamics of their exclusion: as taboos that have the power to deframe the image by "contaminating" it with a radical exteriority. This alone allows them to challenge the falsified documents of a contemporary cinema beholden to the spectacle of the visible; this alone allows the cinema to regain its rightful role as a truthful historical witness.

The difficulty of giving shape to an experience of loss that is being actively *unseen* and rigorously excluded from the visual field is that in these cases, the task is not to make an invisible image visible, but to undo the false testimony of the visual in order to make perceptible the absences or occlusions hidden by the image. What must be grasped, then, is not simply the play of on-screen and off-screen space constitutive of the development of filmic narrative, nor the various confrontations of filmmakers with forces of social, political, and psychic censorship, nor even the dialectic of showing and withholding that is said to constitute desire in the cinema.[4] While film theory and history began tackling the above problems in earnest, the films that I discuss in this book take up another concern: the invention of figures capable of making perceptible, in the absence of representation, a gap internal to the visual field. Within the architecture of the framed image, this gap designates what I will call an internal off-screen, a space defined not as a potential or virtual image, but through its inclusion as an unseeable mark within a given set of images or as a destructive force acting to undo the dynamics of figuration. What distinguishes the internal off-screen from other types of off-screen space is that it concretizes a contradiction. At once in frame and out of sight, the internal off-screen is blocked from and with (in)visibility by a second image that, appearing in its place, designates an original absence. To "see" this dynamic figure of an invisibility within the visible, we will need a new practice of looking, one capable of seeing an excluded and covered-up absence.

It is for this purpose that I turn to the work of Nicolas Abraham and Maria Torok. Abraham and Torok developed the psychoanalytic practice and theory of cryptonymy to help them listen to the silenced and occluded words in their analysands' speech. In case after case where analysands carried the experience of historical trauma within themselves, Abraham and Torok detected the presence of unspoken words that could barely be heard in the rhymes and deformations of speech. In a series of writings published both separately and together, they posited that these subjects were the bearers of an intrapsychic crypt, a structure of the psychic topography where words associated with an unspeakable trauma are buried. Unlike melancholia in which the refusal to mourn a lost object leads a subject to mourn the loss of the self, the crypt is an attempt to undo loss by preserving the object whole. Because the words buried in the crypt commemorate a painful experience, they are rigorously absented from direct speech; however, because they point to an external situation that remains unresolved, these words continue to produce a mysterious proliferation of speech. Unlike the force of repression proper to the Freudian unconscious, the crypt—an unconscious lodged within the ego—preserves the lost objects of trauma in a suspended animation, a living death. The function of the crypt is not simply to exclude these wounding words from the subject's psychic life but also and at the same time to save them from annihilation and to repeat them in myriad cryptic forms. Abraham and Torok called them taboo words, arguing that while they could never be heard directly, they could be sounded out by listening to the array of words that spoke in their place. The resulting speech was composed of cryptonyms, the synonyms, allosemes, rhymes, and other poetic displacements that pointed to the taboo words while skirting their semantic meaning. Only in this way could the subjects continue to speak of the original scene of trauma without ever recognizing, even within themselves, that the trauma took place. Abraham and Torok named this procedure of replacing a taboo word with a verbal metonymy that hides the semantic field of trauma: *cryptonymy*.

The importance of cryptonymy to a reading of cultural, rather than psychoanalytic, speech resides in its identification of structural relations within a text. Cryptonymy isolates those textual experiences in which the unsaid emerges indirectly from within the said through what Abraham and Torok call a "poetics of hiding." This does not mean that the terms of the psychoanalytic practice should be understood as simply metaphors for textual operations taken up in a different register. However, it does free us from the need to posit a psychoanalytic subject in the form of, or hiding behind, a text. A textual cryptonymy assumes that the pathways of symbolic production developed from within psychoanalytic thought apply not only to the internal life of a subject (or even a culture) but also constitute more generally a mode of "listening" to partial or broken symbols in any textual form. The heart of the psychoanalytic project, for Abraham and Torok, is thus not in establishing a set of prefabricated concepts by which to "read" psychic development and conflict. Instead, they define psychoanalysis as a special way of treating language. "Whereas normally we are given meanings, the analyst is given symbols," they write at the conclusion of their rereading of Freud's well-known Wolf Man case. "Symbols are data that are missing an as yet undetermined part, but that can, in principle, be determined. The special aim of psychoanalytic listening is to find the symbol's complement, recovering it from indeterminacy."[5] Acknowledging this more expansive definition of psychoanalytic practice requires breaking not only from the doctrinaire texts of metapsychology but also from the standard ways in which psychoanalysis has been taken up in film and literary studies. Too often the language of psychoanalysis has served as the guarantor of a proper "reading," such that discovering Oedipus, castration, or the death drive within an image is used to explain, retroactively, its origin in psychic conflict. Instead, suggest Abraham and Torok, a "properly" psychoanalytic approach demands that we first listen to the conflictual process of textual becoming present in every work and then uncover, working back from there, the original situation that brought it about.[6] Psychoanalysis thus defined involves uncovering the history of a word, image, or idea and relating it back to an absent origin by listening to and tracing the history of the sayable and the unsayable that surrounds it.

Turning to the situation cinema confronted after the war, we can see how this practice of listening can be used to understand cultural works. Many of the films I consider in this book are concerned, in different ways, with describing the conditions of postwar Europe: the dramatic rezoning of physical space, changes to social relations between dominant and marginalized peoples, and the visibility of the (gendered and raced) body as a site of political and historical struggle. However, two conditions make a simple "representation" of this situation problematic. First, these new conditions are part of a historical process that erased images of the vanished and the dead buried in the ground of the "old" Europe. The proliferation of spectacular images could not help but commemorate in silence the history of disappearance, displacement, and unspeakable violence that it replaced. Second, and just as importantly, these new conditions contributed to a continuing history of the visual and social exclusion of women, the non-European, and the growing population of expendable bodies within global capital. It is by trying to frame this antagonism between an image that shows "everything" just as it appears and the haunting persistence of nonvisible bodies incorporated within the visual that postwar cinema developed, piece by piece, a cryptic history. Like Abraham and Torok's verbal cryptonyms, cinematic cryptonymy creates images that could stand in the place of the missing bodies. For the sake of clarity, I will call these crypt-images, emphasizing their property of figuring a visual taboo in the absence of a direct representation. However, the operations of the crypt-image, the specific relations produced between the visual and unseen, come from the cinematic scene and not from the psychoanalytic one. Specifically, cinematic cryptonymy relates a visible image to a social or historical absence, whereas psychoanalytic cryptonymy involves the relationship between the said and the unspeakable within an inter- or intrapsychic situation. Thus, whereas Abraham and Torok's method aims at hearing a taboo word, cinematic cryptonymy is the figuration of taboo bodies. What connects the taboo word to the taboo body is that both arise from a failed process of mourning, both are incorporated—included as an absence—within symbolic production, and both testify to a desire to simultaneously annul and preserve an unassimilable loss. Cryptonymy, in its linguistic/psychoanalytic practice and in the figural/cinematic form I pursue in this book, brings to light not the taboo elements themselves (whether words or images), since these are truly outside the field of view, but the structures of inscription and the dynamics of erasure that mark any text haunted by the taboo image.

The Cinematic Crypt-Machine: Translation and the Forms of Cinema

The cinema is a crypt-machine in a double sense. At the same time as film captures the absences already present in the world being recorded, some films are themselves bearers of a visual crypt. The visual crypt is a scene, image, or body that, while wholly outside the frame, is nonetheless within the film: a necessary but conjectured element that "completes" the film, filling in the gaps of its narrative and visual order. I call this a pretextual scene because it is a pretext—a lure of spectatorial and critical desire—for the reading of the film while also logically preceding the film; the film, in this sense, exists primarily to cover up and make visible the pretextual aspect. This scene, this image, this body (the last term gives rise to and produces the others because the scene and the image stage the corporeal erasure) is a historical body under erasure. That is, a marginalized body, usually that of a woman or young girl, but also the bodies of racial minorities, of the unemployable youth or the elderly, of the insane—even the bodies of animals, chained up and waiting for slaughter. Any body that, due to its phantom-like haunting of the social field, has the power to unsettle the regime of the visible and invisible, the audible and the unheard, the inside and the outside, may appear within the visual crypt. The crypt arises when cinema confronts the demand to film an image or body whose cultural and social absence cannot be accounted for within history. Written out of the economy of looks, this absent body (singular in its multiplicity) animates a still-living corpse interred within the image, but out of sight. When it functions as an apparatus of visual encryption, cinema perpetuates the invisibility of the pretextual missing image: it produces crypts. When it figures the dynamics of decryption, when it records the topographies of absence, cinema can work to decipher the aporias of figural exclusion. In each case, the critical task is to grasp the relations between a visible image and what is excluded (from) within it.

Giving language to this critical task, to this critical desire, requires translating the words and structures of cryptonymy as developed by Abraham and Torok into a cinematic-critical practice. This involves a radical displacement of cryptonymy and not a simple substitution of the "proper names" of the objects they identified. Alongside his work as a psychoanalyst, Nicolas Abraham was an important translator and theorist of translation, principally through his translations of Hungarian poetry into French. In fact, as the focus on cryptonymy as a unique mode of listening to the cryptic speech of the other suggests, cryptonymy itself can be understood as a mode and theory of translation. For Abraham, translation involves transforming an established text, such as the analylsand's life story, into an invented text—in this case, the dialogic intervention of the "co-signs" as complements to the patient's broken symbols. The invented text is no less true than the established text, which in turn is just as fictional as the invented one. What differentiates the act of translation from the original or established text is that the invented text is a complement to the original, operating in the gaps of nonmeaning it left open. In this sense translation contains the dual meaning of bringing to light what was already there and of creating something new. What cryptonymy translates, what it both brings to light and invents, is a language proper to the silences through which failed and blocked mourning speaks in a given text. Thus, translation displaces the original from its point of origin, from a "first meaning," and treats it as a point of convergence for all possible translations. The original is both what makes the invented text go beyond itself (relating the invented or translated text to a pretextual scene) and the place to which the invented text returns.

This book is organized as a series of translations or displacements of Abraham and Torok's theory of cryptonymy to the cinema. Treating Abraham and Torok's work as an original text, I endeavor to unfold the theory and practice of cinema's confrontation with absent images by translating the verbal and psychic structures discovered by psychoanalysis into the audio-visual and social apparatuses of film. This work or translation is authorized by an affinity between the two cryptonymies, as both strive to grasp textual gaps created by conditions of historical erasure and occlusion. Abraham and Torok turned to psychoanalysis because it offered them a way of listening to the silences of those who have suffered an unspeakable loss. Recounting the trajectory of their research in the introduction to *The Wolf Man's Magic Word*, they reflect that following various studies of symbol formation, their work turned to "cases (of cryptophoria) where the symbolic operation is blocked, where introjection is lacking, and where the libido's encounter with the tools of its own symbolic development is wanting."[7] The symbolic blockages Abraham and Torok studied in cases of cryptophoria resulted in gaps and occlusions in speech. Although the concepts of the crypt, incorporation, and transgenerational haunting seem to aspire to the pantheon of psychic facts that make up Freud's dream of a universal science of the unconscious, their very language betrays their origin in the history of violence and trauma during and following World War II. Having themselves lost their families in the camps, Abraham and Torok developed a method of listening to those who have been silenced by the horror of what they survived and witnessed.[8] The camps do not make their way directly into their writings, but who can fail to hear the stories of dehumanization, ghettoization, and the guilt of witnessing behind the proper names of Abraham and Torok's tropology? Each in their own way, psychoanalysis and cinema were contending with the material scars left by unmournable objects on the social and psychic imaginary.

The language of this necro-analysis bears the crypt of the analysts' own past, speaking their roles as silent witnesses to historical trauma through a series of rhymes and allosemes that say everything without ever uttering the wounding words of history. Jacques Derrida, a close friend of Nicolas Abraham with whom he shared many fundamental ideas, highlights this link between cryptonymy, the analyst's personal history, and the history of historical trauma in his foreword to *The Wolf Man's Magic Word*. There he writes:

> To whom? To what does a name go back? But a *present* going back, a going back to the present, a bringing back to the present, to whatever kind of haunting return or *unheimlich* homecoming. . . . In rushing, at the risk of cutting off, the question "Who signs here?" I am not asking, that goes without saying, *which* of the two, but how are they *first-named*, in their proper and common name(s): Nicolas Abraham and Maria Torok?[9]

Elsewhere, Derrida writes that cryptonymy is always first of all a matter of the proper name, since it recognizes the co-presence within the self of a host of psychic guests (incorporated figures, specters, and cryptic psyches) while seeking to give subjects the tools for writing their own names within this multivocal life-text. His invocation of the analysts' proper and common names as the "first-named" of cryptonymy thus suggests his intuition that the analytic model is haunted by Abraham and Torok's complex and cryptic life story. Furthermore, Derrida posits that this haunting enacts a particular form of history, a "present going back," in which the past is the homecoming of a future time centered on the repetition of trauma. Curiously, then, the silences of the proper name function to open up cryptonymy to the scene of history, even as this scene is rigorously buried by the analysts themselves, for whom the language of analysis provides a whole verbarium of crypt-words, a memorial to the taboo scene of their past.

I emphasize the excluded inclusion of history and trauma in cryptonymy because it demonstrates that the use to which Abraham and Torok put psychoanalysis, listening to the silences imposed by history on speech and writing, is of a piece with the task taken up by the practices of cinematic erasure in the films discussed in this book. This shared desire to decrypt the absences that haunt the present grounds the translation of cryptonymy into a cinematic practice in the historical moment at which both emerged and to which they continually turn back. At the same time, cinematic cryptonymy extends the horizon of Abraham and Torok's method by explicitly turning to the absent images lodged in the social imaginary of the present and not only those deposited there by the history of the war. This demands the invention of new forms of encryption and decryption not present in Abraham and Torok's work; in each case the appearance of the figure of erasure is determined by its moment of historical visibility. In his book *Specters of the Atlantic*, Ian Baucom argues for what he calls a history of temporal accumulation. In a consideration of Walter Benjamin's theses on history, Baucom writes that "as time passes the past does not wane but intensifies; as history repeats itself it repeats in neither attenuated nor farcical form but by 'redeeming' the what-has-been, 'awakening' it into a fuller, more intense form."[10] This understanding of history, continues Baucom, demands that the historian both place historical objects within their situations and invent new situations and periods of time in which to place objects. In line with Abraham and Torok's thinking, to which he turns several times, Baucom stresses that this form of temporal intensification is underwritten by the presence of a lost object displaced from history and which each new moment preserves and erases. In Baucom's analysis, this lost object is the unmournable slave body that lies buried at the origin of finance capital. Although my story starts considerably later, I invoke Baucom's book because it emphasizes the kind of decentering of time around an object of loss that connects cryptonymy as a historical practice with cinema's turn to history after the war.

Georges Franju's films of the postwar period map the dynamics of the city as a reconstructed image that erases *as it preserves* the absences of the past (those who vanished during the war) and the present (women, the mad, and the wounded who were relegated to social erasure). In the first chapter, I analyze several of his documentary and fiction works—focusing on *Blood of the Beasts* (1949), *Hôtel des Invalides* (1951), *Le Grand Méliès* (1952), and

Eyes without a Face (1959)—as sites of internal exclusion, dynamic structures for the expulsion of unmournable bodies into the interiority of the French physical, social, and psychic topography. The enclosure of an absent body within an image of the postwar city means that the traumas of history were at once incorporated as generators of the French imaginary and blocked, at least from active participation, from any direct visual and historiographic account. Although the war dead were certainly commemorated after the end of hostilities, and the conditions of women and other marginalized bodies were increasingly at the center of political debates, this new visibility paradoxically assumed, for Franju, the status of a fetish object that cut these bodies off from the dynamics of history. As Gabriele Schwab notes in the German context, silencing "was not a withholding of facts; it was caused by the absence of any kind of emotional engagement at both personal and collective levels."[11] Franju depicts the bodies incorporated by historical silence as affectless, spectral, and desubjectified, as bodies isolated within the personal and collective history of France's postwar transformation.

To mark the place of this absent body, Franju invented a unique type of image that I will call the crypt-image: an image that appears in place of an absent image and that therefore erases an absence present in the visual and social field. The crypt-image's role in Franju's films that I will analyze is analogous to the role of cryptonyms in cryptonymy. Abraham and Torok posited that while taboo words were excluded from the dynamic symbolic life of the subject, they continued to be spoken by synonyms, rhymes, and allosemes that took the taboo word's place. They called these substitute words cryptonyms, or words that hide. To hear cryptophoric speech, it is necessary to recognize that cryptonyms are related to the prohibited word that they displace through what Abraham and Torok call a "metonymy of words," a purely lexical operation that bears no relation to the word's phonetic or semantic properties. The cryptophore uses words as things, as love objects, rather than as symbols or symptoms.[12] The crypt-image, like the cryptonym, is not a simple substitution but the displacement of an erasure; it takes the place of an image from which the unmournable body has already been excluded and thus signifies (in) the absence of a direct reference to the lost object. Unlike other images that invoke the unrepresentable through a figural substitution or metaphor, the crypt-image repeats the pretextual lost object within the film. For Franju,

I will argue, France's recent "past"—its collaboration with the Nazi Holocaust and its colonial history—actively produce the postwar topographies of visual exclusion in present day France. The films figure the image of a modern France as a displacement of the horrors of the past and also assert the impossibility of representing this condition of a traumatic absence that includes or is created by images. A consideration of the architectural and topographic logic that runs through the director's work will be the basis for a reconsideration of his oeuvre as the invention of crypt-images, each blocking the figure of a body erased and written out of the proper order of social circulation. Franju's crypt-images map the ways in which a series of internal exclusions figure the incorporation of taboo bodies within the social whole.

Whereas Franju's films map the cryptic spaces of postwar France, Mario Bava's genre cinema, especially his early horror films, confronts a different condition: the generational inheritance of trauma that takes the form of an absent image that recurs historically. In the second chapter, I analyze two of Bava's generational horror films—*Black Sunday* (1960) and *Kill, Baby . . . Kill!* (1966)—as films of corporeal encryption in which a crypt is inherited by future generations in the form of a secret, unseeable image. Historically, this situation arose from the split of Italian society brought about by the rapid (and externally enforced) pace of the economic miracle in which a high-tech industrial society was grafted onto the spaces and subjectivities still tied to older forms of life. These older forms continued to exist, however, within the Italian imaginary, and the "modernization" of social life remained haunted by the gaps of the past. This has led to an extension of what Italian historians have described as Italy's "divided memory," the multiplication of divergent and contradictory narratives or memory that not only arise from a single historical event but also are commemorated and remembered without a working through of their contradictions. John Foot describes the process as one in which "different sets of memories have surfaced from and about events, shaping both public and private memory. One aspect of this divided memory is that certain accounts were excluded from historical discourse for long periods of time."[13] In Mario Bava's films, Italy's economic modernization in the 1960s appears in two divided forms. First, the series of gothic horror films for which he is most famous are set in a distant past full of terrible secrets that pass on as violent specters from generation to generation. The gothic setting of these films forecloses any image of modern Italy. In these films, Bava emphasizes the historical recurrence of the premodern subject (a subject, of course, only conceivable as the pretextual if negative scene of the modern Italian state) brought about by a violent but unspoken historical crime. In almost every case, the inheritance of the historical crypt takes place between generations of women who pass along the absent words and images of the past from mother to daughter (or grandmother to granddaughter, and so forth). In other films, however, Bava sets the scene of horror in the modern spaces of capital: a fashion house, a summer beach resort, or an urban apartment building. In these films women (and children) are transformed from the bearers (and reproducers) of the historical crypt into the "absent bodies"—images of their own absence—encrypted within the present forms of capital. As a whole, then, Bava's work charts the inheritance of women's erasure across the divisions of history by way of spectral reproduction.

To give form to this phantom inheritance, Bava invents a type of point-of-view shot that I will call a phantom-image or phantom-POV: a shot that includes its own visual origin, the looking body, as an absence inscribed within the frame of the film. While the phantom-POV does mark the presence of a specter or ghost within the image in a way reminiscent of the figuration of evil in many horror films, it is unique in inserting itself as an absence within a ghostly vision. As both (absent) source and object of the look, the phantom-POV inserts an erasure within a series of gazes. This introduces an enigma into the social body, an enigma that is addressed to a subjectivity that returns from another time. In this chapter, I use the phantom-POV to address a twofold question: How do films themselves contain (rather than merely represent) phantasmatic secrets? How do institutions of film history, such as genre, national cinemas, and authorship, encrypt and pass on these secrets in silence?

These questions translate a concept originating in Abraham and Torok's cryptonymy—that of the transgenerational phantom—into the cinema. In their work, Abraham and Torok develop the theory of the phantom to help them speak about the experience of being haunted by the crypt of another. Phantoms, they argue, do not return from our unconscious like Freud's idea of the uncanny but are the "gaps left in us by the secrets of others."[14] If a crypt remains closed when someone dies, its silences are frequently inherited by family members who continue to protect the secrets of the past without even being aware of their contents. Esther Rashkin provides a concise summary of the phantom in her study of the literary effects of cryptonymy: "The unspeakable secret suspended within the adult is transmitted silently to the child in 'undigested' form and lodges within his or her mental topography as an unmarked tomb of inaccessible knowledge. . . . What returns to haunt is the 'unsaid' and 'unsayable' of *an other*."[15] The phantom thus represents a cryptic history handed down through silences embedded within a family line. While Abraham and Torok restrict most of their consideration of the transgenerational phantom to the dynamics of forebearers and their descendants, this concept has proved fruitful in broader discussions of historical and cultural inheritance of trauma and remains perhaps Abraham and Torok's most "applied" concept. Translating the psychoanalytic concept of the phantom into a cinematic figure means arguing for the role of visual images as forms of cultural and subjective inheritance that can reproduce the unsightly crypts of past generations. In this chapter, however, I do more than add another instance of historical haunting. I also make an explicit argument for the ways in which institutions of criticism and spectatorship are marked by what they do not see in the images they analyze.

The third chapter focuses on *Notre musique* (2004), Jean-Luc Godard's most lucid demonstration of his unique practice of historical montage. For Godard, the power of montage as a historical tool is its ability to mark the place of the "missing images" of historical trauma that were never filmed or seen. In this way Godard responds directly to what he understands as cinema's ultimate failure or betrayal: having abandoned its task of bearing witness to the horrors of the world. Although *Notre musique* applies this montage practice to a broad history of contemporary situations of violence, oppression, and social displacement, Godard's focus is often on the Holocaust as a critical moment of failure. Michael Witt outlines Godard's relationship to the history of cinematic absences in his analysis of Godard as a historiographic director:

> For Godard World War II was the central cataclysmic event of the twentieth century, and it was cinema's *failure to testify* to the unbearable horrors of the Holocaust that resulted in the most damaging reduction yet of its powers: . . . "The concentration camps weren't filmed; people didn't want to show them or see them. And that was the end: cinema stopped there."[16]

This failure to testify and this refusal to film are understood by Godard not simply as an accident of history but as a readable gap and occlusion that speaks to a refusal to show and to see. For Godard, this missing image signals a deliberate looking away that betrays cinema's role as historical witness. As Witt makes clear, Godard's contention is not that there was no representation of the horrors of the Holocaust (and of the French Resistance) in both fiction and documentary films. Rather, Godard claims that these films—fiction and documentary alike—came *too late* and thus could serve only as falsified documents, proliferating images about the Holocaust rather than images of the Holocaust; they transformed the event from a historical truth to a fictional scene. In place of the taboo image of real suffering, cinematic representations of the Holocaust multiplied images of spectacular and melancholic loss, containing the real within a fiction. In the place of the missing but still-living bodies of the present, they multiplied images of the already dead: crypt-images, images buried in history. Unable to show the trauma of history, they left a "catastrophic hole in the cinematic representation of the twentieth century."[17] In the aftermath of this failure to film, cinema itself became spellbound and fixed on its historical failure to properly mourn the dead. Instead of the working-through of mourning, cinema became a machine for the fantasy of the magical reanimation of the lost object of historical representation.

Anasemic montage, as I name Godard's process as articulated in *Notre musique* and practiced in many films beginning in the mid-1970s, aims to return images to their original relationship with the occluded scenes of historical witnessing. For Abraham and Torok, anasemia names a unique property of psychoanalytic language in which a single word simultaneously expresses two contradictory meanings: the everyday sense of the word and the meaning given to it by psychoanalysis, which relates this meaning to its unconscious complement. Abraham offers the example of the word *pleasure*, which expresses, metapsychologically, its usual meaning and also the sense of pain and unpleasure that so often accompanies it in the analytic experience. More than simply signifying a contradiction, an anasemic term *is* the history of the ego's relationship to the unconscious other scene. Reconstructing the history of the psychic contradictions that ground symbolic expression, anasemia thus has two aspects: the isolation and displacement of words from their everyday meaning and the reconstruction of a transphenomenal origin that restores an affective aporia within language. Anasemic montage transforms the linguistic-psychic dimensions of anasemia into aspects of visual historiography. Of central importance in this process is the notion of the interval, an unseen or encrypted term across which a passage takes place: from stillness to movement, from the photograph to the moving image, and from cinema to world. It is by way of the interval as a dynamic, structural, and topographic element that the cinema incorporates the lost object within its particular chronotope.[18] The analysis of Godard's films in this chapter retraces the dynamics of transgenerational haunting discovered in Bava's work, but in reverse: from the present to the decryption of the absent origin. This produces a turn within the history of cinematic cryptonymy; no longer content to reproduce the marks of visual absence, Godard's work turns to practices that return the absent image to visibility.

This turn in the history of cinematic cryptonymy is further pursued in the discussion of Naomi Uman's films in the following chapter. Uman stands out from the other filmmakers examined in this book because she works outside of the European and commercial cinema contexts. Her artisanal films, mostly rooted in ethnographic practice, are produced within and as part of the social spaces that she lives in and documents. As an itinerant filmmaker whose films allow her to incorporate herself as an "internal other" within a variety of communities in Mexico, the United States, and the Ukraine, Uman's cinema is a mode of visual and linguistic translation focused on the role of physical and psychic borders in what gets excluded from sight and speech. The chapter focuses on her "milk" films—*Leche* (1998) and *Mala Leche* (2003)—in which she documents the different experiences of dairy farmers in central Mexico and California's Central Valley. Across the two films, the US-Mexico border looms large as a fault line of cryptic incorporation through which bodies vanish and words fall into silence. Her interest in what remains unseen extends to her embodied approach to filmmaking, where the film material itself bears the scars of intentional and aleatory processes of occlusion such as scratches, weather effects, and the conditions of found footage. Working outside of the context of European cinema's encryption of the war, Uman's films broaden the scope of cinematic cryptonymy and respond directly to the presence of the crypt in the transnational circulation of images and bodies characteristic of the intensification of global capital at the turn of the millennium. In addition, this chapter returns to some of the spatial concerns broached in the first chapter—and away from the historical focus of the previous two—to argue that the new global topographies are as haunted by cryptic bodies as were those of the immediate postwar period.

To locate Uman's practice as a relation between a filmmaker who is included within and also a stranger to a community she documents, I introduce the figure of the internal off-screen: the visual inclusion of an image's exteriority within the frame. Both interior to the frame and exterior to the image, the internal off-screen demarcates the place of what cannot be figured within the visible. The internal off-screen involves the insertion of a figural absence in the image to mark the place where a crypt-image had previously erased a gap. This concept does not have a direct corollary in Abraham and Torok's writing and in this sense is a wholly new contribution the cinema makes to the history of cryptonymy. I will argue that the internal off-screen is a response to the experience of incorporation within social topographies. In Abraham and Torok's work, incorporation names the inclusion, through cannibalistic or phantasmatic fantasies, of an exteriority within psychic space in order to preserve a loss from ever being acknowledged. "When, in the form of imaginary or real nourishment, we ingest the love-object we miss, this means that *we refuse to mourn.* . . . Incorporation is the refusal to reclaim as our own the part of ourselves that we placed in what we lost. . . . The fantasy of incorporation reveals a gap in the psyche; it points to something that is missing."[19] Seen from the perspective of social life, incorporation points to the ways in which bodies that are excluded from the social and symbolic whole are cannibalized and transformed into mute and absent specters. While the previous chapters in the book have registered the effects that the incorporation of vanished bodies have had on the spatial and historical shapes captured by cinema, the internal off-screen names a series of practices aimed at returning incorporated bodies to symbolic visibility. The chapter will thus demonstrate the importance of the cinema as a tool for decryption and broach the social and political powers of cinematic cryptonymy.

Cinematic Cryptonymies and the Challenges to Film Studies

The crypt-image, the haunted-POV shot, anasemic montage, and the internal off-screen name the specific contributions made by the films analyzed in this book to the practice and theory of cryptonymy understood broadly as a mode of listening to gaps in symbolic expression. Each term arises from the specific set of practices belonging to the individual films. Abraham and Torok stress cryptonymy's status as a practice of listening that is truly dialogic: the speech of the analyst constantly inventing new terms to account for the unique silences of the analysand. For them, Freud's insights relating to the dynamics of expression and censorship in the subject, and the clinical elaboration of this history, were betrayed by the search for a set of universal principles or symbols that impose a pregiven developmental matrix on individual experience. This does not mean, however, that each analysis must start anew. Neither idiosyncratic nor generalizable, cryptonymy operates at the seams at which a symbol is stitched to a symbolic system, an individual sutured to a social practice. Moreover, for cryptonymy this demands an account of the ways in which the self is always haunted by the cryptic presence of everything that it excludes; if a symbolic system can be said to have an unconscious life, this is nothing but the order of things external to that system while also being incorporated within it. Within analysis, this means that the analysand is haunted by the analyst; in textual and cultural works, the text is marked by the critical discourse that "overwrites" it; and in social and historical contexts, each time and place is built around the times and places that border it. The words of cryptonymy provide a way to symbolize the dynamic processes that block expression due to the inclusion of these foreign "lost objects," but cryptonymy must use them to reassert the originality of analysis in every case. Hence the importance of translation to Abraham and Torok's thinking: translation relates an invented text to an original, a new expression to an existing text, by allowing two different languages to speak of and to each other. Lacking a master narrative, cryptonymy proceeds along the path of a text toward a conclusion that is nothing other than the dynamics of analysis, the lines of translation. This book follows a similar impulse; guided by the forms taken by taboo words in speech, I have sought to reveal the effects of missing images—and the bodies they (un)cover—within a set of films. These films, in turn, are guided by their encounter with specific social and historical situations of erased and excluded bodies. Thus, taken together, the analysis of these films accounts for a history (not the only possible one) of cinematic cryptonymy and for cinematic cryptonymy as a historical dynamic (which is not its only possible elaboration).

This approach poses a number of overlapping questions to the writing of film history, the practice of film theory, and the specter of psychoanalysis within film studies.

1. *Wild analysis*. It has often been noted that treating texts as if they were psychic formations as defined by psychoanalysis—dreams, symptoms, slips of the tongue—is a method beset with pitfalls. Freud himself warned of the dangers of "wild analysis" that, in staging an analysis outside of the clinical session, can at best "inform the patient of what he does not know because he has repressed it" and at worst intensify and exacerbate the patient's inner conflict.[20] Lacking the dynamics of resistance and transference, wild analysis will never be able to produce new knowledge or to work through the knots of affective and symbolic blockage. If Freud nevertheless often turned to artistic and other texts in his writings, these served as demonstrations of a metapsychology that either emerged from or would have to be tested in clinical practice. In themselves, these texts did not speak. Much the same can be said of a good deal of psychoanalytic film theory in which the danger is not so much the reduction of the film object to the language of analysis as it is the "loss" of the object, its incorporation as mute witness to the scene of interpretation. As Metz argued in his foundational essay, film theory is often aimed at the preservation of the cinematic object and is thus unable to do anything but repeat its loss.[21]

And yet Abraham and Torok, though having frequent recourse to their patients' life stories, are equally at home in a rereading of the Wolf Man case based entirely on documents and previous case histories, or in analyzing the phantom of Hamlet as it haunts generations of spectators and readers of Shakespeare's play, or even in an analysis of the historical writings of the psychoanalytic institution. In turning to their writings as a set of moves by which to understand films, I rely on the central role they give to cultural texts and existing documents to not only "prove" psychoanalytic concepts but also to invent a mode of listening. Cryptonymy's approach to textual and cultural objects, however, is markedly different from the forms of wild analysis that emerged through an application of Freudian and Lacanian psychoanalysis. For Abraham and Torok, cultural documents are not the end products of psychic processes that can be retrieved from the precipitate of the text. Nor are they reflections or analogies of the inner workings of an individual or collective psyche. Texts—be they the notes of a case history or a piece of fiction—are first of all collective practices that place the possibilities, and therefore the gaps, of speech within the social field. "We must not lose sight of the fact," they remind us, "that to stage a word—whether metaphorically, as an alloseme, or as a cryptonym—constitutes an attempt at an exorcism, an attempt, that is, to relieve the unconscious by placing the effects of the phantom in the social realm."[22] Recalling that the phantom is the expression of the secrets of an other deposited unwittingly within the self, it is clear that for Abraham and Torok to "stage a word" is to insist that the unsaid and unspeakable can only be revealed as part of a social exchange that is broader than that created between two people in the clinic. Staged words transmit the history of their nonknowledge, and open the possibility of future speech, by invoking a community of listeners to come. This insight grounds both their rereading of the Wolf Man case, where they are attentive to the moments where Freud "staged" his own hesitations about the case for the ears of future analysts (and thus founded a psychoanalytic *institution*), and of *Hamlet*, where the history of the work's critical interpretation is used to demonstrate an aspect of the play that has remained "out of play," shrouded by nonknowledge, by the many generations of its analysts and critics, whether psychoanalytic or not.

This approach is particularly attractive when applied to film history because of cinema's role, for much of its history, as a mass art and because of its unique relation to the real. As a machine of projection, cinema long served a communal, mass audience. Regardless of the numbers of spectators drawn to any individual film (most of the films discussed in this book were hardly popular), the film image is in part defined by its potential for mass visibility. Cinema, unlike the individual psyche, always involves the social, public staging of images. Furthermore, the technical demands of the cinema and the high costs of commercial filmmaking (and of experimental filmmaking of the era covered in this book, at least when compared to dreaming or writing) mean that its origin can always be traced back to the contradictions inherent in the capitalist mode of production of which it is a commodity. Cinema's origin in the specific antagonisms of capital and its screening within the social space of projection give films a unique role in the staging of collective images that can bear the crypts of historical and institutional trauma. Equally relevant is cinema's special relation with the real, from which it draws its images. It is this evidentiary or even forensic character of the film image that allows it to bear witness to the world. Consequently, the gaps and absences in films commemorate exclusions in the world. This is a fundamental difference from psychoanalytic cryptonymy where the crypt incorporates a taboo word, a signifier stripped of its signifying capacity in speech. Cinematic cryptonymy traces the encryption of taboo, missing bodies, and the film crypt is the bearer of a corporeal absence. This nature of the cinematic crypt justifies the language of Abraham and Torok's cryptonymy, emphasizing its occluded origin in real historical loss. Moreover, staging a taboo body requires that it be placed in the social and historical scene, beyond the family dynamics to which Abraham and Torok so often return.

2. *Authorship*. This book will proceed as if each of its major concepts could be signed by a proper name: *George Franju*'s crypt-images, *Mario Bava*'s phantom-POV, *Jean-Luc Godard*'s anasemic montage, and *Naomi Uman*'s internal off-screens. In this, it would seem to offer a catalog of the great cryptic auteurs of film history. And yet, the use I make of these proper names complicates this proposition on two points. First, although these films will be located within a directorial oeuvre, no claim will be made for the applicability of the analysis to every film or even to the director's work as a whole. Second, the proposition is complicated because I will argue throughout that the cinematic figures I describe pertain, albeit in contingent ways, to larger practices of erasure in cinema and thus constitute elements of a theory of cinematic erasure broadly conceived. The importance of the authorial signature is that it condenses or invokes a variety of determinations—historical periods, modes of production, national contexts, institutional practices—while maintaining the sense of a unique deployment of these contexts. A proper name is thus both overdetermined and singular. For this reason, I maintain the authorial mark. However, in this book, as for Abraham and Torok, the proper name is the first and final cryptonym of a multivocal speech consisting of overheard dialogue, the incorporated dead, and the analytic discourse. The proper name is a *word that hides* this discursive polysemy of a text centered on a shared

secret or mute word. As with cryptonyms more generally, to hide in this sense also means to make this polysemy readable as what remains unsaid in a text. The proper name, because of its fictive resonance (because, that is, of its ability to lend itself variably to any host of individuals or groups, living or dead, without losing its coherence) thus marks the place where the word of the subject no longer designates the unity of the individual and its history. The proper name calls forth the crypts and phantoms that haunt the subject and open it up to the presence of the other. By marking this work of disunity through attention to the auteurist signature, this book reconsiders *la politique des auteurs*, which remains central to postwar film histories—in spite of the many assaults on this critical paradigm.

Abraham and Torok argued that the Wolf Man, even late in life, was trying to make audible the presence of complex dialogues taking place within him and among a whole host of internal characters, a dialogue that has gone unacknowledged in his lifetime of psychoanalysis. By taking on the name given to him by Freud—he signed his memoirs "Wolf Man"—he wanted to insist not only that his real self remained silent behind the interminable speech of analysis, but also that his "self" was itself a fiction encrypting an amalgamation of specters and guests buried in the psyche. And this is precisely the importance I give to the names of directors, industries, and other groupings of films and filmmakers throughout this book. Unlike auteur theory's drive to discover a singular expression, these proper names will in each case indicate a place where the signature, evoking a unity, encrypts a multiplicity and vocal contradiction. In one sense, this means that a proper name will designate not only the work of the filmmaker but also a number of other hands that sign the film in silence: critical writings, the acts of institutional censorship, the cuts demanded by international distributors, and generic and national inheritances, to name just a few of those who often would rather not be called out. Any work that responds to and in some way writes or speaks the films in question can be included beneath the line of the signature. The task of cryptonymic analysis is to place the image within this dialogue, to show how it is always the product of this complex polysemy of discourses.

Complicating this work, however, is the assumption that this complex discourse does not only speak but also contains shared silences that are kept in secret. In fact, I will argue, it is often these silences, these textual crypts of the absent image, that compel critics, censors, distributors, and other filmmakers to return to the films in question. The taboo image is a silence shared by the multivalent speech inherent in this expanded sense of authorship. Thus, reconstructing the dialogue inscribed in the image's proper name depends on making visible an image that, missing from the original film, could account for and verify this chorus of voices. What I am suggesting is not simply that the name will function as a metonymy of larger social and institutional discourses. In each of the cases analyzed in this book, the directors' name (and this includes, of course, their public persona, their visual style, and their critical work in writing or interviews) incorporates a historical absence echoed across a larger discursive framework, an absence commemorating the place where a textual body has been left out of film history.

3. *Criticism*. A direct and unavoidable implication of the expanded context of authorship described above is the importance I will give to the critical literature surrounding the films under discussion. I will, throughout, use the words and silences of the critics to reveal the images absent in the films. An intrapsychic crypt does more than bury an unmournable body in a closed-off region of the ego, it also erases any signs that a loss has taken place by keeping the dead alive, at least insofar as fantasy life goes. This, paradoxically, is what allows the cryptophore to act, outwardly, as if they fully acknowledge the traumatic experience that haunts them. Likewise, the crypt-image and the dynamic and topographic structures built around it function *as if* no visual loss has taken place. A cryptonymic analysis thus encounters not a black screen or white mark where an image has been, but a series of textual operations *signifying* an unreadable text, a text that presents itself in an act of unscreening. The absent image has to be retrieved from behind the cryptic visual field. I argue, following Abraham and Torok, that this unreadability takes one of two forms: either it poses an unresolvable enigma located outside the proper textual body (unresolvable because it is missing a key component), or it presents a text that seems to refer to no enigma at all, to be self-evident.[23]

The films I analyze in this book have all been treated in the critical literature either as aporetic (and this is often ascribed to either an institutional or generic condition of the film, such as the "rules" of art cinema or the cheap and quick production process of b-horror) or as requiring no interpretation. The critical attempts to overcome this dual resistance to dialogue involve the search for an image or figure outside the text that could account for its operations. The critics, in short, draw on pre- or paratextual objects to put the films in order and explain their gaps. The danger seems all too clear; it would be possible to construct almost anything one wants to "complete" the missing image, since the missing objects are connected to their textual signifiers through a "metonymy of words" or of the signifier alone, without any reference to the signifieds.[24] There is thus no "check" on the act of analysis outside of the poetic maneuvers the analyst discovers. Cryptonymy's task, however, is not to discover hidden meanings behind the manifest textual system, nor can we treat films as psychic formations arising from a subjective unconscious conflict. One of the strengths of Abraham and Torok's work is in showing how analysis can bypass the unconscious so important to the clinical session by looking for the twists and turns of avoidance present in a series of documents organized dialogically. Of their work using the multiple case histories about and writings by the Wolf Man, they note: "In our unique experiment, the prolonged repetition of sessions was replaced by numerous rereadings, renewed returns to the same documents."[25] These rereadings allowed them to reconstruct the gaps across texts; the knots at which the Wolf Man remained unheard (the silences in the analytic case histories) because he spoke in secret (the structures of avoidance in the Wolf Man's speech). Thus, throughout this book, it will be crucial for us to listen to the hesitations, the twists and turns, the sudden reversals of the critical literature so that we can reconstruct the shared silences and discover what remains unseen. In this way, cryptonymy depends on a "third ear" that can hear a silence shared between two or more people rather than on an absence within a unified work.

For this reason, the analyses undertaken in the following chapters will proceed by staging a critical dialogue between a film and the scene of writing, hoping to thus sound out the silences and visual erasures that pass from image to writing, from text to commentary, from an original to its translation. It is this alone that can verify the validity of analysis, indicated by its actions in another scene that puts it into play.

The Crypt-Image and the Taboo Body in the Films of Georges Franju

> The "shadow of the object" strays endlessly about the crypt until it is finally reincarnated in the person of the subject. Far from displaying itself, this kind of identification is destined to remain concealed.
>
> Abraham and Torok, "'The Lost Object—Me': Notes on Endocryptic Identification"

> What the case called for was a doctor qualified to treat the living, not the dead—perhaps even a psychoanalyst.
>
> Henry Rousso, *The Vichy Syndrome*

The Crypt Image and the Taboo Body

Franju's work poses a unique problem within film history; while he is central to the development of French cinema, founder and leading figure of a number of its key institutions (he cofounded the Cinémathèque Française in 1937 and served as secretary general of the Institut de Cinématographie Scientifique from 1944 to 1954), he remains marginal and displaced within the history that he helped to shape. As a filmmaker, Franju is at once too inside film history—too recognizably industrial, institutional, and generic to constitute a sustained unique vision—and too outside of it—old-fashioned, cut off from the liveliest currents of contemporary cinema, bereft of any heirs, and too inconsistent to be exemplary. In response, many critical studies of his work hold out the promise of historical reparation. What is at stake in this critical response, however, is not merely the relative neglect of an important director, a problem of historical due, but something of the nature of an enigma unsettling the historiographic drive. There is, it seems, something *unfathomable*, almost taboo, about Franju's presence in the annals of French cinema. *Positif*'s sigh of disappointment with the filmmaker they once championed, in a review of *Thérèse Desqueyroux*, suggests the sense of loss that haunts Franju's authorial trajectory: "there's something very saddening in Franju's career and his steadily widening distance from all the hopes we placed in him, his *self-burial* in conventional productions, in five-finger exercises in style, and in Selected Classics."[1] For the writers of *Positif*, and for many others who celebrated Franju's daring early documentaries, the director's vision was soon occluded by his reliance on adaptations and conventional production practices. While this sense of loss can be read as a cautionary tale about the power of the film industry to contain even the most radically subversive auteurs, the language of loss and mourning associated with Franju's career also testifies to the continuing power of his unique oeuvre. For, in both the documentaries and the fiction films, Franju created a singularly funerary cinema. His films often center on a critique of the entombment of marginal figures and painful memories in spaces demarcated, both visually and psychologically, from social life. But they are also films of preservation and commemoration, films that keep alive memories that have been marginalized by official discourse and bodies that have been excluded from visibility. If Franju's work is "out of sync" with film history, this is due, at least in part, to the singularity of his ambition, throughout his career, to create images capable of figuring the condition of absence and loss preserved within and erased by institutions of the cinematic imaginary.[2]

For Franju, this condition of visible absence was, first and foremost, mappable to an emerging spatial order of postwar France. In his films, everyday spaces—a country estate, a Parisian street, the woods and fields that surround them—frequently give way to hidden chambers of violence, clandestine burial, and extrajudiciary imprisonment. Echoing with the horrors of World War II and the Algerian conflict, the films chart the relationship between a silenced history and the postwar moment onto landscapes of in-visibility, of the inclusion of what is kept out of sight within the image of a new, modern France. The interior spaces in question may be a tomb, a mental hospital, a medical clinic, a war museum, an abattoir, or even a pound for abandoned dogs. In each case, behind their facade of social propriety, they hide bodies that have vanished from sight. They are an interior ground of the visible that is cast out from the field of vision. In an influential account of France's postwar period, historian Henry Rousso explains the significance of absent bodies for the national imaginary of the time. Of the 600,000 dead, he notes, only a third died in battle. "The rest had *vanished* in bombardments, executions, massacres, and deportations or had fallen victim to internal combat in France or its colonies. Traditional forms of commemoration were inappropriate to such circumstances. Hence authorities maintained a discreet silence about the war and its memories."[3] Excluded from the historical register, the vanished dead were also cast out of the image that France presented of itself after the war. France was haunted not only by the absences left by these missing bodies but also by the impossibility of mourning them and by the silences erected to conceal their fate. In this situation, silence itself becomes an object of history that must be retrieved from the archive of historical events that perpetuate it. Ceremonies for the fallen in battle, scandals in political life, debates about city planning, each referred back to the occluded silences without ever speaking them directly. Rousso describes the peculiarity of this historical undertaking: unlike a history that deals with the documents of the dead past, the silences of the Vichy period continued to play an active role in French social life and identity, and thus the story of war became a history of its continued existence as gaps in the present. Rousso's book narrates the preservation of silence within national discourse: the commemoration of what is officially forgotten. Likewise, Franju's films can be contrasted with traditional depictions of haunting in which the past returns to torment the present. What Franju enacts are situations in which the living return to live in (the) place of the unmournable dead, haunting the grounds of an innermost spatial crypt.

This topographic artifice of an interior space constructed to both hide and commemorate objects of historical absence transforms France into an image of the intrapsychic crypt found in Abraham and Torok's work. In their writings, the crypt names a sealed-off enclosure, lodged within the ego, in which a loss is entombed, cut off from any contact with the self and thus preserved as loss. "Created by the self-governing mechanism we call *inclusion*," they explain, "the crypt is comparable to the formation of a cocoon around the chrysalis. Inclusion or crypt is a form of anti-introjection, a mechanism whereby the assimilation of both the illegitimate idyll and its loss is precluded."[4] The crypt protects a lost object from being recognized as lost by blocking the paths of introjection and mourning.[5] It withholds the lost object from the self, excludes the interior from the psyche that surrounds it, and casts the innermost interiority outside of the self. This serves a double purpose: ensuring that the crypt-bearer never has to confront the trauma of loss, the crypt preserves the lost object as a necrotic foreign body within the self. To access the crypt, one must follow the twisting paths of a taboo word: a word that has been excluded from speech because of its relationship to the traumatic scene of loss. Although the taboo word is never spoken, at least as an active part of speech, the cryptophore—one who bears an intrapsychic crypt—never tires of repeating it in the forms of rhymes, allosemes, and other poetic displacements at the level of the signifier. Abraham and Torok call them cryptonyms, or words that hide. A crypt preserves a lost object by both denying that it has ever been lost and allowing it to be repeated with other words.

In Franju's work, images often incorporate sites of invisibility within their frame. I call them crypt-images to emphasize their role as images that hide and preserve other images that have been excluded. Like the cryptonym, the crypt-image displaces a taboo through a series of figural or visual deformations operating without any direct reference to the lost object. However, in contrast to the verbal taboo, the crypt-image is a visual restaging of a taboo body. The taboo body is a special kind of image. It is an image that refers to a real body that has been excluded from sight. Kate Ince points out that when Franju made *Mon chien* (1955), a short pedagogical movie used to highlight the cruel fate awaiting abandoned dogs, he regretted that he did not film the actual extermination of the animals in the pound and that he felt that because of this omission the film tipped too far into melodrama.[6] Putting aside the clearly provocative intent of the statement, it is emblematic of the director's treatment of the taboo body as a piece of material evidence that is excluded from the film while grounding its fiction. Showing the gassing of the dogs, a truly taboo image within the institutional context in which the film was made, would have negated any pedagogical value of the work. Aside from likely foreclosing it from its intended exhibition circuit, the excessive visual horror would have overwhelmed the film's message warning its bourgeois audience against abandoning their pets. Raised to the level of fiction, we can be treated to the full pathos of a young girl mourning the loss of her favorite pet, and we can vow to never be in her place. Thus, an unmournable body, a true taboo excluded from the circuit of domesticity, is replaced by a mourned loved one. And yet, for Franju, the film fails precisely because it saves the taboo body from its proper place in the innermost exteriority of social visibility. Made mournable, the dead dog reenters the circuit of the living (child) by being buried within the family plot, cast out as a fictive, and thus assimilable, loss. Rather than saving the unwanted pets from extinction, *Mon chien* inscribes them outside the social image by encrypting a documentary within a melodrama. The film's failure highlights the great importance that Franju afforded the taboo image as a pretextual image that commemorates a loss external to the visual frame while setting the film's imaginary in motion.

The taboo image has three distinct facets in Franju's body of work, which are developed throughout his career. The first is the *unwatchable taboo*, an image of extreme visual horror. While Franju rarely makes use of it, the unwatchable taboo image defines much of his critical reception, due both to its shock value and to its importance in the history of the horror genre and the documentary. Crucially, however, what defines this image as taboo in the sense I explore here is not the violence or shock of the visual but the inscription of the spectator's refusal to see within the frame. Incorporating the look away from the camera, the unwatchable image includes or accounts for the spectator's body as it physically turns away from the image, refusing to see. The *figural taboo*, by contrast, characterizes strategies of active defiguration either at the level of the object (scars, occlusions using masks and costumes, and such) or on the level of the image (out-of-focus shots, sudden cuts, and deframings). In these cases, the image or body is treated as an object, a screen (in both the sense of barrier and surface for projection) for the taboo body. Lastly, Franju makes use of a taboo image characterized by its foreignness within the filmic system. This image may appear to enter as if from another movie or another scene to interrupt the flow of images, or it inserts a gap of quietude that cannot be assimilated into the film. I call this the *foreign taboo* to indicate that it marks the eruption of "elsewhere" into the film's topography. Textually, it presents the viewer with an image that is readable in itself while disrupting the unity of the scene in which it is incorporated. It is a part of a film that, delinked from its total assemblage, cannot be accounted for within the filmic unity. Thus, it too commemorates the place of a (textual) body that has been cast out of the frame of vision.

This chapter traces the development of these three kinds of taboo images through Franju's body of work. Because they often appear together in a single image, this development does not follow a chronological trajectory. Instead, I will trace the paths of social and textual encryption, starting with Franju's depiction of the city as a topography of internal exclusion (focusing on the figural taboo), then tracking down his use of generic textual forms to embed taboos within conventional images (revealing a foreign taboo), and finally opening the crypt onto a historically embedded loss (which is the site of an unwatchable taboo and of a hesitation constitutive of the foreign taboo). This move from topographic crypts to historical encryptions emphasizes the proliferation of the unseen across multiple experiences of social life in France after the war. For, while the crypt-image harkens back to those bodies vanished by the war, it also points to a new condition of invisibility that emerged partially as a response to these historical horrors and partially as the consequence of a new visual culture tied to global capital. In his essay "Postscript on the Societies of Control," Gilles Deleuze posits a "generalized crisis in relation to all the environments of enclosure."[7] He argues that there has been a historical break in the disciplinary societies Foucault described that were characterized by the seriality of environments of enclosure: prison, hospital, factory, school, family. These enclosures enter into crisis when the new flows of global capital and the needs of flexible labor that come along with it create a "variable geometry" of social relations that can no longer be enclosed within a definite boundary or reconciled into a single state of affairs. This gives rise to a new social order characterized by a more flexible system of circulation and a new organizational model, what Deleuze terms the societies of control. Here, the role of disciplinary institutions of enclosures gives way to networks of externalized control based on self-monitoring feedback loops. Franju's films are prescient in capturing the early emergence of this new biopolitical situation and showing how it entails a transformation in the relationship between the visible and the nonvisible. Part of the function of the enclosure was to keep the disciplined bodies within a space that blocked sight, situating them outside of social visibility. The crypt-image is the avatar of a new situation that involves, instead, the proliferation of the unseen *within* the visible frame, an indetermination of the visible and the nonvisible. No longer marked off in a separate region or extravisual zone (an "off-screen"), the unseen becomes the first, and absent, term of a substitutional series of images that both repeat and obscure its absence. Thus, for Franju, the unseen, the taboo body, corrupts the entire visual field, becoming the condition of visibility itself.

The White Mask

Before taking up the forms of the taboo, I turn to Franju's second and best-known feature film, *Eyes without a Face* (*Les yeux sans visage*, 1960), to bring out the unique properties of the crypt-image, since it is only from within this image that the taboo body can be staged. The crypt-image is an image of misdirection and containment; it blocks sight. Thus, the crypt-image designates another, absent image not through a metaphorical substitution or an off-screen space but as a spatial incorporation. *Eyes* reveals this structure as a figural, corporeal situation: the external inclusion of the dead within the body of a (still) living girl who is kept out of sight. The film is best known by the haunting figure of a young woman, Christiane (Edith Scob), dressed in white, her face covered by a smooth, white plaster mask reminiscent of a burial shroud. This image circulates to this day in the film's promotional materials, DVD covers, and in the memories of spectators. As an instance of figural erasure, it can serve as the paradigmatic instance of a crypt-image: an image that deflects sight in order to hide another image. For the mask not only defigures Christiane's face, but it also covers up a previous facial disfigurement caused by her father in a horrible car accident before the film's opening scene. The white mask preserves the original violent scene in the past while erasing its scars for the present; it testifies to a "utopian wish that the memory of the affliction had never existed or, on a deeper level, that the affliction had had nothing to inflict."[8] Abraham and Torok's formula for the fantasy of incorporation foregrounds the unique temporality of a situation in which a loss in the past is erased by being preserved as a present absence. This temporality proper to the crypt-image structures much of the film's narrative logic.

At the time of the film's release, this cryptic image was also evocative of the French state's official erasure of the horrors of torture in Algeria. *Eyes* was released in France in the same year that the government banned from exhibition Jean-Luc Godard's *Le petit soldat* for, among other things, depictions of torture and explicit reference to the Algerian struggle for independence.[9]

Franju's film, like Godard's, depicts scenes of clandestine institutionalized violence reminiscent of acts of torture that were rising to general consciousness through reports of the conduct of French forces during the Algerian revolution. These scenes bore a double taboo, for they cast light on acts of Nazi medical experimentation, reinscribing the historical silence surrounding French collaboration during World War II. Franju, however, avoided Godard's fate by inserting his violent images into the context of a horror film rather than a political thriller. Franju recounts his experience making the film as a series of subversions or deflections based on what he was not allowed to show: "No sacrilege because of the Spanish market, no nudes because of the Italian market, no blood because of the French market and no martyrized animals because of the English market."[10] Christiane's white mask may thus stand in for a series of visual deflections of bodies that could not be shown, while the missing image of state torture is retrieved only by way of the historical censorship that befell other films at the time.

In the United States, however, the film did not escape the knife. *Eyes* was released to American screens in 1962 in a dubbed version from which the notorious scene of facial removal surgery was excised.[11] Significantly, the film's US exploitation title, *The Horror Chamber of Dr. Faustus*, emphasizes the link, central to the narrative, between horror and a secret chamber, unseen to the outside world. The American distributors seem to display a real intuition that the deletion of on-screen violence matters less than the evocation of the horror chamber as a secret site capable of hiding any number of unseen horrors. The title aligns well with Franju's approach to horror as primarily a structural or even architectural affect. It arises when an interior site, constructed with the express purpose of keeping its interiority secret, opens up and pollutes the exterior in which it is enclosed. In *Eyes*, Franju multiplies these inner spaces to include not only the "horror chamber" itself, an underground lab in which Christiane's father performs horrific skin graft experiments on dogs and young women, but also a family crypt, Christiane's bedroom, and the interior of the doctor's black car. Each of these spaces are sites of horror due to their containment of a taboo body that crosses their interior boundary. They are crypt-images that preserve the scene of horror by excluding it from social visibility behind a veil of a secret.

We are introduced to the black car, one of the film's most enigmatic horror chambers, in the film's opening scene as it snakes its way along a wooded road at night. Adam Lowenstein's description of the scene captures its anxious energy as well as its inscription of the first of numerous taboo-POV shots in the film.

> After the titles end, we join a woman who is driving at night. She appears nervous and apprehensive. A shot from the car's backseat, facing forward toward the driver, implies that the woman may not be alone in the car. And, indeed, she soon adjusts her rearview mirror to reveal a mysterious figure in the backseat.[12]

The mysterious figure turns out to be the corpse of Dr. Génessier's latest victim. After disfiguring his daughter in a car accident, he becomes obsessed with discovering the secrets of facial transplants. To perform these experiments, he has his assistant, Louise, abduct young women from Paris and lure them back to his secret medical chamber. In this scene, Louise is taking the body of a girl, killed during a failed experiment, to dump it in an inky black river cutting through the landscape. The scene, overlaid with a jarringly carnivalesque soundtrack, establishes several elements that will recur throughout the film. First, the "impossible" POV shot of a corpse tears a hole in the order of looks by allowing for the possibility that the looker may not be alive, and thus may not be able to bear an active look. This hole or gap in the vector of points-of-view is fully realized in a later scene in which Christiane hides from her father behind the same car, this time when it is parked at the home. Franju frames Christiane's head behind the rear window in a shot that echoes this opening one. Christiane's look in the later scene bears the gap left by the dead girl in the opening shot, inscribing an identification between the living and the dead women. Second, this opening sequence places the camera, claustrophobically, not only inside the car but also beside the corpse. The car is the first of the inner chambers containing the horror of the proximity (and identity) of the living and the dead.

Franju ironically fetishizes this car throughout the film. It glides noiselessly along the road, framed from a high angle so it looks like the elongated body of a stalking animal, to transport victims to and from their death. This scene, in its attention to the car as a cursed object, introduces a third theme into the film: that of the death-bearing nature of mechanical transport. Kristin Ross has argued that the automobile was *the* modern object around which Paris was rebuilt after the war.[13] As an object it is emblematic of a new modernity of smooth surfaces that, like the white mask, reflect and refract the historical gaze. Later in the film, however, Franju reminds us that the car also displaces the train, an earlier form of transport that carries the indelible shadows of Europe's traumatic past. Driving in the same car to Génessier's rural estate with Edna Grüber, a young student from Paris who thinks she is going to see an apartment for rent, Louise stops suddenly at a train crossing. As the train cuts violently across the landscape in front of the car, filling the frame with white smoke, Edna stiffens with sudden horror, mimicking rigor mortis. In this identification with her own corpse, Edna seems to be responding to the image of the train that took nameless and forgotten victims from Paris to their death in the Nazi gas chambers. At the estate, Edna will be administered chloroform before being tied down for the doctor's experiments.

We see here another of the properties of the crypt-image: its temporalization of a traumatic scene that is excluded from sight by way of an identificatory affect.[14] In this scene, the stiff horror of death encrypts the vanished victims of French collaboration *within* the modern topography of *Eyes* but *outside* of the film's narrative order. The historical silence erected around the acts of collaboration is displaced from the story but entombed in the image. This temporalization of history functions not by connecting different historical traumas to establish a metaphoric chain of horror, but instead by isolating the taboo body from within the figural and narrative frame. The crypt is the petrification of time, the isolation of an unmournable body as a fetish object just before its loss or death, such that it continues to live in suspended animation in a secret chamber of the self. Franju uses a similar formal strategy to extend the chain of substitutional crypt-images of mechanical transport during a later scene of nighttime burial. In this scene, Dr. Génessier and Louise bring a body to the family crypt in secret in order to bury it in the tomb bearing Christiane's name, where it will escape discovery. Franju plays up the generic markers of the gothic horror: an unlit cemetery at night, a young woman's frail body draped in white, a mad scientist working alone to probe the limits of nature and the law, and the sense of the untimeliness of the scene. While set in postwar France, then, this burial bears the hallmarks of an atavistic scene. The scene is interrupted, however, by a sudden and unexplained shot of a jet airplane passing overhead.

This shot is surprising as much for its peculiar framing as for its unaccounted disruption of the figural and narrative unity of the scene: Franju frames the airplane from below, a sudden cutaway within the act of burial, emphasizing its gleaming underbelly like an ancient monster floating among the stars. Further adding to the disorientation, this shot enacts a sensual confusion between the audio and visual bands of the film as the silence of this misfit image "answers to" the deafness of the visual: below, Louise has retreated outside of the crypt and is stopping her ears with her hands to cover up the rhythmic sound of Génessier's pickax. The misfit image is highlighted through this leap across the cinematic bands; it is as if the sound of the burial became so intolerable that it produced a tear in the visual field from which the airplane emerged as the silent image of an unbearable materiality against which Louise could, without acting against her master, stop her ear. Fused completely to Louise's point of view, dissociated from the surrounding milieu, and expressing by other means the terror of false burial echoing on the soundtrack, the airplane is both a real object and a hallucination, an external thing and an internal fantasy. The silent image entombs Louise's anxiety while again establishing a connection between a corpse in the fiction and the anxiety of modern transport bearing unseen bodies. The phantasmatic airplane, at once more real than the obviously generic markers of the scene and an intrusive hallucination caught within the circuit of Louise's affective panic, completes the series of mechanical crypt-images that cut through the topographies of internal exclusion in the film. Carrying the bodies of the vanished dead in its hull, the airplane links the clandestine burial of the girl and the gothic crypt in which it is hidden to the technologies of silence and death that run through the film.

Whereas the various forms of transport contain corpses that have no proper place in the narrative, either because they embody a not-seeing or because they are the unseen corpses of history, the family crypt is a site of false burial that structures a substitution of bodies within the fiction. Although bearing Christiane's name, the family crypt entombs the bodies who die in her place, die so that she may continue to live and—eventually—regain her face and return to proper social visibility. This entombment of false bodies sets up a series of cryptic displacements as Christiane is forced to live on through the fiction of her own death. One of the film's strangest scenes occurs after the police uncover the bodies of one of Dr. Génessier's victims from the river. To cover up his crime, Génessier (mis)identifies the corpse as that of his still living child and buries her body in the family plot, in his daughter's grave. At the funeral, as well-wishers offer their condolences, his acts of mimicked mourning condemn Christiane to become a phantom, haunting the family estate. "I have to come back to life for others," she tells Louise in despair before begging for her own death. To come back to life for others and for her father's pleasure means that Christiane has to return as a still-living, silent corpse in (the) place of her father's original crime; she must return as the object of his false mourning and as the image of his desire to erase his own past. This cryptic demand placed on the child by her cryptophoric father transforms her into a taboo body, an image of a loss buried in her father's cryptic wish to erase his crime of corporeal disfiguration. But also, and at the same time, she must come back to life for those interred in her grave, come back to life to repeat the crime of unmarked burial, come back to life to cover-up for her own un-death. In each case, she returns to life *from the living*. She lives, an inside-out phantom, only insofar as she can occupy the place of those who have died.

As the crypt fills with bodies of abducted victims who are denied their proper mourning, Christiane's name becomes a taboo word, a word tied to a scene of unspeakable loss that is kept secret and passed only in silence within the family home. Marked with her own dead name, her white mask represents a covert form of identification between her and the dead girls. In "Mourning and Melancholia," Freud provides the metapsychological formula of the melancholic: "the ego in the guise of the object."[15] This means that, in cases of unworkable grief, the bereaved transform their very "self" into a lost object of eternal mourning. For the cryptophores who preserves their desire for the lost object by denying that a loss has ever taken place, however, a new formula is necessary, one that allows the lost object to continue to live through a secret identification with the living. Abraham and Torok differentiate the crypt from melancholia—which Freud defines as a mourning for a lost part of the self—by emphasizing that in the crypt it is the object that "carries the ego as its mask. . . . The mechanism consists of exchanging one's own identity for a fantasmic identification with the 'life'—beyond the grave—of an object of love, lost as a result of some metapsychological traumatism."[16] A living identification with the dead allows the dead to appear in the guise or facade of the living. This situation describes perfectly Christiane's conundrum of wearing the death mask that belongs to faces of nameless girls buried by her father in her tomb. Only in this way can the dead live on beyond the grave ("looking in the mirror," says Christiane, "is seeing someone who comes from the beyond") in order to wash the father's hands of his crimes.

Through this series of crimes and the substitution of women's bodies, the film hints at a pretextual scene that will never be named. By transforming Christiane into a crypt-image of a taboo body, a corpse buried within herself, Génessier may be mimicking an earlier scene of consummated desire, a scene that must truly be excluded not just from the film (as the car accident has been) but from the fiction. A secret buried within the exteriority of the fiction, wholly fictitious and outside the family plot, this scene can only be a fantasy of analysis, an invention of the hermeneutic procedure. It suggests a child conceived in incest and dead in the mother's womb. In spite of the phantasmatic nature of this scene, it would account for the father's intense desire to return his daughter's face to an original wholeness, intact in spite of his violent drive, as well as for Christiane's feeling that she bears within herself the victims of her father's crimes. I will not insist on the truth of this intuition. As a pretext to a fiction, it is of course no more or less fictitious than the original film.[17] The value of this scene cannot, in any case, be sought in the truth of a fiction.[18] I invoke it only to emphasize the nature of a cryptic text as a lure of interpretation, the site of an unfinished chain of figural displacements demanding a dialogic intervention. The crypt-image testifies to the presence of an absent body (a series of absent bodies) that, unmournable, is truly excluded from the figural economy of images.

How should we understand this new condition of visibility as the barrier of the unseen and unshowable? As a theory of readability, Abraham and Torok's work begins at moments in the clinical dynamic when speech is blocked. They posit that in these cases silence is not merely the absence of speech or even an act of resistance, but a real object for analysis. Under these conditions, silence designates the speech of a taboo word, a word that was the condition for, or deeply imbricated in, an earlier trauma. The taboo word is replaced by an entire lexicon of other words and actions that allow the cryptophore to speak it in silence, to repeat it through lexical, sonorous, or visual substitutions while rigorously avoiding the pathways that lead from the word to the original scene of trauma. The cryptonym names the verbarium or body of words that hide the taboo word. Cryptonyms, they posit, are created to take the place, and maintain the absence, of a silent, unspeakable word. The crypt-image, as I have been developing it in the analysis of *Eyes without a Face*, defigures a taboo image by erasing a corporeal disfiguration and shrouding it in an image of visual deflection. This is the role of the white mask, the black car, the family home, the crypt, and other images that enclose a taboo body. Under these conditions, the film at once shows too much and withholds everything from sight. The seeming excess of corporeal cruelty and bodily horror masks an image in which there is nothing to see: an absent-face covered by a mask or glimpsed in an out-of-focus shot.

The analytic task is precarious: to discover, invent, or produce a missing body that completes the film, fills the gaps in the image. But where should we look? Genre and the family plot provides one answer. Franju's reliance on the melodramatic tropes of the gothic horror film urges us to seek an original crime within the monstrous form of Génessier and to discover in his overriding desire to make his daughter *whole* the acting-out of a shameful but consummated desire. While this new scene of incest may complete the fiction, it leaves unexplained the historical resonances that return time and again in the critical literature on the film. Traditionally, cinematic psychoanalysis has taken the text, the author, or even the spectator as its object. In such a situation, the task is simply to decode the manifest images, to discover the latent content to which they allude, and to substitute an unseen (truthful) image for the visible (false) one. In the absence of an unconscious latent field, however, the verification of the truth of analysis cannot come from within the text, since a text offers no resistance to the speech of the analyst. In such cases, we may turn our attention to the critical discourse, and to what is unsayable within it, trusting this intuition of the other scene. To do so, I leave the family plot and turn instead to the scene of social history, specifically to the cinematic (re)mapping of Paris after World War II. This shifts our attention from the crypt-image and the taboo of defiguration to the topography of encryption and the spatial exclusion of an unwatchable taboo.

The Crypt-City

A decade before he portrayed the French countryside as a graveyard haunted by the bodies of vanished and unmourned women in *Eyes without a Face*, Franju directed a documentary in which he showed that the city of Paris was built around its own cryptic interior.[19] Emerging from the shadows of World War II, *Hôtel des Invalides* (1951) is a portrait of a city as a memorial for forgetting. Henry Rousso describes how the shock experienced by the French when the first trainloads of camp survivors returned to Paris after the war quickly led to the erasure of these scenes from official French life: "Spectators at the earliest French parades had glimpsed the striped pajamas worn by deportees, but these were soon banished from official commemorations. The return of victims from the Nazi concentration camps was the event most quickly effaced from memory."[20] Although spared the physical destruction that scarred so many European cities after World War II, traces of occupation and collaboration cut through the streets of the capital city in silence. The process of urban renewal that was about to begin not only retrofitted the urban environment to the new flows of global capital but also remade urban space with the clean surfaces of a modern architecture untouched by history. M. Christine Boyer calls this new urban topography "The City of Spectacle." She writes of the postwar period in Paris:

> Redevelopment projects . . . taking place in historic centers soon revealed a new paradox: the look of the traditional city with its vernacular styles of architecture, the fabric of its enclosed squares and picturesque streets, its civic and ecclesiastical monuments suddenly appeared to contrast sharply with the representational insertions of

open spaces and cool abstractions appearing in the reconstructed city of modernism.²¹

In Franju's documentaries, this uneasy proximity of two different time periods and architectural styles appears as the enclosure of the city's history within an unmappable space that thwarts direct access to this forgotten history. As Kristin Ross argues, this process turned Paris into an incompossible image containing, without contradiction, chronotopes of destruction and of (re)construction.²² Commenting on the mobility demanded by the postwar economic order, a mobility both actualized and fetishized by the cult of the automobile, Ross writes that it caused a revolution that "saw the dismantling of all earlier spatial arrangements, the virtual end of the historic city, in a physical and social restructuring that matched the transformations of a hundred years earlier. Parisians of the 1960s . . . saw with their own eyes and lived one Paris intersecting and colliding with another in the process of demolition and reconstruction."²³ By the time of the New Wave, this modernization becomes a major theme of French cinema, Godard's *Two or Three Things I Know about Her* (*2 ou 3 choses que je sais d'elle*, 1966) being only the most explicit critique of its emerging dislocations.²⁴

Franju's early documentaries, predating this period by a decade, testify to the moment of forgetting and burial that preceded and cleared the ground for the historical reconstruction Ross discusses. His documentaries of the late 1940s and early 1950s reveal topographies of entombment and death, condemned sites of a metropolis of forgetting that will soon be encrypted within the new city of circulation and gleaming facades. *Hôtel des Invalides* locates the monumentalization of war at the center of a surreal milieu composed of visual and auditory scraps of a broken image. Franju depicts these cryptic spaces of death as visible occlusions within the city. Hidden behind an official image of the orderly and reanimated metropolis and closed off beyond a series of gates that join them to the surrounding space, the dead zones are also institutions for the deflection of sight and the erasure of the bodies of the historical dead. These are crypt-images enclosing the topographical taboo of an unbearable image, an image whose excess of horror inscribes a spectatorial nonlook within the frame.

The films pose the problem of impossible mourning as a visual and topographic situation inherent in the urban architecture. Although I evoke the psychic topography of the crypt to describe the crypt-city as a place in which the unmourned bodies of the vanished dead are buried without ritual, the crypt here takes on new meanings not available to it in the psychoanalytic discourse. For Abraham and Torok, the crypt is a foreign structure in Freud's psychic topography, "a kind of artificial unconscious, lodged in the very midst of the ego."[25] The crypt stands out as much for its status as a false or artificial unconscious as for its noninclusion as an interior exteriority. This artificiality is evident in the complex poetic devices the cryptophore employs to ensure that the taboo word never follows its ordinary path toward the traumatic scene. Cryptophoric language lures the analytic ear away from the buried scene by staging artificial scenarios that mimic the work of repression.[26] When mapped onto the city, as it is in Franju's films, the crypt functions as an institutional force of silence within the history of social space. This silence is commemorated using an architectural artifice that blocks the natural paths that lead into the excluded city center. In one sense, Franju literalizes the cryptic metaphor, revealing that within social space the crypt takes on the full architectural and topographic dimensions inherent in Abraham and Torok's vocabulary. At the same time, Franju's films make plain the real continuity between psychic and social experience, showing how the two overlay each other as spatial maps. This cinematic mapping of the cryptic city entails a transformation of the sayable and the unsayable (the *language* of psychoanalysis) into the register of the visible and the invisible (the *look* of the film), a translation that is not without its displacements and deviations.

In a revealing statement quoted by Raymond Durgnat, Franju remarks on the importance of spatial incongruities in his choice of subject matter. "If the Hôtel des Invalides hadn't been situated in Paris," he says, "if the Seine didn't run alongside, I'd never have shot *Hôtel des Invalides*. If the Lorraine steelworks weren't surrounded by wheatfields, I'd never have shot *En Passant la Lorraine*."[27] This should not be taken as a penchant for the pastoral or idyllic scene in Franju's work. Rather, it reveals the incongruity and artificiality of a war museum as part of a capital city, a poisonous factory set within agricultural wheat fields. In each case, the first space is only readable within the map or geography of the second, which grounds and locates the first. However, this location is precisely that of a beyond and outside of the natural order of the milieu. Natural, in this sense, indicates an organic part of the topography, a space or even building that belongs within the active and living rhythms, whether social or environmental, of the place. Both the war museum and the poisonous factory (as well as the hidden lab in *Eyes* and a whole series of other spaces in Franju's films) are institutional formations of death operating, clandestinely, within the living spaces of the city and the field. It is in this nonbelonging, and the regressive history suggested by the allegorical enigma of the urban crypt, that Franju uncovers an artificial vision as a gap in the frame, a hesitation in the hermeneutic quest, and a death drive in the life of the city.

This artificial vision is especially evident in *Hôtel des Invalides*, ostensibly a celebration of the war museum and monument to France's military glory, the Musée de l'Armée, which houses both Napoleon's tomb and the veterans' hospital of the film's title. Like many of his documentaries, *Hôtel* was initiated by a government commission and thus, on the surface, was meant to provide an official image of the museum located within Paris. "I've always tried to make natural locations look artificial," says Franju, and in this documentary the interior of the museum is rendered strange through the codes of the horror film.[28] Although the film is primarily a "guided tour" through the museum—only at the very end are the maimed bodies of the veterans shown during a church service—Franju's camera angles and ironic juxtapositions challenge the landmark's status as a national monument by superimposing it with a second image: what Robin Wood calls a "monument to pain, cruelty, ugliness, [and] death."[29] This second image is not contrasted to the first as a truthful image opposes an official lie, although the recitation of the numbers of the war dead and recreated footage of World War I does suggest such a counterhistory. Instead, it creates a double inscription of the museum of death within the official image of Paris and of the living within the tombs of the dead. These two topographies, at once spatial and psychic, produce the museum as a crypt-image, an artificial image erected as an edifice to a gap in the proper image of Paris.

The documentary begins with an iris out on the museum's dome, around which circle flocks of sparrows and pigeons. A voice-over intones the official history of the monument's founding and construction, followed by a description of its exterior, "guarded by a triumphal battery of 12 cannons." The next few shots of the surrounding walls, the cannons at the perimeter, the visual splendor of the artifice inverted on the watery surface of a pond, the gates seen from outside, and a coat of arms generate a catalog of the monument as a crypt-image. Each of these images relates an exterior barrier or boundary that guards the inner space and turns away the inquisitive camera's eyes. The camera rests for a moment on the fenestration known as "le loup voit" before traveling through the wolf's eyes to show the city's surrounding landmarks, each presented in a clichéd postcard view matched by an equally straightforward and digestible narration: "The Place de la Concorde and the bridges over the Seine. L'arc de Triomphe de l'Étoile. And the tower of the engineer Alexandre Gustave Eiffel which surround the Hôtel des Invalides where are housed those gravely wounded and the illustrious fallen." This short tour places the museum within the official visual discourse of Paris, an image of an image, while transforming Paris into a city weighted down by its past, by monuments to its history that loom, with the gray skies, above its lifeless present.

When the camera finally enters the gates of the museum, it does so by following a group of visitors who each embody a different form of mobility through the halls of the crypt. Through the hallways lined with suits of armor, the camera trails these living visitors—the skipping girl, the limping man, and the gliding lovers—past historical relics and finally to a church service attended by the still-living veterans of war. What stands out is not only a critique of the false face of war but also the figures of the living entombed in the place of the dead, an unnatural burial highlighted by the artifice of the image. Shown in the mirror of an old periscope, a young woman admires her reflection as it is projected, in an organic composite image, into the tableau of busts of (dead) war heroes. Walking past paintings depicting the glories of historical battles, the visitors' shadows, including that of the child and her mother, stretch and ooze against the walls like so many Nosferatus emerging from the twilight of legend.[30] And, going into the old church, an old man shambles through the doors to join the crippled and defaced bodies of the veterans inside, corpses returning to the places they knew in life, repeating the compulsions of the living dead while their medals gleam on their old uniforms in parodic glory. These strange images create a reciprocity and substitution of the living and the dead, as each visitor takes the form of a monster from the grave: the phantom woman in the mirror, the vampire in the shadows, the shambling and lurching zombie. Through the modulations of corporeal mobility, the bodies pass from the condition of the still living to that of the living dead. When the visitors exit the doors of the museum, along the circuit of singing schoolchildren that retraces the flight path of the birds at the beginning of the film, it is as shadows spilling into Paris, as living ghosts emerging to haunt the city.

The architecture of the crypt-city destabilizes the clear distinctions between past and present, living and dead. Crossing the artificial boundary

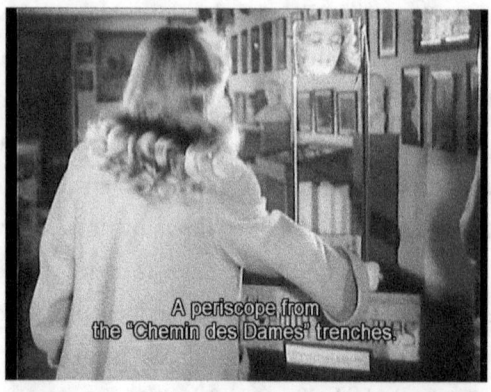

between an official, proper image and an artificial, cursed interior transforms the living into shadows and memorials of the dead. And, similarly to Christiane in *Eyes without a Face*, the identification of the living and the dead allows these shadows of the still living to exit the cryptic enclosure and pollute the space of the city. The significance of this substitution is that the condition of the inside, an interior chamber built just out of sight to house the bodies of the still living, escapes into the outside, distorting it with ghostly refractions of erasure. Exiting from the tomb, the living come back from life, crypt-images with the blank, white faces of the dead. Thus, the figural taboo generates a topographic situation of spatial encryption. A further implication of this situation involves Franju's destabilization of the boundaries of reality and fantasy, realism and fiction. As I have argued, by angling the camera and manipulating the lighting, Franju transforms the real interior space of the museum into one haunted by the fictional monsters of the horror film. We can now ask what role reality has in Franju's elaboration of the taboo image. In their essay "The Topography of Reality," Abraham and Torok argue that in psychoanalysis, reality appears in the patient's life as that which is masked, disguised, and, above all, avoided. "Reality can then be defined as what is rejected, masked, denied precisely as 'reality'; it is that which *is*, all the more so since it must not be known; in short, Reality is defined as a *secret*."[31] Franju's apprenticeship in documentaries is often contrasted with the fantastic form of his later fiction films. This critical break in the oeuvre, however, masks the continuity that Franju imagines between these two modes. The figures of the fantastic reveal the hidden aspect of the real places that are kept secret, avoided, and masked by the fictional image of a city without secrets, a city of memory and commemoration. *Blood of the Beasts* returns to the theme of reality as an image of avoidance while redefining the taboo from a merely topographic space to a historical-spatial one.

The Historical Crypt

No film in Franju's oeuvre is more identified with the horror of a taboo image than *Blood of the Beasts*, a documentary of Paris abattoirs dripping with the blood of animals killed in front of the camera. For many critics, the extreme cruelty of the film's images evokes a metaphorical confrontation with the Holocaust. However, the historical metaphor is encrypted within an image that blocks its full realization and writes the erasure of history within the postwar city. Thus, the historical dead are buried out of sight in the heart of Paris.

So far, I have been considering Franju's use of figural distortions and defigurations to figure the presence of a taboo body within topographies of internal exclusion. While the interior spaces in both *Eyes* and *Hôtel* are designed to keep a secret loss hidden, Franju's use of masks and disfigurations generates a series of corporeal substitutions by which the living appear in place of the dead and the lost object identifies with the still living. In *Blood*, however, the situation seems to be reversed: we are confronted not with an unreadable series of substitute crypt-images hiding a figural taboo, but with a direct vision of the lost object, the taboo body of sacrifice operating in the heart of Paris. Abraham and Torok indicate two ways of detecting a crypt in their patient's words. Sometimes it presents a riddle or enigma where the terms of the solution are missing. This is exemplified by the series of corporeal displacements in *Eyes* that call out, due to a marked incompletion, for the intervention of a scene outside of the fiction, but where the clues to the contents of this scene are never given. At other times, however, the crypt takes the form of absolute visibility, an image in which there is nothing (more) to see. Although this image may, precisely for this reason, be unbearable (be, that is, of the order of the real), it nonetheless insists that here the film is showing everything. The crypt is opened, the taboo body is splayed out for sight, and every critical intervention can only either repeat the obviousness of the seen or construct a capricious reading of another scene. And yet in some cases we cannot escape the intuition that something more needs to be said. This intuition is often strengthened by the presence within a community of listeners or viewers of an enigma deposited by the text. Abraham and Torok, for example, detect an unmarked enigma in Freud's case history of the Wolf Man. When Freud describes a scene of sexual play between the young Wolf Man and his elder sister, he describes this play as a "seduction," a word that, Abraham and Torok point out, is much more appropriate to a scene between an adult and a child than to games taking place between children.[32] This misplaced word, they posit, was spoken by the Wolf Man in the analytic session but remained unheard by Freud, at least as to its real implications of sexual abuse. The shared silence between the Wolf Man and Freud indicates a gap in the analysis born not out of an enigma but from a complete scene that appears to show or say everything but that hides another scene. In such cases, the crypt-image functions as a foreign element, a misplaced or misspoken word, shared by the textual system and by the critical-analytic speech.

Franju's film contains a number of these isolated, misplaced images that stand out precisely for their exteriority in relation to the film as a whole. These shots implicate the viewer in an interpretive labor that is then thwarted by the "obviousness" of the taboo images of real violence and suffering. Adam Lowenstein turns to *Blood of the Beasts* as an example of shock horror that links, through affective juxtaposition, the horror film with historical trauma. For Lowenstein, the mysterious image of a barge framed by Franju to appear as if it is floating on land is notable because of its foreignness and marked displacement within the film's documentary vision.

> Franju composes the frame in such a manner that the barge, like a ghost ship, seems to trace an unnatural path between land and sky, with no water visible. . . . In this sense, I argue that the "barge is more than a barge" because it undermines its own everyday appearance and forces a reckoning with the disturbing experiences which inhabit it almost invisibly: the long shadows of World War II, specifically the German Occupation and the Holocaust.[33]

This shot is further associated with Franju's surrealist "signature," his imposition of his point of view on the naturalness of the scene. As in Abraham and Torok's uncovering of the Wolf Man's speech in the word "seduction" incorporated as a foreign element in Freud's text, here the mysterious shot traces Franju's angle of perception within the "obviousness" of the documentary film. If the barge carries in its tow an unassimilable and unshowable historical trauma, it is because Franju inscribes it out of its proper place (on water) and thus allows it to resonate with an authorial inscription of another scene. The failure of the slaughterhouse to fully figure and make visible the horror of historical violence allows the misfit image to absorb the spectator's anxiety, and this "unreadable" image must now carry the affective burden of the vanished dead.

Nonetheless, we may very well ask what it means to bear witness to historical trauma through an image of a barge floating impossibly on land. For, if this reading evokes a historical taboo, it does so by the sudden and fantastic evocation of a second scene, and thus suggests the very paths of the avoidance of censorship that Franju used to ensure that *Eyes* remained in circulation by not showing the real conditions of violence and torture. Maria Torok has called such an image a fantasy. Here, fantasy does not designate a false or fanciful image, but one that actualizes an affective situation while leaving the real situation that leads to the troubling affect untroubled. A fantasy appears when there is an intrusion of a repressed image that corresponds to an experienced affect. It thus cuts across and displaces content that arises in different regions or locations of the psyche: an unconscious affect intruding on the ego's imaginative stage. In the image of the barge, this shift occurs through a topographic displacement (inside/outside, land/sea), a shift in "tenses" across historical periods, and a shift in "voice" between the documentary and authorial image. As Lowenstein shows, the presence of fantasy indicates more than a movement between cinematic bands, geographic spaces, or filmic tense; it creates an experience of critical-textual synesthesia—even of (textual) derangement—through which sensations and images that are unrepresentable in one experience appear in another.

Both the fantasy and the foreign taboo appear as intrusions into the unity of the ego (or text) in such a way that "even though the ego does participate in this representation . . . it does not recognize itself directly as the active source of fantasy."[34] Textually, we encounter an image that is incomplete without being partial, readable in itself while disrupting the unity and readability of the scene in which it is incorporated. The foreign taboo is a part of the film that, delinked from its total assemblage, cannot be accounted for within the filmic unity. This kind of image demands a hermeneutic intervention from outside ("fantasy is expressive of an attempt at working through a problem and is combined with a desire for collaboration") while figuring an analytic aporia within a fully visible and readable image.[35] The originality of Franju's taboo image emerges from its insertion within a series of real images that it proceeds to derealize or unmoor from the stable anchor of the codes of realism. What is at stake is not an opposition between documentary and fiction but the encryption of an object signifying an anxiety from a scene outside the film. The misfit, the foreign taboo, is a calculated intervention that decomposes the too-visible and knowable film. Thus, it is associated with the work of the death drive, a drive to dissociate meaning and unmake social and psychic order. The foreign taboo is a cinematic object, an image-thing, blocking the continuous flow of images. Like the misfit of Maria Torok's model of the psyche, it is immediately posited as imaginary and as a product of a hallucination or a trick of framing.

When we find this taboo in the very heart of the abattoir and as an interruption of *Blood of the Beasts*' most realistically gruesome images, it takes the form of a muteness, a silence in the charnel house. The shots of animal slaughter create a visual excess in which the spectator's inability to look seems to demand the presence of an image elsewhere. It is as if turning away or masking the eyes with a hand placed over the face revealed a reverse field, a countershot of historical horror. The film's violence is commonly used to link the work of the Parisian abattoirs to the trauma of the Nazi concentration camps; the brutality of the documentary—its agonizing shots of animal suffering—is said to produce a traumatic affect that rhymes with the repressed memory of French collaboration. Siegfried Kracauer's influential reading of *Blood of the Beasts* in *Theory of Film* draws out the redemptive value of this violence. The horror of the image, he claims, allows spectators to indirectly confront historical horror by luring the eye into a scene that would otherwise be too terrible to witness. Kracauer relies for his interpretation on the allegorical story of the Medusa, the monster whose paralyzing gaze could only be confronted and defeated when looked at through the angle of Perseus's reflective shield. Although Perseus used the shield to see, and thus destroy, a real horror, Kracauer suggests that the cinema's projective powers may instead be used to master history through a process akin to introjection: the symbolic inclusion of reality within the ego.[36] The "mirror reflections of horror," argues Kracauer, may thus allow the spectator to "incorporate into his memory the real face of things too dreadful to be beheld in reality."[37] Kracauer's theory of the mirror effect of horror suggests that when spectators are unable to account for their experience of panic—in a film whose content doesn't match the affect that it produces—they turn to history for a more sufficient cause, decentering the text in relation to an absent scene.

Both the metaphoric displacement of the abattoir by the death camps as argued for by Lowenstein and the introjection of horror through the film frame analyzed by Kracauer depend on a hermeneutic model that replaces the manifest text by a latent one that is better able to account for the critical experience the film generates. If the affect of horror, or the surrealist appearance of the barge, is in obvious excess of the banal facts of food production or the realistic framings of the film, then this situation must be accounted for by a second scene to which the affect seems more appropriate. This affective mismatch explains why, for Kracauer, the camera's unflinching gaze in the face of horror demands a supplement in the film's critical reflection. And, indeed, everything is present for the supplemental figures to take shape. Trains convey animals to and from the killing chambers. A wooly traitor leads his fellow sheep to their death to avoid becoming mutton himself. Workers dispassionately attend to the daily labor of mass extermination, seemingly devoid of any moral pangs. Butchered flesh hangs from hooks as, below, beheaded calves kick and shudder their final bodily spasms. And, throughout, Jean Painlevé's narration—suggestive in its evocation of the banality of instrumentalized violence—introduces the tools of the trade (the rush or the reed, the English ax, the pneumatic gun), describes the work-related injuries suffered by the butchers, and recounts the history of the French meat-packing trade. The weight of this evidence leads Adam Lowenstein to conclude his discussion of *Blood of the Beasts* and *Eyes without a Face* by stating that "Franju's films remind us that splatter does not preclude shock horror and that the modern horror film may well be the genre of our time to register most brutally the sediments of historical trauma."[38]

Abraham and Torok warn of the dangers of a speech whose readability appears too clearly to erase the painful work of mourning. A refusal to mourn may at times, they argue, lead a subject to construct a crypt-screen, a secret *in place of a silence*, luring the analytic drive toward completion. In these cases, they warn, "it is as if speech did not refer to any enigma at all, as if it needed no co-symbol."[39] Two things suggest that it may be necessary to treat the metaphoric invocation of the death camps as a crypt-screen and to search, behind it, for a cryptic taboo at the heart of the film. The first is the significance that Franju gives to the topography of the city and its enclosure of the abattoir. Although the place of the slaughterhouses is given, the film approaches them through a series of irrational cuts framed by a surreal invocation of a city of ruins. The series of images does not map a direct route into the crypt, and this spatial disjunction, so important to the film, cannot be accounted for by the historical metaphor. Second is the persistent critical unease in relation to this reading, a continuing sense that something remains *unsaid* in the historical metaphor.

Without invalidating the power of the abattoir to invoke the Nazi death camps, it is important to treat this unease as a true critical intuition and to search for an image that will account for its haunting presence in the speech of the film and its readers.

The unearthing of the historical substrate of Franju's horror images has been contested in various ways, principally by opposing a discourse of "realism" to that of metaphorical poetics. In spite of this contested criticism, the fundamental readability of the film—our ability to transform its images from symptoms of anxiety to the expressive traces of the sayable—remains central to most discussions of the work. Thus, whereas Stefanos Geroulanos, for example, questions the overtly metaphorical reading of history in *Eyes*, he also reads the failed facial transplant as signifying a moment of the historical loss of the ideals of transparent identity and beauty following the bodily disfigurations of the two world wars.[40] The allegorical readings that accrete around *Blood of the Beasts* have also been challenged by the seeming "obviousness" of the images. Jeannette Sloniowski, for example, responds to Raymond Durgnat's and Roy Armes's interpretation of *Blood* as a parable of authority and obedience by arguing that the denotative precision of the text—its clear concern with locating the abattoir in a particular place and time—withholds these larger allegorical significations. "The butchers are not the authorities, but just workers who, as the film is careful to point out, do a difficult, dangerous, and unpleasant job. This is part of the problem raised by the text: it does not give away too much, and because critics always seem to look for some justification for films of this kind, they tend to fall back upon the idea of the moral and political parable."[41] Here, too, then, the charge of "over-reading" is grounded on the self-evident "readability" of the image as denotation of a real situation. In any case, the image speaks, and then some, by inscribing the specular drive into the critical text. It is this readability of the taboo that suggests that we are in the presence of a crypt-image, an image that covers an absent image. At the same time, what we read in response to this absent image is a multiplicity of contradictory voices. Accounting for this critical enigma, and not for the textual metaphor, is the task that cryptonymy takes up.

We can begin by noticing that for Kracauer it is not the shots of cruelty and violence that motivate a historical reading. It is, rather, the presence of what he calls an *unfathomable image*, an image that produces the same effect on him as the films made of Nazi concentration camps. The analogy, then, is not figural but affective, not symbolic but corporeal.

> Puddles of blood spread on the floor while horse and cow are killed methodically; a saw dismembers animal bodies still warm with life; and there is the *unfathomable* shot of the calves' heads being arranged into a rustic pattern which breathes the peace of a geometrical ornament.[42]

Like the foreign taboo of fantasy already analyzed, the unfathomable ornament seems out of place in the abattoir, a breath (of life?) within the instrumentality of death, an aesthetic ornament among the disfigured and dismembered bodies of animals and workers. That its presence seems almost accidental, the chance arrangement of calves' skulls thrown out of the way, only enhances its shimmering strangeness. Are we to understand it as the insistence of beauty, however aleatory, within even the cruelest of scenes? Or as the uncovering of the skeletal figure of death inscribed within all human labor, even that which strives toward beauty?

The image confronts the critic with an aporia, a missing term that cannot be reconstituted from the elements of the film alone. It is in order to account for this aporia, suggests Kracauer, that the critic must search for an *elsewhere* to which the unfathomable image belongs. This image appears in the place where the film has erased its own erasures, excluded its own exclusions, and repressed the act of repression. The taboo image, like the pleasure word, is buried in a crypt, which is to say: outside of the body of the text, in a missing scene. Since it cannot be sought out in the return of the repressed, traditional reconstructions using the tools of displacement or condensations will not suffice to open its secrets.[43] This image indicates a place where part of the signifying chain along which a traditional psychoanalytic procedure follows the windings of the symptom has been blocked. The unfathomable image thus confronts any figuration with the formal limit of its own power to give shape to horrors of the real: a crypt is stumbled on only when it produces a silence in the other. In the case of the Wolf Man, his original silence was inherited from an overheard dialogue between his Russian mother and his English governess, a heated conversation about the danger posed to the family by the little boy's witnessing of a rape between father and daughter. His transformation of the scene into a silent word and its cryptonymic text, however, remained unreadable until Freud himself stuttered, in his written case history, over the *terms* of the seduction of the child by his elder sister—a stutter that revealed (to Abraham and Torok) both the presence of the adult behind the children's play and the repetition of Freud's own silenced seduction theory. Playing the role of third ear attuned to the stutter of the analyst, can we discover an unfathomable crypt not in "Franju's" film, but in Kracauer's verbal reconstitution of the images? It is in the written text that the taboo image appears as a warp in the weave of images, a tension that holds their threads in place while disappearing behind the ornamental figure.

Encountering the unfathomable shot of a peaceful ornament, Kracauer's writing takes an unexpected turn: "In experiencing the rows of calves' heads *or the litter of tortured human bodies in the films made of the Nazi concentration camps*, we redeem horror from its invisibility behind the veils of panic and imagination."[44] What is striking is that, to the extent that the rows of calves' heads afforded a certain geometric peace within the cryptic erasure of figuration (animal bodies flayed open, decapitated, and separated limb from limb, eyes without faces, skin without flesh), the conjunctive itself passes over the noninclusion of the historical image within the documentary. For whereas the ornament inscribes a certain excess of pleasure, an aesthetic surplus within the butchery of bodies stripped of form, the litter of tortured human bodies is meant to evoke the experience of framed horror and panic through which the historical real of Nazi concentration camps is reflected. Far from grounding a historical dialectic that would turn the film into an allegory for the concentration camps, the taboo image *interrupts* the chain of signifiers leading from institutional slaughter to historical slaughter with a necrotic pleasure that dismembers the official discourse of the modern city as the rejuvenation of France following the Holocaust and the occupation. That is, this taboo image, this geometric peace, marks the limit of the official function of the image as the reconstruction of the picture of the city as a crypt-image, an image blocking a visible history of slaughter. Kracauer's aporetic "or" suggests that the abattoir encrypts a buried pleasure in the form of a silent ornament within the innermost tomb of the city. This is a fantasy of analysis, no doubt, but one that speaks to the tension, often repeated in the critical discourse, between the horror of Franju's images and the poetic beauty of their formulation. Ultimately, what Kracauer cannot quite say except in the form of an "or" that brackets history both within and outside Franju's film is that the taboo marks the place of the *erasure* of history by the urban topography of postwar Paris, and with it the erasure of the bodies of history that have been displaced into the innermost memorial of a city without mourning. The cryptic insight of Franju's films maps the city as the order of the noninclusion of images of its past, except when they are interred as unfathomable images of fantasy and desire. The film preserves the silence of history through the cryptic image of an aesthetic breath.

An unfathomable image followed closely by its rhymes, the taboo is this critical hesitation, this palpable uncertainty (in the writing), not between the image and a spectator (the unbearable image and its grounding of a metaphoric displacement) or between an image and the world (the unfilmable image and an absence registered by topographic metonymy) but suspended within an image. On the one hand, the visible crypt-images stand in for another, invisible image covered over by a "most powerful taboo." This is the image of a historical trauma that negates the visibility of bodies: the films of Nazi concentration camps that erase, through their very visual excess and the horror of "turning away," just as much as through their clichés, the bodies of the dead. On the other hand, however, crypt-images make the place that they occupy unreadable except as the site of a critical substitution—from slaughter to concentration camp, from image to written word—that inscribes a corpse within the innermost topographic enclosure of the modern city. The slaughterhouse is not only a space enclosed structurally and figuratively in the center of *Blood of the Beasts*, a deadly parody of the city center as the postwar circulation of exchange and commerce, but is also the site of the displacement of its figuration, the denaturalization of the urban topography. Within the slaughterhouse, a single unfathomable image—visible but unreadable, out of place in the mise-en-scène—both realizes the logic of the realist unveiling of the dead within the city and is the insistence of an encrypted silence in the hermeneutic project.

Without speech, the taboo image is, like the taboo word, always spoken for by another. It is the cipher that opens up the critical discourse while escaping its determination. It is the love-object given to the reader, the analyst, as payment for the speech of analysis; given, but encrypted, entombed within a cryptic text composed of the rhymes of the missing corpses.

The Author and the Mark of History

Franju's films put all interiorities into crisis. The family, the museum, the city, the text, the body: each becomes a topography of cryptic mourning (that is, of a refusal to mourn). Each incorporates a lost object, a taboo body, by casting it in a secret inner recess and guarding it with unreadable images that block sight and divert the eye. Each preserves this loss by cutting off the critical paths connecting the object to a traumatic, pretextual scene. For Abraham and Torok, certain words are expressions of a taboo word that can only be avoided by burying or encrypting it in other words, so it may be spoken in secret, curled up in the tongue and turned around into rhymes that mimic the taboo word's speech. Likewise, Franju's images encrypt a taboo body within a condemned interior grave. When the crypt is opened, it is not with an image of the lost object itself, which is rigorously excluded from sight, but through a series of substitutions that chart a path to a missing, unseen image. The sexual economy of the daughter's body, the border and genre crossings of the war museum, and the aesthetic breath within the slaughterhouse each put a lost body into circulation, opening the crypt toward a missing scene. At the same time, this scene is constantly repudiated and blocked from sight, transformed into a taboo buried within a spectatorial flinch, a conventional shudder, or a hermeneutic aporia.

To describe this situation, I have focused on the topographic order of Franju's work, especially those films focused on institutional critique. I have thus been largely silent about those hagiographic films, remakes of literary and cinematic works or documentaries of famous people, that Franju made throughout his career. These films inscribe the conditions of the crypt within history, as acts of temporal rather than spatial preservation and loss. Among the strangest is *Le Grand Méliès* (1952), an homage to the pioneering filmmaker whose influence Franju considered to be largely forgotten, in spite of his place in the opening chapter of most film history books. In the place of a permeation of an enclosure by everything that it is meant to exclude, here Franju inscribes a historical re-creation within a present-day commemoration, animating the past with the spirits of the present. Paying tribute to Méliès in a sketch of the best-known moments of his life with the cinema, *Grand Méliès* enacts a truly cryptic transgenerational drama through its use of the director's immediate family to both frame and enact his story. The Méliès family plot is the story of history's refusal to mourn the dead patriarch. Incorporated into history as a figure of historical loss, Méliès becomes an object of commemoration. By inserting himself into the story as an heir to the tradition of fantastic cinema, Franju writes his own name within the family crypt of French film history.

The first sequence of *Le Grand Méliès* is narrated by Méliès's granddaughter, seen inside the house where the filmmaker died. His widow portrays herself, silently and spectrally gazing out of the window while his son (who will later play his father) sits at the piano: the living tarrying in the antechamber of the dead. As the scene shifts to the past, the son reenacts his father's life as a stage magician, his first encounter with the Lumière machine, his development of trick cinematography, and his final job as a toy salesman, forgotten to history. The film closes by returning to the frame of the present, as his widow buys flowers to place on his grave. The familial displacement of the magician's body—first as memorial words, ashes in the granddaughter's mouth, and then as the reanimated corpse of the son's body—opens up a generational crypt, turning a family inheritance into an abyssal series of incorporations by which all future bodies are entombed within the body of patrilineal origin. A funerary film entombing a nostalgic hagiography, the images revive the living in the words and actions of the dead patriarch. Truly no longer himself, Méliès appears only as his son's specter, his granddaughter's echo, an absence in his descendant's place. Thus, a narrative and figural gap is incorporated within the family order, suspending the living dead in the still living. The return of the dead is an allegorical and metaphorical structure by which an absent, unspoken history can be revisioned in generic images that lift the veil of historical silence. But in this case, Méliès's living heirs return to life in order to commemorate the erasure of the loss, the refusal to mourn the absence of cinema's origins. The hagiographic film bears all the signs of the cryptic structures I have been analyzing.

I opened this chapter by noting Franju's displacement in relation to film history, his "shadowy presence" as a specter of French cinema.[45] We can now put this problem in its proper historical context. The historical identification of the lost object, the dead filmmaker, with his still-living descendants as imagined in Franju's film can be extended to Franju's cryptic inclusion of film history's past: his authorial name bears the hand of a dead filmmaker.

However, this is not a matter of influence or imitation but of the identification of the dead filmmakers of the past with Franju's signature. A true cryptophore, Franju transformed himself into the grave of film history. This situation appears through the artificiality of the authorial signature and the erasure of the proper name. I have argued that throughout his films Franju reveals the artificial or fictional nature of spatial enclosures incorporating erased bodies. Thus, the white images in Franju's films—the mask, but also the white horse in the abattoir, or the white train smoke that fills the frame, or the white doves that figurally deform Christiane's spectral white body in the final shot of *Eyes*—are images of a literal deflection of sight, where the loss of a name figures the exclusion of unmournable bodies from history. In a different register, the son's body in *Grand Méliès* literally enacts his father's body, bearing the continuity of the family name as a false and doomed inheritance: a transgenerational debt paid by the inclusion of the child as a corpse within the name of the father. At the same time, the figural disembodiment so beloved by Méliès signals the exclusion of the flesh from the place of narrative meaning. And, perhaps, if you will grant me this analytic fantasy of coherence, Georges Franju's place in film history is the material signature of the archive of images whose incorporation within film history signifies both the refusal to mourn the death of the image and the enigma of his proper name, an unmarked grave in the Cinémathèque Française.

Mario Bava, the Phantom-Image, and Transgenerational Debt

> If you asked me to tell you the plot of any given Mario Bava film, I don't think I could.... Why? Because the films are simply too entrancing.
> —Martin Scorsese, introduction to *Mario Bava: All the Colors of the Dark*

> As the curtain falls, only corpses and riddles are left, silent like the night of Elsinore. Having lost all hope of seeing the mystery unraveled, the spectator remains bewildered.
> —Nicolas Abraham, "The Phantom of Hamlet"

The Burned Letter

In one of his rare interviews, published in 1971 in the horror fanzine *Terror Fantastic*, Mario Bava recounts the story of an unread—indeed, it would turn out, of an unreadable—letter he received from the grave:

> Just this morning, I found a letter, still sealed, from a dear friend who has since died, written about 10 years ago. It was like receiving a letter from a dead person. What would you do in my place? I burned it.[1]

Bava's story, like Franju's remark about the scenes of canine euthanasia that he didn't film during the making of *Mon chien*, is intentionally provocative; it draws attention to a missing image and an absent writing. Revealing the existence of this missing document, whose contents are not known even to himself, Bava casts the lure of critical desire by drawing the reader's attention to an unfillable biographical gap in the authorial sign. What horrible secrets does the letter contain, that it must be destroyed before reading? What ghosts from Bava's past does the director wish to bar from ever returning?[2] These questions are even more insistent in light of the plots of some of Bava's most exemplary films. For, especially in the horror films in which he made his most personal mark, Bava frequently stages situations in which the dead return in the form of a secret inheritance that is borne, unknowingly, by those still living. For the psychoanalytically inclined critic, the story of the burned letter evokes the traditional symptomatology of the return of the (authorial) repressed, the mark of a guiding unconscious linking text to signature, fiction to biography. Nor was Bava, notoriously camera shy, overly hesitant to play this public role and to assert, even if in the form of a disavowal, the presence of an unreadable authorial specter haunting his films.[3] Asked if the presence of violence and horror in Italian cinema could be attributed to him, he responds: "Not at all! Maybe they come from my subconscious, but I'm quite a meek guy. Maybe the cinema was an outlet for me, otherwise I would have become another Jack the Ripper."[4] Who can resist paying a small pittance as an entry fee to a screening of Jack the Ripper's unconscious?

And, indeed, generation after generation of spectators and critics return to Bava's films to find there the frisson of a unique vision and personal style that unsettles the creaky clichés of genre filmmaking. It is as if the images themselves were haunted by a mystifying and entrancing eye, and the truth of their enchantment would therefore have to be found in his unique vision and its reflection of the secret depth of his, on the surface, unassuming life.[5] "For many filmmakers," write Alain Silver and James Ursini, "the 'fixed and dead' objects are the conventions of the genre.... That one man working against such limitations could become one of the most striking of genre stylists may seem hard to believe.... The proof... is in the images themselves."[6] And yet, if the proof of Bava's unique vision—honed at the feet of his father, the famous special effects master of early Italian cinema who never tired of sculpting fake corpses in the family's basement—is to be found in Bava's images, the images are in turn the bearers of an absent knowledge. The story of the letter withholds as much as it reveals, insinuating the unreadability and inconclusiveness of the authorial archive. By burning the letter whose story he recounts, Bava announces the document's absence from within the critical scene, a piece of the puzzle that will remain forever unknown to future scholars and fans at precisely that place of a letter to which he draws our attention. The burning of the letter becomes more than an accident of history. It can stand in for a gesture of refusal, a withholding of a secret, that is repeated time and again across Bava's films as well as (and inseparably from) his critical and authorial self-fashioning. Excluded not only from the authorial archive but also from the director's own conscious knowledge, burned before it is read, the letter is a truly unreadable sign, a mark only of its irretrievable absence.

This act should be understood not simply as the refusal to allow the dead to return but also as an alchemical transmutation of a dead letter into a spectral sign, what Abraham and Torok have called a secret or transgenerational phantom. In the previous chapter, I argued that although the crypt is primarily a topographical edifice built into the psyche, it can also appear across generations as children and grandchildren grow up to incorporate and recreate the traumatic scenes of their predecessors. In his horror films, Bava stages the condition of cryptic inheritance as the cause of familial and social haunting. The transgenerational phantom and the cryptonymic secret that it bears should, however, be differentiated from standard accounts of hauntings and secret returns. Traditionally, secrets are understood as pieces of information that are passed on in hushed tones from mouth to ear, withheld from general knowledge but hoarded by a select community of listeners. In contrast to this notion, Abraham and Torok define a secret as a piece of information that is transmitted without any party—neither bearer nor receiver—ever being conscious of its contents. They call this secret and its effects on the psyche a phantom. The phantom is passed on from parents to children without ever being spoken, even by or for the "original" bearer of the traumatic cryptic knowledge. The phantom, in other words, indicates the transgenerational inheritance of the spatial crypt lodged within the ego, the transmission of a cryptic absence from ancestor to descendant. This kind of secret is neither a consciously withheld piece of information nor a bit of repressed knowledge. It is, instead, a gap of nonknowledge, the product of a trauma arising from an unmournable loss, that has been transmitted from generation to generation or within a community of "empty mouths."[7] Abraham puts it thus: "what haunts are not the dead, but the gaps left within us by the secrets of others . . . the phantom that returns to haunt bears witness to the existence of the dead buried within the other."⁸ Unlike most standard accounts of the phantom as a spirit that returns to demand reparations for a repressed historical crime for which the living must answer, Abraham and Torok's phantom haunts the self with the shameful crimes of the other. The existence of a phantom in speech or a text indicates a situation of unresolved mourning in a past generation of which the present is merely an unconscious repetition or beholden puppet.

In this sense, the burned letter is a phantom, a crypt in time that incorporates the past (the words of the dead) as a mute absence within the present (understood both as the psychic life of the filmmaker and the critical and historical narrative). Strictly speaking, the letter's silence could not refer to Bava's psychic life, nor can it reveal the secrets deposited in the films by his unconscious. The letter's silence is the silence of the other, the unnamed friend buried within the generational inheritance of Bava's auteurist archive. It denotes Bava's secret debt to the foreign words of the dead. By burning the letter, he allows us to hear the presence of this other, mute voice within the films. Undoubtedly, this leaves open the possibility that a biographical analysis, if expanded to account for the life of his father Eugenio, would reveal a past trauma that the director's oeuvre conceals. In fact, we know that, due to his innovative special effects work at the birth of Italian cinema, Eugenio was recruited to work in Mussolini's Instituto Nationale LUCE doctoring war footage of fantastic Italian victories on the battlefield. Having learned the secrets of the trade in his father's dark workshop, Bava's own reputation as a master of special effects cinematography is thus linked to the cinematic erasure of a historical crime whose origin remains just outside of his own life story.⁹ Just as crucially, however, as Martin Scorsese's comment in the epigraph of this chapter suggests, the presence of the cinematic phantom in Bava's work clarifies the importance of incoherence and unreadability for the films' spectators. For, I argue, the enigmatic nature of the films is a constitutive aspect of the critical work. It is in this inscription of an unreadable secret that passes from director to image and from image to spectator that a specter comes to haunt the oeuvre of one of Italy's most prolific filmmakers of the postwar period; at the same time, it also inscribes a nescience in the very heart of film history.

In this chapter I argue that Bava's cinema is haunted by a phantom-image, an absent image whose origin is not in the film but that rather originates in a pretextual scene (ultimately, that of postwar Italian history) that has been excluded from the text. Like the transgenerational phantom uncovered by psychoanalysis, the phantom-image is an image that is incorporated within the film but whose secrets belong to another scene. I will look at two paradigmatic films from Bava's early horror work, *Black Sunday* (*La maschera del demonio*, 1960) and *Kill, Baby . . . Kill!* (*Operazione paura*, 1966) to situate Bava's figuration of the return and repetition of a visual and figural absence that signifies a historical secret. In contrast to Franju's cryptic topographies, I will show how Mario Bava develops a temporal and transgenerational image of corporeal encryption. His cinema figures the way in which a crypt is passed on historically in the form of a secret or unseeable image whose recurrence displaces the present, transforming it into a repetition of the past. In Franju's films, what horrified was the paradoxical inclusion of an outside within an interiority in such a way that the very boundaries between the proper and the improper, the internal and the external, ceased to hold. This reflected the topographic transformation of Paris as it was reconstructed to erase the repression of the historical past, encrypting the repression within an interiority whose access roads could no longer be mapped. In Bava's films, horror arises from the preservation of the past image of a social hole within a fractured present. It is history itself that is haunted by what it cannot figure.

The Phantom-Image

Black Sunday, Bava's solo directorial debut, thematizes the historical condition of the phantom as an absence lodged within a transgenerational inheritance. The film opens in seventeenth-century Moldavia on the night of the torture and execution of the vampire-witch Asa at the hands of her brother, the Grand Inquisitor. After condemning Asa to death for the crime of a "monstrous love" committed with her attendant Igor Javutich, the inquisitor orders that the "S" of Satan be branded on the soft flesh of her back and that a heavy iron mask, whose interior is lined with sharp spikes, be driven into her face. At the moment of her impending death, Asa turns to her brother and condemns his lineage with a terrible curse: "My revenge will strike down you and your accursed house, and in the blood of your sons and the sons of their sons I will continue to live immortal." Keeping her promise of generational revenge, Asa returns to life every hundred years by draining the blood from a female descendant who is born in her exact image. In fact, throughout the film the family is haunted more by this visual repetition, the image of a child born with the face and body of the dead witch, than by the return of the dead from the grave. As with *Eyes without a Face*, this is the story of the living who unconsciously identify with the dead and thus adopt the mask of the lost object, except that, for Bava, the generational gap distances the unmourned body from those who live in their ancestor's place. When, two hundred years after the prologue, the young princess Katia, Asa's spitting image, turns eighteen, her father bemoans her fate: "[Katia] is Asa's living image," he ruminates over a glass of hot toddy, "it's as if [Asa] tormented her victims with her own beauty before killing them. And it's this resemblance, this repeating of Asa's vengeance, which terrorizes me." Thus, for Bava, the return of the dead is intimately linked with a visual and figural situation: the recurrence of a female image that carries in itself a dreaded transgenerational curse.

Bava cast British actress Barbara Steele to play the roles of both Asa and Katia, and her dual performance quickly raised her to cult-horror stardom. "One image haunts the history of Italian horror cinema more than any other," writes Patricia MacCormack, "the face of Barbara Steele in *La Maschera del Demonio*."[10] Steele's face, punctured by holes from the cruel iron mask, continues to circulate as an emblem of Bava's film and, indeed, of Italian horror, adorning DVD cases, posters, fan websites, and illustrations in academic books. There is an inherent tension between Steele's image as the driving libidinal-economic force of the film and the critical-historical wish to assert Bava's unique vision as the cause for the film's appeal and continuing importance. Framed by the directorial lens, it is her image as an excess of the visual that haunts the film's reception. This paratextual circulation mirrors

the image's function in the film, where portraits of Asa hang throughout the Vajda estate, including a full-figured nude that serves as a secret door within a passage leading from the family home to the abandoned crypt. Steele's image is the visual threshold leading to the crypt where Asa is buried: a literal crypt-image whose circulation and visual excess guard the tomb of the taboo body. And, as Carol Jenks has shown, the visual repetition of Steele's face in the film transformed her image into a true fetish object, the lure of desire that stood in for the Italian horror film as a whole.[11]

Steele's dual role also allowed Bava to play with a certain indetermination throughout the film between Asa and Katia, as both characters and spectators are sometimes left to wonder which is which. At the end of the film, Asa is destroyed when a cross is pressed to her forehead and her body dissolves into its skeletal remains. As the camera captures a slight, enigmatic smile of triumph on Steele's face, however, we are overcome with a shudder of doubt that perhaps it is Asa who has triumphed and that Katia was accidently killed in her place. In this way, the visual likeness functions as an enigmatic horror unsettling both the family line and the spectator's perceptual grasp of the scene. While functioning as the libidinal lure for both spectators and characters, Steele's image unsettles the look through an indetermination of the living and the dead, the pure and the polluted, the proper and improper sites of desire. Steele's body was thus transformed, as if by witch's curse, into a *machine for reproduction* by which her image continues to circulate, undead, in the imaginary of spectators and critics alike due to its enigmatic and even aporetic presence in an image that exceeds authorial vision.

I emphasize the role of visual reproduction for two reasons. First, because the return of the witch's cursed image explicitly structures a narrative of matrilineal inheritance. By appearing in the witch's image, each new generation inherits a secret identification between women, an auto-reproduction outside the circuit of male sexuality. The curse insinuates the woman's body as an image of its own reproduction and the exclusion of male power. For Jenks, this articulates the image of a noncastrated woman against whom the entire apparatus of patriarchal force is mobilized. "For the horrible—the truly horrible—fact of sexual difference is the repressed knowledge that the mother is the uncastrated, not the site of lack but of too much body.... Asa had so much desire, so much body, that the inquisition ordered its complete disintegration, that it should be consumed to ashes."[12] When, in the film's final scene, the townspeople once again burn Asa's body, the fire spreads to fill the entire screen and her disintegration consumes the text, erasing the body like a dead letter from the past.

At the same time, however, the narrative emphasizes that the cause of this visual reproduction is a cursed or unresolved scene of failed mourning. The witch's death at the hand of her brother and her interment in an unmarked tomb both exclude her from the proper order of reproduction and preserve her image as a death-dealing sight of generational substitution. The prologue stages a scene of historical incorporation of an unmourned body within a family line. This incorporation of a dead body within a family lineage hints at one of the film's central enigmas: the true nature of the crime for which Asa is initially put to death. In the scene, she, along with her serf Igor Javutich, is accused of a crime of "monstrous love." Adding to the inconclusiveness of the scene is an ambiguity as to the relationship between Asa and Igor. Tim Lucas has discovered Italian promotional material from the time of the film's release that describes Javutich not as Asa's serf but as "brother to the witch," a relationship that helps explain the presence of several large portraits of Igor in the Vadja home.[13]

While this original and perhaps incestuous relationship is covered up by the dubbed English soundtrack, its echoes reappear in a scene late in the film when Katia and a young doctor, Andre Gorobec, share a rare romantic hiatus on the grounds of the Vadja estate. Although the romance plot initiated during their unexpected meeting outside of Asa's crypt early in the film is given very little narrative space, its importance in the gothic story is based on the promise that a proper generational descent arising from their union could undo the cursed history of incestuous repetition brought about by Asa's words. As Gorobec tries to convince Katia to leave these haunted grounds with him, however, he is rebuffed by her melancholia. "I feel a sense of terror, a presentiment of death, of being destroyed by something that's inside of me," bemoans the young princess. By situating the curse of death within Katia's body rather than on the surface of the image as her father fears, this scene conjures the specter of a "monstrous" (read: incestuous) pregnancy as the original crime for which Asa was put to death. The body that Asa carried within her would thus return, in secret, to haunt the family line as a reproduction without a future.

The dual sense of female reproduction I argue for here—as subversion of patriarchal authority and as a cryptic inheritance of an unmourned body—is manifest in the figure of the female monster. As Andrea Bini remarks, Bava's originality was to locate the female monster as the source of anxiety within a family line, threatening the patriarchal order from the inside.[14] This new role of the female monster comes into focus by comparing *Black Sunday* to Hammer Studios' *Dracula* films, whose then recent success in the Italian market—generally skeptical of tales of the supernatural—convinced producers to finance Bava's film. In their figurations and their narratives, the *Dracula* films of the time emphasized the seductive power of masculine monstrosity. Linda Williams has argued that in the traditional horror film, not only is male monstrosity seductive, but also women are punished for, and mastered by, their curiosity and their look at the phallic image.

> The monster or the freak's own spectacular appearance holds her originally active, curious look in a trancelike passivity that allows him to master her through *her* look. At the same time, this look momentarily shifts the iconic center of the spectacle away from the woman to the monster.[15]

Bava's generic innovation was not merely to place a female monster at the heart of the horror film and allow her look to dominate the male characters but also to place the look within a series of female views from which the masculine look is excluded or castrated.[16] Just as crucially, however, the origin of this play of female looks is a visual absence that punctuates a hole in the social order. In *Black Sunday* and his other gothic films, Bava constructs a direct link between a visual erasure and a phantom. The effect of this is to provide a visual and figural representation for the death drive, allowing it to appear for itself in a way that eluded Freud in his writings.[17]

The phantom-image in Bava's films is constituted formally through a POV structure that, in some way, obscures its corporeal origin in a character's look while incorporating this absent body within the vector of the gaze. This absence is then *inserted* within a series of looks, where it constitutes a hole and absence in the social field. This absent-presence denotes the place of the missing body as an object of historical encryption within the generational plot of the gothic horror. *Black Sunday* conjures up a phantom-image in its very first scene, the depiction of witch burning already discussed. For much of the sequence, the camera remains at some distance from the witch who occupies the focal center of the shots. At times—such as when Bava switches to close-ups of Asa's flesh as it is being branded or pauses on her heaving body as the fire is lit beneath her feet—the spectator is encouraged to occupy the position of the anonymous townspeople who, encircling the conflagration, revel in the torture. A key series of shots in the middle of this sequence, however, disrupts the camera's social exteriority and salacious pleasure. As the hooded executioner approaches Asa, holding the spiked mask of Satan in front of him, the spectator is momentarily aligned with Asa's terrified gaze as the iron mask is brought toward the camera, its inner spikes threatening to puncture the screen. Just as our vision is filled with the deadly mask, the camera smoothly slips out, as if through the mask's thin eye-slit, and we are again placed at the comfortable distance of the gathered crowd to watch the executioner hammer the mask into the witch's face.

For Carol Jenks, this sequence was at the center of the film's assault on the masculine eye. "If . . . a film whose own hypothetically constructed spectators are male places a woman about to have her eyes put out as the figure to whom they are sutured in the text, there is an obvious point of crisis, an almost literal ravishment. . . . The conventional interpretation would be that it is raising the *spectre* of castration."[18] While recognizing the presence of a specter in this scene, Jenks's analysis displaces it from its proper place (both grammatically and figurally) by aligning it with the threat of castration and the power of the monstrous-feminine to threaten the masculine subject. What is striking in this sequence, however, is not so much the alignment of the camera-eye with the suffering woman (a trope of horror films) or the reassertion of the masculine/social look in the next shot, but the special effect of a seemingly impossible tracking shot that displays Bava's bravura technique as a master cinematographer by eliding the presence of a cut. The shot carries Asa's look into the social field by phantasmatically displacing it from her body and granting it the status of a "special effect." Moreover, the erasure of the cut "misaligns" the spectator from within the woman's gaze, as the spectator no longer occupies either the witch's look (the place of terror and social death) or that of the townspeople (since this look is now haunted by the witch's disembodied vision).

The socially displaced vision thus signifies the place of a woman's body that, in the scene of witch burning, had been excluded from the social field and relegated to the status of social death. This nongaze is both a hole in the textual fabric of the images and the lever of spectatorial displacement and disorientation within the film's narrative and figural economy. From this point on, and throughout the film, Bava will return to this displaced POV shot, this phantom-image, to indicate Asa's spectral presence. Shortly after the prologue, but two centuries after Asa's death, two doctors are on their way to a medical conference when their carriage mysteriously breaks down near the Moldovan crypt where Asa's body lies entombed and largely forgotten. Provoked by the strange sound of the wind playing in the ruins, the doctors enter the underground sepulcher. As the elder Doctor Kruvajan, a skeptical man of science, descends the stairs and looks around the tomb, the camera adopts his curious look and begins to circle slowly around the chamber, picking up details of the ruined crypt and gothic set design. As the camera completes a 360-degree circle, however, Kruvajan unexpectedly *steps into the shot* that had begun as his POV image. Displaced from within the look, Kruvajan is captured by a gaze that is no longer his own, prefiguring his eventual succumbing to the witch's potent spell to "look into these eyes." Announcing the witch's spectral presence in the tomb, the displaced vision also inscribes the doctor's (masculine) scientific incredulity within the undead look, displacing it from its mastery over the scene (of knowledge). And, as in the phantom-image in the prologue, this sequence ultimately displaces the spectatorial look, jarring us out of our complacency and giving the camera a material, haunted force that Bava will continue to exploit to locate the witch as an absent presence. As the camera stalks the halls of the estate (knocking ancient suits of armor to the ground in its passing), trawls the desolate woods kicking up a whistling wind, or snaps into a sudden close-up of a character's terrified face, it manifests this corporeal absence incorporated within a POV structure that slips through and within any definite point of origin. When the doctors exit the tomb, they encounter Katia, Asa's twin image, lit against a gothic background of a moon-filled sky with two large mastiffs at her side. Gorobec, the younger doctor, is held in the spell of her vision, unable to move or speak as she stares gloomily toward the crypt. It is as if Katia were reincarnated by the witch's look, a fantasy that, occupying the place of the absent gaze, is nothing but a fascinating crypt-image that displaces, through a rhyme or pure repetition, the hole in the generational fabric where the woman's body is buried.

Phantom-Image as Absent Point of View

The specificity of the phantom-image comes into focus when compared to two other affiliated images: the ambiguous POV shots of the *cinefantastique* as defined by Mark Nash and the free indirect POV shot analyzed and used by Pier Paolo Pasolini. Both these shots, like the phantom-image, articulate the complexity of POV structures when they are used to account for social relations in which a particular subject position is displaced from any (direct) access to the center of the look (as both subject and object, bearer of the look and image of the gaze). The first touches directly on the genre of the fantastic and thus has a generic relationship to the phantom-image, while the second is developed within an art cinema practice contemporaneous with Bava's work. However, in each case they differ from the phantom-image in that the phantom articulates a historical and transgenerational situation rather than a generic or politico-aesthetic one.

Nash draws on Tzvetan Todorov's discussion of the literary fantastic to argue for an analogous cinematic type: the *cinefantastique*.[19] Like the fantastic, the cinefantastique depends on maintaining a structure of ambiguity in which *both* the possibility of a supernatural and of a natural explanation remain (more or less) equally plausible accounts of strange narrative events. Nash supports his claim with evidence from Dreyer's *Vampyr* (1932), in which the "reality status" of certain narrative events is made ambiguous by an indefinite use of the "pronoun function" of POV shots. Specifically, Nash points to Dreyer's reliance, in key sequences, on POV shots that either have no clear subjective origin or where the looking subject is for some reason an "impossible" source of the look. Crucially for the present comparison with the phantom-image, Nash's key example of an impossible POV is a subjective shot from the position of a corpse. Describing the scene, Nash writes that:

> There is a series of shots in which we see [David] Gray looking out of the coffin, his eyes staring, alternating with shots of what he "sees." The shock of the transition in point of view . . . is increased by the gliding

motion of the camera, so clearly marking the shots as subjective that it is as if all the previous displacements of subjective shots existed to contrast with this matching of seer and seen.[20]

Like the phantom-image, the visual ambiguity at the heart of the cinefantastique can be associated, at least in some cases, with the filmmaker's attempt to present the "look" of the dead. In *Black Sunday*, it is only on the point of death that the camera assumes Asa's subjective POV, a perspective that then haunts the film even in her corporeal absence. Thus, like the image of the cinefantastique, this haunting takes the form of a subjective camera position or movement that, lacking a proper subject, disturbs the order of looking relations as it is commonly articulated in classical narrative film. In both *Vampyr* and *Black Sunday*, the spectator is aligned with a camera that *embodies* an absent or impossible subject.

For Nash, the subjective ambiguity is ultimately resolved through the assertion of authorship. Lacking a stable reference in the film, Nash reads the ambiguous shot as an instance of an authorial discourse, a signature, that disturbs the film's textual realism by embedding the director's absent vision at its origin: "This suggests a theoretical model of the 'art cinema' in which a system of authorial intervention clearly distinguishes the film from the 'transparency' of the classical realist text . . . and facilitates readings in terms of the 'truth' of the authorial subject as origin."[21] This use of authorship as a pretextual sign around which textual enigmas cohere is familiar from Franju's use of surrealist gestures to insert himself within the documentary film. As I have argued, however, in *Black Sunday* the fetish-image of Barbara Steele functions to *de-author*, and in fact to de-authorize, the film. As a machine for self-reproduction, her image wrests the textual center of the frame from the (male) auteur to the (female) look while transgressing the generic categories of the horror films of the time. Undoubtedly, this is partially due to Bava's work in the *filone* cinema, traditionally understood as a generic and thus unauthored cinema (at least in the sense that the young critics of *Cahiers du Cinéma* defined the politics of authorship). Ultimately, however, the de-authoring role of the fetish image is due to its continued reproduction as the bearer of spectatorial desire in contexts that exceed those of Bava's oeuvre. As phantom-image, Steele's body displaces the auteur as much as the spectator from the centrality of the gaze. Where, then, do we locate the origin of the phantom-image? Neither generic nor authorial, the phantom-image is a social disruption; it indicates the place of the woman's exclusion, her social as well as her physical death. This exclusion is buried in the series of crypt-images (the visible body of the woman as witch and her figural return through the family line), but this burial merely incorporates the original unmourned absence and the crime that instigated it. If the image of the woman's body did not serve as a fetishistic lure within the libidinal economy, then the phantasmatic appearance of her incorporeal look would not play the role of an enigma or hole in the text. Thus, unlike the avant-gardist construction of an authorial countercinema in *Vampyr*, the phantom-image emerges directly from the presence of a spectatorial wish or desire that is both articulated by and excluded from *Black Sunday*.

The phantom-image is different from the generic ambiguity of the fantastic film because it exceeds the textual operations of perspective, linking the text directly to a pretextual and an extratextual situation, a "missing scene," and the gap left in the audience by this absence. This transmission of a gap is also useful in differentiating the phantom-image from the free indirect POV shot analyzed by Pier Paolo Pasolini in his now canonical essay on the cinema of poetry.[22] Pasolini uses this figure, which he draws from the literary tradition of free indirect discourse, to argue for the sociological and political valence of the leading edge of postwar European film aesthetics. Like the images analyzed by Nash, the free indirect is defined by a certain displacement of the camera in relation to the looking body. However, the free indirect does not embody the look of an impossible subject, nor is it simply an authorial mark. When Pasolini references the cadaver's POV shot in *Vamypr* (though he does not name the film), he does so only to dismiss it for its formalist extravagance and, by implication, lack of social content. By contrast, the free indirect appears when a director takes up the way of looking proper to a character in the fiction, or, conversely, it occurs when the director's style expresses a character's interior condition.[23] The free indirect POV is thus a "mixed" or impure shot, encompassing at once a directorial and characterological, an objective and a subjective, vision without clearly differentiating the two. As Louis-Georges Schwartz emphasizes in his article on the history of the free indirect, Pasolini focused on the device's manifestation of social antagonisms.[24] The free indirect interrelates two irreconcilable gazes and two antagonistic ways of understanding the world.

> The "gaze" of a peasant, perhaps even of an entire town or region in prehistoric conditions of underdevelopment, embraces another type of reality than the gaze given to that same reality by an educated bourgeois. Not only do the two actually see different sets of things, but even a single thing in itself appears different through the two different "gazes."[25]

By allowing the camera to adopt the way of looking and moving that belongs to a character, the free indirect resolves, at least momentarily and stylistically, the differences between two incompatible ways of seeing the world: that of the peasant and that of the bourgeois. This is, however, a dialectical "resolution" that emphasizes the need for a new world born as a consequence of the conflicts inherent in the different social positions of the present.

As a product of the witch's displaced look, the phantom-image also embodies a gaze that does not belong (fully) either to the character or the director. The phantom-image thus unsettles the boundaries of the objective and subjective poles of the camera in a way reminiscent of art cinema's use of the free indirect. However, the phantom-image does not articulate two contrasting social views, but instead incorporates the absence left over by the social annihilation of a taboo body within the circulation of vision of the social order. By including its own looking subject as a gap within the line of sight, the phantom-image "objectifies" the subjective gaze while manifesting the unseen (that is, subjectively absent) presence of a spectral body. Moreover, since the phantom-image arises from the witch's death, it materializes the presence of a corpse, the living dead, *within* the bourgeois family. Thus, while the free indirect promised a dialectical resolution, at the level of style, to the social conflict made manifest by the unequal economy of the gaze, the phantom-image *incorporates* an erased body *within* the social gaze. The cadaver's gaze (as developed by the cinefantastique) is *encrypted* within the free indirect of art cinema and is given a sociological valence: it rends a social hole within the dialectic of the look.

Narrative Enigmas and the Absent Body

Thus far, I have linked the encryption of the woman's body as phantasmatic point of view to two conditions of *Black Sunday*. First is the tension between the generic codes of horror and the critical desire to retrieve Bava as an Italian auteur to his "proper place" in film history—as the father of special effects cinema. While the horror film privileges the female body as a lure for libidinal vision and commodity circulation, the auteur discourse grants Bava's vision autonomy over the play of the text and transforms the woman's body into a "special effect," an image of Bava's unique prowess as a cinematographer. This tension figures Steele's body as both an image of absolute visuality (a crypt-image) and an erased origin of the camera's place in the scene (a phantom-image). These two poles are fused in the narrative of visual and generational reproduction, as the repetition of Asa's image through witchcraft transgresses the sexual function by transmitting a phantom pregnancy across a line of women who bear the accursed image without having any knowledge of the (primal) scene of conception.[26] This primal scene, it should be stressed, is not a scene Katia or the other women in the family line witnessed, but it is a secret, pretextual scene that Asa took with her to her death.

There is, however, a third condition determining women's absence within the social scene as a cursed secret inheritance: the historical link between witchcraft and the economic transformations in Italy in the early 1960s. As Silvia Federici has demonstrated in her analysis of the transition to capitalism, the witch trials functioned to erase women's resistance to communal dispossession and to place them as bodies of reproduction enclosed within the family. The witch, "the embodiment of a world of female subjects that capitalism had to destroy: the heretic, the healer, the disobedient wife" was disciplined by the horrendous violence of the trials into an image of proper social reproduction.[27] In the 1960s, within the radically different conditions of the "economic miracle" and the transformation of Italy into a global capitalist society, women were facing a similar erasure. Due to the mass displacement of Italians from the agricultural south to the industrial north, many Italians found themselves looking for work in unfamiliar environments. And while southern men were able to get low-wage factory jobs, "the majority of the women who had been registered as active in agriculture before the rural exodus did not find full employment in their new urban environment. Some . . . especially the young and single, did go into the factories of the North; most, however, remained at home, and became officially classed as housewives even if they did part-time or piece-work at home."[28] Moreover, strict antidivorce and antiabortion laws—which Italian feminists were actively challenging at the time—condemned women to their roles within the family in perpetuity. My point is not that the two periods of the transition to capitalism and the economic miracle were the same, but that as massive shifts in modes of production, they both depended on the erasure of women from social spaces and their burial within a family home and as the excluded origin of a generational line. Deborah Willis, in her study of the witch in Italian cinema, notes that the torture and execution of witches is the "'undead' crime of the Renaissance, the past that won't stay buried."[29] It is this historical form of the undead crime, understood as the inheritance of an absent origin as a form of narrative and social disruption, that I argue the phantom-image figures from within the generic text. By metonymically pointing us back to this historical moment, *Black Sunday*'s prologue ties the phantom-image directly to the figure of women's social death within the capitalist order, and it is this social death that is inherited through the witch's curse of consumptive return. In her very image as inherited through the history of the witch trials, a history that is emphasized through the prologue's torture sequence, the witch figures women's bodies as bearers of the violence of social exclusion.[30]

Because it transmits the POV of an absent body, the phantom-image creates a haunting narrative effect on the generic text: that of an irresolvable incoherence. This effect transmits the secret not just as a missing narrative scene but as a gap in knowledge for generations of spectators and critics. In an analysis of the phantom effect in Shakespeare's *Hamlet*, Nicolas Abraham argues that when cultural texts stage cultural phantoms, they do so to exorcise the ghosts of the unconscious by placing them in the cultural realm. This means that a textual phantom is shared by author, text, and reader or spectator. "The state of mind that is provoked [by *Hamlet*'s enigmas] endures long after the play has ended. . . . The tragedy's aim . . . is to spur the public to react unconsciously to the enigmas that remain."[31] Without accepting the notion of textual intent (which seems more appropriate to the dynamics of transference in the clinical situation), Abraham's work suggests that so long as the conditions that gave rise to the phantom are shared by the audience and the film's dynamics, the gaps left by the phantom will continue to resonate with the spectators and address them as an unknown knowledge received from elsewhere. So long as the spectators remain in an ambivalent relationship to the absence of the woman's body, treating it as both a site of pleasure and a mere effect of the authorial/generic system, then the witch's place will remain as the absent body included in the film's POV system, and, so long as this ambivalence responds to the historical condition of women's incorporation as the reproduction of dead labor, then the film's enigmas will continue to elude the viewer's historical grasp.

The critical repetition of narrative and figural incoherence can, at times, betray the presence of a textual phantom. In an epigraph to this chapter, Martin Scorsese speaks of his experience of being entranced by Bava's images in spite of, or even due to, his inability to make sense of the plots. In a recent monograph on *Black Sunday*, Martyn Conterio is even more direct in summing up the mixture of pleasure and exasperation characteristic, for him, of *Black Sunday*:

> Today, whichever version of the film you choose to watch one thing you will note—that carries through regardless—is that it is consistently incoherent, to the point of being utterly bizarre and achieving what can only be read as surrealist gestures. . . . An entire alternative monograph could be written purely on its inconsistencies.[32]

The "inconsistencies" Conterio mentions all center on Asa's body as the bearer of a monstrous secret that is encrypted within the generational structure of the social order that she haunts. These enigmas arise primarily from three unresolved questions in the film's prologue: the precise character of the crime of "monstrous love" for which Asa and Igor have been condemned to death, the real nature of the relationship between Asa and Javutich, and, finally, the figural inconsistency of Asa's character: witch or vampire? The first two enigmas point to the incestuous relationship between Asa and her brother Ivan—a relationship concealed by the English dubbing—and to the secret pregnancy produced by this relationship as the monstrous crime for which the couple is put to death. The efficacy of this pretextual scene resides in its ability to knot together many of the film's loose strands: in addition to the narrative enigmas, it also accounts for the pregnant glances passed in silence between Katia and *her* brother Constantine, as well as for Katia's presentiment of a death arising from within her body. The scene also figures the problem of reproduction as the generation and transmission of the dead, and thus it sets the stage for the historical dialectic of women's entombment within capital. The feminist struggles for the rights of abortion and divorce are also invoked by the secret nonbirth in the scene.

As for the figural enigma, Tim Lucas observes that the confusion of witchcraft and vampirism is, for horror fans, "the film's most obvious fallacy."[33] While Asa is frequently referred to as a vampire, and her need for living human blood to restore her flesh is clearly taken from vampire lore, she is burned as a witch, and her enslavement of men is always at the service of creating a community of women. According to Mario Bava, this confusion is due to his lack of familiarity with the horror film and its established codes. In spite of his important contributions to the genre, Bava always maintained that the shadowy monsters of gothic fiction were unknown to him until he started making films. Moreover, he claimed that the likes of Nosferatu were foreign to Italy's sunny climate, and that as a child his maid tried to frighten him not with ghoulish shadows but with "fables about Sardinian and Sicilian bandits."[34] The vampire's presence, then, would be attributed to the film's producers, who were trying to capitalize on the recent success of Hammer's *Dracula* series in Italy. However, this explanation fails to account for the persistence of the figural enigma in the critical discourse and for the importance of the transgenerational curse to the film's lore. These aspects point to the importance of generic subversion caused by the composite figure of witch and vampire as it both troubles spectatorial expectations and transforms the nature of haunting from that of the curse of male blood to the repetition of a visual image. The film surreptitiously registers this in the difference between Asa's curse, when she promises to feed on the *blood of the sons*, and her actual return through the *flesh of the daughters*. Whereas the traditional gothic tale is based on a curse of origins that pollutes a male line, *Black Sunday* reframes haunting at the incorporation of the dead within a female genealogy. This combines the rupturing power of the vampire with the reproductive circulation of the witch.

Moreover, reading the figural enigma as constituting a vampire-witch, rather than a textual confusion of the two, emphasizes the status of the witch as the bearer of a historical secret. Whereas the male vampire is classically portrayed as a *foreign* presence that invades the proper (European) domestic space from without, the female witch is excluded *from within* the social order.[35] More specifically, the witch was historically accused of using her body and its reproductive potential against the continuity of the social order in which she was incorporated. "By the 17th century," writes Federici, "witches were accused of conspiring to destroy the generative power of humans and animals, of procuring abortions.... The witch-hunt expropriated women from their bodies, which were thus 'liberated' from any impediment preventing them to function as machines for the production of labor."[36] As a compound figure marrying vampire and witch, Asa can be said to be a foreigner excluded within the social body—a taboo image encrypted within, and thus expropriated from, the social world of the film. It is precisely this situation of an interior exclusion encrypted in a generational plot that necessitated the invention of the phantom-image, an incoherent image of an absent body incorporated into and transmitted by a cursed transgenerational look.

This fictional image of the vampire-witch should not be confused with a meaning repressed by or within the text, even though the evidence for its existence is drawn from within the screen(ed) images.[37] Wholly the product of a critical desire, the function of the image is to grant the value of a textual reality to the enigmas that have haunted *Black Sunday*'s spectators since the film's release. Accounting for Asa's expulsion from the social sphere by being placed beyond mourning and for her return in an incestuous likeness in the bodies of her descendants, the missing scene objectifies the absent body at the origin of the phantom-image as the expression of a historical crime: the appropriation of women's power over their reproductive bodies in order to institute the mode of generational inheritance proper to the family within capitalism. Thus, this scene links two historical moments: that of the narrative prologue and the setting of the witch trials, and that of the film's release and the changing roles of women in postwar Italy. By linking the two times, the scene reveals the power of the film's enigma; it haunts the generations of spectators as the historical condition that is buried within the imaginary circulation of postwar Italian cinema.

> The phantom is summoned ... at the opportune moment, when it is recognized that a gap was transmitted to the subject with the result of barring him or her from the specific introjections he or she would seek at present. The presence of the phantom indicates the effects, on the descendants, of something that had inflicted narcissistic injury or even catastrophe on the parents.[38]

If we expand the scope of those afflicted by the phantom from the family line to a community (of critics, spectators, or national subjects), as Abraham suggests in his analysis of *Hamlet*, then we can conjecture that the presence of the phantom manifests the continuing gap left in communities by the presence of the woman's look as the bearer of her own absence.

Kill, Baby . . . Kill! and the Missing Historical Scene

In one of the most memorable shots from 1966's *Kill, Baby . . . Kill!* (*Operazione paura*), Bava extends and complicates the phantom-image that he introduced in *Black Sunday* six years earlier. The shot begins with the camera swinging to and fro near a graveyard, as if possessing the point of view of a child swinging idly on a playground swing. However, this shot is initially not attributed to any character, and only the laughter of a young girl on the soundtrack puts the phantom at/in the scene. As the camera's swaying motion gains force, a girl's shoes, feet, legs, and entire body eventually emerge from the bottom edge of the screen, framed from behind. Like the phantom POV in *Black Sunday*—where the camera initially traced Dr. Kruvajan's inquisitive look within the crypt before catching up with him from behind and including him within his gaze—this shot from *Kill* inscribes the body of the character within her own haunted point of view, incorporating an absence that doubles the body. The phantom appears both inside and outside the image, as subject and object of the camera's look. Released after three years of working outside of his preferred genre, *Kill* was Bava's return to supernatural horror, and it develops many of the themes and imagery that the director had introduced in *Black Sunday*.[39] For many critics, it is the epitome of the Italian gothic horror cycle. Tim Lucas calls it "the purest of Bava's horror films: it was made without American stars and without American International [Pictures] interference, on less than half its allotted budget: it reflects the kind of horror film that could be made, as Bava liked to say, '*solamante in Italia*.'"[40] For Troy Howarth, *Kill, Baby . . . Kill!* is the film that "best evokes the classical mood and style of *Black Sunday*," while managing "a coup that is relatively rare in the genre: [making] the supernatural elements seem wholly credible."[41] And, indeed, while the film's story and atmosphere evoke Bava's directorial debut, it is also characterized by a new relationship to Italian cinema on the one hand and to genre filmmaking on the other.

At the formal level, *Kill, Baby . . . Kill!* develops the phantom-image in several important ways. First, the split between the image track, where the absence of the body is located, and the audio track, where its presence is suggested, introduces a new way of figuring the cinematic phantom. In earlier films, such as *The Whip and the Body* (1963), Bava had already started experimenting with dividing the representation of the body along the seam of the voice. But in those films, the soundtrack was eventually restored to its traditional function when, in the absence of a corresponding image, it designated a hallucination or false image. In *Kill*, the soundtrack at times plays a much more radical role of denoting an absence *within* the image, the encryption of the absent body within the gap opened by the visual representation of the ghost. As Bava repeatedly returns to the child's laughter to indicate the ghost's unseen presence, he de-realizes the phantom and relates it to an off-screen space that is wholly within the visual field. Second, whereas in *Black Sunday* the phantom-image embodied the witch's gaze in her body's absence, here a displaced or unarticulated POV shot is retroactively occupied by the ghost's presence. The image "tremors in place," capturing in one frame both the body and its absence, the look and its missing center or origin. This double vision, in fact, allows the shot to mark the inscription of a double look: that of the dead child *and* of her grieving mother. It thus expresses directly the generational inheritance of loss that is articulated narratively in *Black Sunday*.

The perspective of the dead child, Melissa Graps, and the mourning mother are joined by another pretextual scene: a crime whose repercussions echo through generations. During a night of revelry that the film doesn't show, the girl was trampled to death by horses while the drunk villagers witnessed in stunned inaction. Shamed and fearful of the baroness's anger, the townspeople buried this event in a collective silence. Unable to mourn this death cloaked in communal silence, the Baroness Graps entombs herself in her mansion just outside of town, swearing vengeance on the townspeople. The curse seems to be fulfilled when a series of unexpected suicides, mostly of young women, strikes the town. According to the superstitious townsfolk, this is the work of the ghost of young Melissa Graps. However, the town is haunted by the silence surrounding the original scene as much as by the violence of retribution. To cover up their role in the child's death, the town's inhabitants bury each dead body in silence, under cover of darkness, and retreat to their separate homes.

The impossibility of mourning Melissa due to the secret surrounding her death condemns all the town's dead to secret burial and impossible mourning. To this point, the story can be understood as a straightforward case of communal guilt given form and taking its revenge on those responsible for an unpunished crime. However, we eventually discover that the phantom does not appear either of her own volition or as the manifestation of the villagers' guilt. Rather, she is the manifestation of her mother's inability to mourn her child's death. The mystery of the ghost's origins deepens even further when it is revealed that a young medical student, Monika Shuftan, who mysteriously arrives in town in the film's opening scene, is (without her knowledge) the youngest daughter of the baroness and sister to the phantom. Baroness Graps sent Monika away with her last remaining servants after Melissa's death to protect her from the wrath of her undead sister. Raised outside of Karmingen, Monika never knew of her fate until, discovering her grave in the Graps family crypt, she is forced to recognize her place within a deadly genealogy.

For Bava, the supernatural has always indicated not so much the resolution of the fantastic hesitation between the real and fantasy as the presence of a still-unresolved enigma that cannot be smoothly integrated into the cinematic scene. This is why his early work in gothic horror so clearly demonstrates the power of the cinematic phantom as the bearer of the crypt of the other. When Monika reads her name on the family tomb, she enters a spectral lineage as the bearer of a family secret. Thus, like her sister, Monika is a textual phantom, someone who haunts the grounds of her name. It is this discovery that finally tips, for the spectator, the fantastic into the supernatural and the murder-mystery film into a ghost story. However, rather than resolving the narrative aporias, this generic shift indicates, by way of a fantasy (the same fantasy through which the mother incorporates her daughter's dead body within her desire for revenge) the unresolved enigmas of the daughter's death. For, even at the very end, this inside-out detective film *withholds* both the true events that led to Melissa's death and the reason for Monika's banishment from her mother's home.

At heart, *Kill, Baby . . . Kill!* is a detective story that follows Dr. Paul Eswai—a coroner called in to help solve the string of apparent suicides—as he struggles to uncover the source of the crime in spite of the townspeople's silence. Although ultimately he—and the spectators with him—must abandon his faith in rationality and accept the supernatural cause at the heart of the town's malaise, his devotion to science leads to a number of additional deaths. Most memorably, he forces Nadienne, the innkeeper's daughter, to abandon the treatment of leeches prescribed by the local witch-healer, Ruth. Later that same night, Melissa appears at the inn's window and compels Nadienne to impel herself on a sharp iron stake. The series of narrative dead ends as we follow Eswai's search for a cause to the suicides are set in spaces that evoke the topographic and visual crypt; the streets of the town and the interior spaces of the mansion snake and coil, barring access to the places in which the crimes take place. Ewa Partyka connects the film's impossible, unmappable spaces with Bava's dizzying visuals:

> This consciously concocted illusion of reality leaves the audience in a half-dreamy state of abandon. They forsake the rules governing the world as they know it; they suspend their natural tendency towards disbelief; and become submerged in Bava's baroque, dark-hued realm. Just as the doctor in *Operazione Paura* becomes lost in a maze of staircases, labyrinths, and mirrored rooms, so the observer loses himself completely within these worlds.[42]

Bava uses the combination of narrative incoherence and visual confusion to turn Karmingen into a cryptic space in which all paths wind their way into the Graps family graveyard. The crypt itself is further enclosed within the Graps estate, reachable only by a secret passage first shown in surreal superimposition of the family home and the haunted tomb, a transition that violates spatial coherence and locates the one within the other. While this spatial organization is in many ways an extension of the secret passageways built into the Vadja estate in *Black Sunday*, here the topography of internal exclusion dominates an entire social field, as the whole village is placed both outside of space (an internal exclusion) and beyond time (in a mythical past).

Thus, at every turn, *Kill* frustrates spectatorial mastery over space and story. The strange space of the cryptic *narrative secret* is no more in the film than it is in the spectators who are captured by it, piecing together fragments of a story that do not cohere in the text. Derrida argues that a cryptic discourse is at once sealed and porous, whole and fractured.

Is this strange space hermetically sealed? The fact that one must always answer *yes* and *no* to this question . . . will already have been apparent from the topological structure of the crypt, on its highest level of generality: The crypt can constitute its secret only by means of its division, its fracture. "I" can *save* an inner safe only by putting it inside "myself," *beside(s)* myself, outside.[43]

Narratively and visually *Kill* locates a secret within an inner space that is also the place of spectatorial incorporation, where we are included as the film's exterior gaze, unable to find our ways to the inner chamber or see the original crime. The secret can be articulated only by its relation to an outside that is not wholly foreign, an externality that is included as a gap within the film. It is this gap that I have been calling a pretextual missing scene.

Clues to the shape of this missing scene must be gathered, then, not from the screened images but from those images that *Kill* explicitly expels and marks as other. The crypt is defined by what it excludes, and the other side of Italian genre filmmaking of the 1960s was undoubtedly the critically celebrated art films of the times. Riccardo Freda, Bava's cinematic mentor and the man who introduced the cinema of the fantastic to postwar Italy, was explicit in insisting that genre films were meant as repudiations of art cinema, especially of its basis in neorealism: "Realism in general is the worst possible for of artistic expression. . . . Realism is but a mechanical reproduction of real life."[44] As Carlo Testa points out, Freda drew on Hollywood adventure films, which he claimed were films of the "imagination," to concoct an elixir of simple generic plots mixed with characters that are easily identifiable by their (excessively visible) body types. This formula defines many of Italy's popular films of the period, from the horror film to the sword-and-sandal epic and the spaghetti western. Undoubtedly, Freda's celebration of the fit and visible body placed within simple plots (often set in a mythical past) harbors a nostalgia for the aesthetic qualities of films made under Fascism. Angela Dalle Vacche writes that the peplum, or Italian sword-and-sandal film, "revamps the spectacle of the male body and the passion for antiquity promoted by Fascist historical films like Gallone's *Scipio Africanus*."[45] Likewise, the female body in Freda's films (and those of Bava) tended toward the figure of the operatic diva, full of the theatricality of spectacle and ornament.[46] Thus, Freda uses the body as a historical allegory contrasting the spectacular bodies of genre cinema with the more psychological and interior gestures used in art cinema, the fantastic heroism of the Fascist imaginary with the realist observations of postwar film.

However, the relationship between these two great modes of production—popular genre cinema and the various realisms of art cinema—is not one of simple antagonism. Rick Worland notes that the success of Hammer's gothic films in Italy was a key driving force in the emergence of a robust genre film industry and that this success was the economic base on which the production of more critically celebrated art films depended. Citing the absence of a strong tradition of Italian gothic literature (an observation supported by Bava himself when he says that he had no knowledge of the genre when he started making films), Worland proposes a different explanation for the sudden, and short-lived, prominence of gothic films in Italy: the return of the repressed. "Horror films had been largely prohibited in Fascist Italy even though many American movies were distributed on the peninsula until 1939," he notes, arguing that it was precisely the absence of the supernatural from the Fascist imaginary that made it so appealing to postwar audiences.[47] The gothic film in particular, then, operates as a kind of internal exclusion under Fascism: a crypt in the institutions of cinema.

Angelo Restivo is even more direct in tying art cinema to the popularity of genre films. The two modes, he shows, were not only economically dependent and figurally differentiated. They figured two different audiences and thus two different conceptions of the Italian nation.

> The Italian art cinema of the sixties thrived in part because the Italian film industry as a whole had such a secure economic base. But it would be a mistake, I think, to view the Italian art film *solely* as a differentiated product defining "Italy" for an international elite. . . . The Italian art film of the sixties [also] differentiates itself from the "low art" of the period insofar as it self-consciously addresses itself to a national cinematic tradition: the tradition of neorealism, so crucial to the process of national reconstruction after the war.[48]

While genre filmmaking in Italy arose from a specific rejection of the ambiguous realism of art cinema, the art film tried to lay claim to a national audience by denying the economic and libidinal power of popular filmmaking. To the extent that the 1960s films of Michelangelo Antonioni, Pier Paolo Pasolini, Federico Fellini, and the other art film auteurs remained in dialogue with neorealism—even if by seeming to reject or overcome it—they did so through the problematics of a national cinema. These filmmakers extended cinema's role in the (re)construction of the Italian state from the period of postwar rebuilding to the age of the economic miracle and the massive shifts in population, topography, and media that it brought about. The "low art" films of the time, of which Bava's are key exemplars, were addressed, by contrast, to a provincial or international audience driven primarily by nostalgia for the lost object of the Fascist body (politic) and "essentialist worldviews . . . not yet modernized by the changing international economic structures."[49] In this way they resisted the notion of Italian cinema found in art films on two fronts: by addressing on the one hand a multiplicity of regional audiences and on the other a fully commodified global media circuit. It would be a mistake to understand these films as addressing *only* a desire for a past image. Instead, they put into circulation an image that is at once within and outside of the Italian nation while being foreign to but marketable within global capital. What the theory of cryptonymy makes visible on a historical scale is the way in which the return of a lost object speaks to an encrypted continuity in which the present is unable to introject or make sense of the continuity of the past. The past is then preserved beside(s) and outside the present.

Kill, Baby . . . Kill!'s opening sequence articulates this encryption of history through a muted evocation with Roberto Rossellini's *Germany Year Zero* (1948). Bava's first job in the Italian film industry was as Rossellini's assistant in the 1930s, and in *Kill* he pays his debt to his mentor in a cryptic dialogue. Rossellini's film famously creates an identification with the vision of a child witness to historical horror, a horror whose world he has inherited but of which he cannot make sense. Bava's film begins similarly by showing a young woman's suicide due to her inability to confront the phantoms of the past that seize her. In both films, the young act out the death of an earlier generation without having personally witnessed the crimes of the past. As we watch, the young woman runs in terror from an unseen force, reaches the side of a building half in ruins, and begins to climb up the derelict stairs as if in a daze. Bava then cuts to a sudden and unexpected close-up of her face as she sees, half waking from her sleepwalker's dream, an iron fence below. A quick zoom onto the fence seems to mimic her coming to attention a moment too late, and as she falls, impaling herself on the metal spikes below, a child's shadow can be glimpsed at the top of the ruins. A young girl, giggling, leaves the scene. This sequence recalls, in inverted form, the famous final sequence of Rossellini's *Germany Year Zero* (1948). In the neorealist film, Edmund wanders the ruins of a haunted Berlin after hearing his sister call his name. His sister's voice, and his name wrapped up in it, signifies for Edmund the guilt of the past. Having just murdered his father, the (female) familial voice haunts him like a specter of guilt, a debt that cannot be repaid. This marks his name, in his ears and for the spectators, with the unspeakable crimes of history. Climbing to the top of a ruined building on a set of crumbling stairs, he looks down to the streets below as his father's coffin is carried away. Rossellini then cuts from a shot of the ruins to Edmund's face, and the boy, seemingly compelled by a sinister force of death that lurks over the destroyed city, approaches the edge of the tall building; closing his eyes, he falls to the concrete below.

These two sequences rhyme across the missing body as a signifier of a haunted history. In Rossellini's film, the sister's absence is conveyed by her voice as it reaches to seize hold of young Edmund and fling him to his suicide. In *Kill, Baby . . . Kill!*, Melissa Graps's unmourned absence is manifest through her giggling voice and fleeting shadow, a nonimage that drives a number of young women to suicide. Abraham and Torok offer a very precise definition of a *rhyme* in cryptonymy: it refers to the speech of the taboo word as it moves along lines of visual, audible, or semantic transformations without any direct reference to the hidden *meaning* of the word. These rhymes can take any form, "from perfect rhyme to assonance, from audible to sight rhymes to rhymes by meaning and even rhymes for lack of rhymes like a textbook on poetics."[50] What makes them rhymes, in each case, is that they are transformations of a taboo word whose absence they preserve. Understood as cryptonymic rhymes, these two scenes are united not only by the dramaturgy of the fatalistic gesture or the mise-en-scène of ruin, but also by the absent body of a woman or young girl. This absent body is given "voice" in each scene—by the sister's call and the dead girl's giggle—as the force of an external compulsion that takes hold of and haunts the characters, sealing their fate. In *Germany Year Zero*, this compulsion is explicitly equated with historical loss. Edmund's sister's voice is the haunting echo of a history that has become at once intolerable *and* unmournable, full of unthinkable horrors and yet still living and incapable of passing on. And it is, we gather, the reverberations of this lost familial voice within the historical ruins—more than what little Edmund sees on the street below—that drives him to his final, radical act.

In *Germany Year Zero*, Rossellini transformed neorealism from a cinema of the present tense to one that directly confronts the historical past. This shift in tenses also suggested the commercial limit of neorealism, as the film met with relative commercial and critical failure on its release. According to David Cook, this was due to neorealism's reliance on a historical dialogue that was increasingly being forgotten or even erased. "In the end," he argues, neorealism "proved nontransplantable in alien soil, and the relative failure of *Germani* . . . foreshadowed the larger failure of the neorealist movement to transcend its specific social and historical contexts."[51] Neorealism, in this reading, is a specifically Italian and specifically postwar cinema, and its mode of realism was unable to capture the ghostly shapes of history haunting the German landscape. Hence Cook's complaint that all of the aesthetic "trappings" of neorealism—location shooting, nonprofessional actors, a newsreel or evidentiary quality to the images—could not overcome the "rather contrived story of a young German boy corrupted by Nazism who murders his bedridden father and commits suicide in the wake of the German defeat."[52] If we recognize here a complaint very similar to the one leveled (in a more celebratory tone) toward Mario Bava, this is not because *Germany* is in some sense closer to a genre film than the director's earlier works. Nor do I want to suggest that Bava's films have been misplaced as genre cinema and that they should instead be treated as "accented" art films. To the extent that the division between the *filone* as a mode of inheritance and art cinema as a national practice maintains a critical value, then Bava's own insistence that he worked entirely within generic traditions should be taken seriously. The importance of the rhymes between the two sequences is in the *displacement* of the image, from the ruins of neorealism to the gothic decay of the horror film, and from the voice as marker of a historical absence to the voice as bearer of a cryptic other scene. Rossellini's narrative contrivances are the result of his attempt to use neorealism to document the unfinished fiction of the past and to gesture toward a missing scene that, in the other films in the war trilogy, constituted the films' future, what came *after*: the Italian nation. Bava, inspired by his mentor Riccardo Freda, rejected neorealism for neglecting the imaginary life of the past, the past's inheritance as imaginary fantasy. For him, it was necessary to show history as it appears within the present: as a phantom that occupies an impossible origin of the social relations expressed by a series of POV shots.[53] In this way, Bava directly *staged* the historical phantom, made it an object for the camera and for the spectators.

In such cases, the analyst must create a missing scene able to account for the taboo body contained by and excluded from the rhymes. I have already noted that the reasons given in *Kill* for the absence of the baroness's daughters are not only manifestly insufficient to account for the events of the film but are also themselves shrouded in silence. Why, audiences are compelled to ask, do the townspeople refuse to speak of the night of Melissa's death? This silence would indicate the presence of a secret guilt, a guilt that would be out of keeping with the accidental nature of the death. Perhaps more telling is the silence surrounding Monika's birth and the presence, in the family crypt, of a gravestone bearing her name. This silence is better suited to events involving the baroness's own shame rather than a desire to protect the girl from her undead sister. Further support for this interpretation may be found in the mode of haunting: the baroness turns her dead child into a vehicle for her vengeance, encrypting her child's body as the revenant of the mother's impossible mourning. The rhyme with *Germany*'s narrative of generational guilt appears as more than an homage or reimagining; it brings to light the role of the phantom in *Kill* as the manifestation of the guilt of the older generation passed on in visible form across generations.

While Melissa embodies her mother's vengeance, the film's true specter, I argue, is Monika. Her return reveals that the narrative of Melissa's death contains a second secret, that of Monika's expulsion from the family line. The true cause of this event is never clarified in the film, but it does circulate as a silence. Her birth certificate, which places her as the missing child of the Graps family, is kept in secret by the local burgomaster. Just before the official can reveal this secret document, he dies in the fire that consumes the birth certificate. Thus, Monika's birth and relationship to the ghost takes on the status of an encrypted nonknowledge, much as Bava's burned letter from the past enclosed his own nonknowledge outside of the auteurist text. Both unread and burned, the fire turns the past into a fragment of nonknowledge whose very existence as a gap is destroyed. What would account for the need to erase not only the events of the past but also any indication that the past contains a secret? This arises from a situation in which the denied knowledge points to a scene that must be both preserved and excluded. We can only conjecture a pretextual scene implicating the baroness. The most likely such scene would suggest that the child may have been taken by the servants not to protect her from her sister's vengeance but because she was consummated in an illicit affair. The absence of a father in the narrative suggests that perhaps she is the child of the baroness and the male servant, a violation of the social order that surrounded her birth with shame and drove the baroness to silence. This fictional pretextual scene, hinted at without ever being stated in the film, would account for the appearance of a phantom in the Graps family line. For, while the dead daughter could at least be buried and thus introjected within the ancestral plot, Monika's absence left a gap in the family crypt. Moreover, having been taken by the servants and, presumably, raised as their own, her situation foregrounds the uncertainty and porousness of the aristocratic social system and its dependence on a law of inheritance.

This missing pretextual scene may also account for the silence and mystery surrounding Melissa's death. Tim Lucas offers the following description of the event: "As she rang the bell in the town's church tower for help, the villagers came . . . but not to her rescue, watching her bleed to death—as though astonished that a blue-blood bled red like anyone else."[54] Troy Howarth likewise treats Melissa's death as an accident and then postulates that the baroness's vengeance is a mark of displaced guilt at having let the seven-year-old child wander the streets alone at night.[55] What is clear is that, although the exact scene of death is never shown in the film, it returns to haunt the critical text in the form of a hermeneutic enigma. And, while both Lucas and Howarth accept the official version that its cause was an accident, the villagers' unexplained paralysis as witnesses of a child's agonizing death insinuates a darker event, an unspoken crime of class-motivated murder or even sacrifice, that took place during the night of the dark festival. This violent rage toward the aristocratic child may perhaps have been inflamed by the discovery of the affair between the baroness and her servant. Although just as fictional as the other events, the missing scene of the crime has three benefits for understanding the film. First, it explains the silence on the part of the villagers surrounding the events of that night. Second, it accounts for the phantasmatic presence of a secret from the past whose inheritance defines the community bound together by a historical shame. This phantom staged in the national imaginary marks the condition of a community bound together by a secret that conceals a taboo, lost body. Third, this missing scene makes Monika's secret identification with her mother explicit, as she returns to haunt the crypt of her dead but unmourned sister.

Although fully within the generic traditions of postwar popular cinema, Bava's gothic horror films do not merely rework tropes of the past. With the phantom-image, Bava was able to develop a way of seeing the gaps and absences of history. His films are haunted by the silences that secrete the past into the present and not by the events of the past themselves. Both *Black Sunday* and *Kill, Baby . . . Kill!* propose that these secrets are borne by and within women's bodies. This figures women's bodies as the possessors of a generational power, directly associated with the look, from which they are excluded. Women appear, in Bava's films, as phantoms encrypted within their own vision, as the absent origin of a generational curse. Lesley Caldwell writes that "the *renewal* of Italy was an obsessive concern of the postwar cinematic imaginary, one that was frequently embodied in the role of mother and linked with an association between strong female characters and landscape or place."[56] If women were used as symbols of national renewal within a patriarchal national imaginary centered on reproduction, they were also at the forefront of social and political struggles in the labor market, laws governing the family, and the struggle for full possession of their bodies. Félix Guattari argues that Italy found itself, after the war, in a situation in which two temporalities were superimposed in the present, a situation in which "high-tech industries [were grafted] onto a collective subjectivity, while retaining ties with a sometimes very distant past [of patriarchalism]."[57] The collective subjectivity of postwar Italy, in this model, depended on the encryption of women's roles within the double site of social and reproductive labor. Such a situation requires that women's bodies appear as both the internal ground and excluded image of the national imaginary.

To the extent that the new economy of consumption elevated the economic and social role of the woman's look (through regimes of advertising aimed at women) *and* enforced traditional social structures that incorporated motherhood within a patriarchal family structure, it encrypted the woman's body and look as machines for reproduction. Women's continued social enclosure within the family as bearers of dead reproductive labor is the specter that haunts the narrative coherence of both *Black Sunday* and *Kill, Baby . . . Kill!* If the matriarchs in these films bear the burden of a dead child, they also pass on the history of this cursed labor to future generations in the form of an inherited crime of past generations. The missing textual scenes, I propose, are useful because they fictionalize (that is to say, they stage in cultural terms) the conditions by which an absent, unmournable body is inherited as a transgenerational phantom. However, this encryption also figures a historical inheritance between women, the return of desire as a counterhistory to the patriarchal plot. Thus, on the surface, Maggie Günsberg's observation—"when the films depict female objects of incorporation by female vampires, femininity becomes pitted against femininity"—describes the relationship between Asa and Katia, as well as that between Baroness Graps and her daughters.[58] At the same time, I have been arguing that locating the missing scene, in each case, reveals a secret identification between the younger generation of women and their female ancestors, an identification that, while organized around a lost body, nonetheless imagines the crypt as a transgression of the domestic, patriarchal economy of the woman's body in Italian culture.

Bava's films focus on the lineage of and between women, a lineage haunted by an unmourned body whose point of view both encompasses and excludes the body at the source of the woman's look. What is inherited is this look without a "proper" body or, rather, the spectral form of the body's encryption within its own look. The visual repetition in *Black Sunday* and the dissociation of the voice from the image in *Kill, Baby . . . Kill!* express, on the formal level, the condition of the phantom as an avatar of a "lost" body incorporated within the image but outside of the visible frame. The phantom-image figures, visually, women's internal exclusion within Italian society. Gabriele Schwab also uses the concept of the phantom to explain traumatic collective or communal inheritance. "The collective or communal silencing of violent histories," she writes, "leads to a transgenerational transmission of trauma and the specter of an involuntary repetition of cycles of violence."[59] Schwab is addressing the haunting legacy of communal guilt related to World War II in the German body politic. What Bava's films perform, however, is not so much the repetition of a violent history as the inheritance of structures of social exclusion. While these social exclusions were themselves, of course, accomplished through horrific violence, it is the woman's body as excluded and displaced from herself and from her active look that persists in the phantom-image. This makes the phantom a witness to the history of what cannot be seen, a spectator to an image of nonsight. The phantom does, indeed, bear witness, but it is witness to the dead within the other and, crucially, to itself *as* this lost object encrypted in the tomb of the other.

Anasemic Montage and the Cinematic Interval in Jean-Luc Godard's Late Cinema

> These were unsayable words that he posted in the form of a rebus, making sure to add at the bottom: "You will never guess . . ." to show/hide. Walk around with a rebus and pretend it is undecipherable.
> —Abraham and Torok, *The Wolf Man's Magic Word: A Cryptonymy*

> But look closely at these shots from the Hawks movie. You'll see that it's the same thing twice. That's because the director is incapable of seeing the difference between a man and a woman.
> —Jean-Luc Godard, *Notre musique*

Grave Images

Although Jean-Luc Godard does not make use of the generic figures of gothic horror that are found in the works of Georges Franju and Mario Bava, a similar haunted melancholia pervades his films starting in the 1980s. For Godard, a meditation on his own death is frequently intertwined with an extended eulogy for cinema. This affect has been noted by many critics, who frequently register what Nora Alter, writing about *JLG/JLG—Self Portrait in December* (1994), calls the "pervasive funereal quality" of the audio and visual tracks in Godard's later career.[1] Daniel Morgan suggests that this melancholia is a product of Godard's sense "that cinema as he knew it was coming to an end, that he had outlived it, and that it was no longer the privileged site for artistic innovation."[2] Implied here is that in an age when history, and especially the history of cinema, is increasingly used not to explain the present or commemorate the past but to market DVDs and retrospective exhibitions, cinema would fade from history without being given a proper mourning. Michael Witt is even more explicit in linking Godard's late work to a work of cinematic mourning when he compares the director's films to a "graveyard, peppered with image-tombstones of those [great directors of the past] who have 'died in action.'"[3] As Godard has often argued, the cinematic image is akin to resurrection, a reanimation of the shadows of the past into the vital forms of motion and change. Thus, the tombs of cinema's past in his films are not merely elegies but attempts to bring back to life a history of images that has not found a proper place of burial. This is a truly phantasmatic citational practice that transforms large portions of the films into a crypt for film history.

As I have been arguing throughout this book, the crypt-image is not defined solely by its affective charge, and images of mourning can at times merely mimic an experience of loss that a film refuses to confront. Two additional characteristics of Godard's late work, however, align it with a truly cryptonymic discourse while revealing a profound shift that Godard's work marks in the history of cinematic cryptonymy. First, Godard's crypt-images do not enclose a lost object, but only *other images* that have, in some way, been excluded from their "proper" place in history. At stake is not an image of loss, but the encryption of a lost image within the visual register. Sometimes these lost images are the preserved fragments of a "true history of cinema," the history of artistic innovation that begins with the great directors of the silent era and ends with neorealism.[4] Encrypted within Godard's work—as material fragments of the past—these images mark the place of an unfinished mourning not only for film history but also for Godard's love for the cinema and of his faith in its capacity to project history. At other times, however, Godard's crypts incorporate a truly absent image. These are unfilmed or else buried and unseen images of historical trauma that for Godard are emblematic of the betrayal of cinema's function as witness following its wholesale incorporation into an industrial, commercial style: the cinema of sex and death. This idea appears especially in Godard's insistence that images from inside Nazi death chambers exist but have been repressed from circulation. His films from this period return frequently to this "absent" image of trauma as both ground and horizon of cinema in the modern age.

Central to Godard's discourse is the idea that cinema can act as a spectator to history but that this alone does not ensure that films can see or frame the historical scene. Witnessing is thinkable only in relation to a blindness or absence that cannot be accounted for within the camera's gaze. Whereas Mario Bava's horror films incorporated the condition of the unseeing witness into generic texts of haunting, Godard treats the cinematic apparatus as a haunted confrontation with the role of a historical witness. Christopher Pavsek argues that "what is 'invisible' in Godard is not only that element in the given, visible world which somehow exceeds the grasp of pictures, but is also something which is literally invisible in the real profilmic world.... The lack in the filmic picture is twofold: that of the picture vis-à-vis its object, as well as that of the object vis-à-vis the image and its perceiving subject."[5] The missing image is not an absent image, but an image of what cannot be grasped visually, either because it has no proper place within the visual order, such as the images of film history, or because its taboo nature marks it with the bar of a true repression, such as in the images of historical trauma. Whereas, however, for Pavsek this twofold lack is principally understood as a formal property of the image, I will emphasize that these missing images figure a body whose death cannot be represented and whose fate it is to remain unmournable. Whether an image of cinema's past preserved in a future work or the image of an unfilmed absence incorporated within the frame, Godard encrypts images within images, provoking a critical game of connoisseurship centered on identifying the source of an obscure origin. The missing image, however, is more than the lure of cinephilic desire; it motivates the entire Godardian text, which displaces this fetish image from its "proper" place in film history or the historical document in order to reincorporate it within an auteurist text spanning films, lectures, and biographical fragments.

Another property of Godard's crypt-images is a direct consequence of this setting into play of images within images: the films and Godard's statements concerning them appear as audio-visual and textual aporias, eluding the grasp of interpretation and displacing the critical scene either to the margins of non-communication or into the innermost interiority of the films where the critic piles on more references or citations in a dialogue that cannot be separated from the work. The relatively large amount of critical attention that the films from the 1990s have garnered should not deceive us; in continuously insisting on the limits of interpretation, the critics are often the first to announce the interminable quality of the analysis. In this, we act like Freud as he returns, throughout his life, to the Wolf Man case, appending footnotes to new editions of the case history or including details of his life in masked forms in the metapsychological writings. Each new piece of evidence only added to the mystery surrounding this strange case until the Wolf Man ended up as the uncredited star of Freud's "Analysis Terminable and Interminable."[6] Nora Alter, for example, complains that Godard's work presents the critic with a "rebus" composed of "vague and unilluminating" images.[7] Michael Witt, among the most perceptive readers of Godard's work in this period, chafes at the director's often repeated claim that cinema is dead: "On the face of it, [this is] neither a very clever nor original thing to say. On the contrary, in the context of the diversity and sheer quantity of films currently being made worldwide, such a claim seems *vague, unilluminating* and, frankly, rather silly."[8] Undoubtedly, Witt goes on to use this unilluminating idea to great effect to explain the historiographic qualities of Godard's work, but the textual resistance is not so clearly swept away. The rebus is not simply the mark of a difficulty in reading but the construction of an interpretive lure that resists the critic's speech at every turn. The critical desire to make sense of the films is always tracking the edge of an abyss, a ruin of meaning, bedeviled by a "nagging suspicion that it may all be, in a sense, a sham, that we have gestures of seriousness instead of the genuine article."[9]

The critical anxiety these statements betray is akin to the analyst's position in relation to the Wolf Man's cryptic speech as described by Abraham and Torok in *The Wolf Man's Magic Word*: "These were unsayable words that he posted in the form of a rebus, making sure to add at the bottom: 'You will never guess . . .' to show/hide. Walk around with a rebus and pretend it is undecipherable."[10] The structure of the rebus is that of a crypt within which the cryptophore has incorporated the body of a pleasure that can neither be enjoyed nor grieved. The rebus should be understood not so much as a code standing for the taboo word but as the alliteration of an unfulfilled desire for an unmournable body. The cryptophore's puzzling stratagem is to speak the words of desire in a form that excludes them from the psychic economy of the text. Similarly, the many "gaps" in Godard's texts—the importance his later films give to the interval over the image, and the ways in which these gaps rhyme with a critical anxiety about what is unseeable or unsayable in the films—should be understood not simply as missing images but as monuments to the desire for film to speak, a desire that has been, for some reason, blocked. Unlike Franju and Bava, who figure the gaps in the visual, Godard opens the cinematic crypt and lets the images of the past speak, even if it is only to insert a silence within a flow of "readable" images and a gap of the unseen within the frame of the visible image.

For Godard, what is missing or unseen is not simply what escapes cinematic presence but a body whose death is unfilmable and, at the same time, is the proper internal limit of the film. Godard understands the invisible as a figure of historical loss encrypted within film history and its function as audio-visual witness. In a discussion of the structure of montage in Godard's *Germany Year 90 Nine Zero* (1991), Christopher Pavsek writes that for Godard:

> Montage suggests that what is missing in the picture . . . is not some tangible plasticity beyond the grasp of photographic reproductive technology, but rather something *invisible* in the object itself that can best be understood as a *lack* in the object filmed and which can only be called forth through montage.[11]

Pavsek proceeds to define the image (as opposed to what he calls the "picture") as the invisible face of the world that is revealed through montage. Following from Pavsek's argument, Godard's images relate an unknowable (the invisible in the object) to an unknown (the lack in the image of the object) by way of a relation (the interval) that allows the invisible to resonate within the visual field. In Pavsek's analysis, however, this invisible is simply a constitutive aspect of the world, an obscurity inherent in the object's relation to human perception. What Pavsek doesn't address directly is the relation between the profound sense of failed mourning inherent in Godard's late work and the unknowable, unfilmable face of the world.

Anasemic Montage and the Elsewhere of Failed Mourning

To give shape to this blockage in cinema's ability to bear witness to history, Godard invents a new form of montage in which an image is placed in relation to an unseen origin of signification or to an occluded figure. I call it anasemic montage to align it with Nicolas Abraham's concept of anasemia in which psychoanalytic terms signify not only themselves or their everyday meanings but also another, often seemingly contradictory, signification. Jacques Derrida identifies anasemia as the fundamental method of cryptonymy, arguing that it is an approach to language that consists of "going *back* toward the rightful place and proper meaning" of a word.[12] Abraham writes that certain words may be used in such a way that they encrypt—reference by hiding—their relationship to a previous meaning or even to a whole scene from which they emerged. The term names the property of psychoanalytic language in which words hold together contradictory meanings, one clearly articulated and the other occluded, without negation.[13] Therefore, retrieving a word's proper meaning is not to suggest that language can be traced back to an essential and univocal relationship between signifier and signified. Rather, the "rightful place" of a word designates a situation or scene in which the word had a particular meaning that was then silenced in future use. Abraham calls anasemia a figure of "antisemantics" because the anasemic gesture reveals the ways in which the semantic field of a word is constituted through an exclusion of a particular meaning that is thus kept out of active speech.

Godard's montage practice, developed during his work in the late 1980s and through the 1990s but culminating in a particularly clear way in 2004's *Notre musique*, involves a similar use of montage. Anasemic montage wrests images from their everyday or their position in a filmic chain, relating them instead to a historical scene from which they have been taken but whose significance they hide. Whereas for Abraham anasemia was a function of language and worked on the relation between a symbol and its silences, anasemic montage operates between an image and the historical process that brought it into being. Thus, anasemia becomes a fully historical mode of analysis and not merely a clinical-linguistic one. This also means that the loss to which the interval testifies refers to a particular figure: the unmourned social/historical body that remains unfilmed or excluded from the image.

Before turning to *Notre musique*, in which Godard explicitly works out and describes this montage practice, it will be useful to examine an earlier work in which he explores the limits of his previous method. In *Ici et ailleurs* (*Here and Elsewhere*, 1976) Godard and Anne-Marie Miéville rework and recontextualize footage of the Palestinian struggle—filmed by Godard and Jean-Pierre Gorin—to bring to light the relationship between a scene of impossible historical mourning and the contradictions between the visible and the non-visible in the cinematic image. The original footage was supposed to have been the basis for a movie called *Until Victory* (*Jusqu'à la victoire*), commissioned by Fatah's Information Service Bureau. Based on a model of political filmmaking that had been successful, at least aesthetically, in earlier works such as the omnibus film *Loin du Vietnam* (*Far from Vietnam*, 1967), *Until Victory* would have positioned the European filmmakers as engaged conduits for the circulation of images of revolutionary struggle "elsewhere" while reflecting on their own position vis-à-vis these images.[14] This plan was abandoned when, after filming had concluded, many of the Palestinian fighters were killed in the raids of Black September. Shown discussing the possibility of their own impending death, the revolutionaries haunt the footage like the still-living memories of their future corpses. It was, as in previous films discussed in this book, the living who haunted the dead. Furthermore, the military and political crisis on the ground meant that Godard and Gorin's images no longer adequately spoke to the historical situation, and, having already returned to Paris, they were unable to record the silences and absences left by the dead. As images of their still-living corpses, the Palestinians became unmournable and their (non)presence in the film made the completion of the original work impossible. As Shai Ginsburg asks, in light of the barrage of images and sounds of political struggle captured for the film, how "can the very real death of Palestinians—just one sound bite, one image among a throng of others—be salvaged and grasped for what it is?"[15] The problem Godard and Gorin confronted, however, is even more scandalous than that suggested by Ginsburg (namely, how to give the deaths of the Palestinians their proper weight among all the other images of preparation for conflict and ideological training). For, in the *absence* of images of their death, any attempt to edit together the filmed material in a way that would be consistent with the historical reality would have to account for the place of the missing images of the unmourned bodies—bodies twice erased from history, first through their expulsion and murder and second by being unfigurable in the document of their own struggle. It is in this sense that the unfilmed death of the Palestinian fighters should be understood as an encrypted image relating the visible to a missing scene.

In *Here and Elsewhere*, Godard and Miéville strive to bring out the visual and auditory absences of this historical crypt and thus begin to define a montage practice of cryptic mourning that relates cinema to history. The crypt indicates two distinct losses that *Until Victory* couldn't register: the loss of the revolutionary subject of history and the loss of the cinematic object as a form of direct historical-political engagement, a historical loss and a loss embedded within historical representations. To emphasize the fractured topography of "here and elsewhere" on which history and its representations are inscribed, Godard and Miéville place fragments of the original footage next to newly filmed images of a middle-class French family watching TV, arguing over child care, and other domestic activities. The unmournability of the historical dead "elsewhere" is, in this way, inscribed within a domestic refusal to look symbolized by televisual noise. The interior of the home, where the zombified family gathers around a television set, exemplifies the spaces of postwar Europe in which the failure of political struggle appears as a "corporium" or embodied lexicon of dead images and words.[16] Combining the crypt-cities of internal exclusion documented by Franju and the haunted generational lineages narrated by Bava, the domestic interior of the postwar home is both a here and an elsewhere—an enclosure made possible only by the radical expulsion of the exterior (the colony) from the interior. Kristin Ross has shown how this cryptic language of exchange worked in the 1950s and '60s when "the colonies are in some sense 'replaced,' and the effort that once went into maintaining and disciplining a colonial people and situation becomes instead concentrated on a particular 'level' of metropolitan existence: everyday life."[17] Godard and Miéville's image of 1970s France is one in which this substitution, the incorporation of the colony within the metropole, has enclosed the French family within a space of internal exclusion where all traces of the exterior are relegated to the domesticated flows of television. Whereas Godard and Gorin's original film was to be animated by the search for a political mode of production, *Ici et ailleurs* interrogates the circulation of media within the context of a vanishing social and political horizon. For Godard, cinema is unique because it creates a mode of communal reception. He uses the term *projection* broadly to refer to this quality of shared vision at the heart of the cinematic image. This experience of communal perception, rather than any ontological relation to the profilmic world, produces a truthful image.[18] In *Here and Elsewhere*, the historical fracturing of projection by the domestication of the image in the television set is partially attributed to the presence of an unmourned loss that leaves a gap in the visible field.

This new condition is expressed throughout the film in relation to montage. How, Godard and Miéville ask, can one edit together images of "elsewhere" with images of "here" in a way that brings out what has been lost between these two spaces? To develop this question, they introduce a third series of images consisting mainly of projected slides and isolated frames in which they explore editing as a relation between the seen and the unseen. This series of didactic images works through the problem of image relations necessary to make the absences incorporated both "elsewhere" (the unmourned dead) and "here" (the failure of representation) visible. Whereas the films undertaken with the Dziga Vertov Group use this cryptic mourning to mark what is unseen in the world itself, whether it be the forces of mediated control or the spaces of organizing and resistance, *Ici et ailleurs* reformulates the problem around the image as being, in itself, the site of a loss that can only be recuperated by montage. In order to create a radical form of montage able to express the place of the unmourned dead, Godard invents a de-synced cinema in which fragments of images and sounds are isolated into blocks of material reality that refer to a pretextual scene that cannot be reconstituted by the in-frame image alone. The lost object haunts the images, hovering just below the surface of an audio-visual rebus. To reconstruct the image's relation to reality, to decipher the rebus of material fragments, demands a new, broader and richer approach to montage that refers to an entire poetics of "postprocessing," including multiple exposure, videographic manipulation, and the organization of autonomous image and sound bands in addition to the selection and linear ordering of shots. Montage thus designates any process by which isolated fragments are manipulated in relation to a second image: the figural "monstrosities" born of multiple exposures, the hidden body revealed by slow or fast motion, the auditory unconscious of the visual. Moreover, this new understanding of montage emphasizes the gaps and discontinuities within the frame and between images, rather than the continuity or contextual/intellectual unity by which montage normally operates. As the example of *Here and Elsewhere* demonstrates, however, this is not mere play or formal experimentation for its own sake. To fracture the image is to seek out the taboo kernel of an absent mourning that, installed in the heart of the image, blocks it from a proper historical project(ion). Godard's late cinema tirelessly repeats, reworks, and revises images using an evolving set of tools for postprocessing, such that the films resemble a cryptonymic subject's obsessive process of working on, reforming, and deforming the material signifiers of a real but unfigurable loss.

In *Notre musique*, and in many of the films after *Ici et ailleurs*, Godard de-figures the traditional "grammar" of montage as it operates between and within the frame. Unlike traditional montage, Godard's aim is not to contextualize images within a new series of signification or to give a precinematic image a value within a cinematic text. Instead, he begins by making visible the essentially spectacular nature of all images in contemporary society; the fact that the regime of the image has already passed through the apparatus of ideological framing and projection of which the cinema is just one technological mode. The visible has already become a kind of cinematic, televisual, or virtual errata and thus cannot be simply retrieved from behind the image. Godard then proceeds to convert the cinematic given into a new set of images structured like a database. Each image in the set is related to an absence and erasure at its origin, to that aspect that was lost when it became spectacle. Montage, in Godard's practice, *isolates* rather than connects images, all the while emphasizing that between these newly discrete fragments of visual reality lies an unfilmed (and, in some senses, unfilmable) image coextensive with an unmourned body.

In *Here and Elsewhere*, Godard and Miéville first decouple the Palestinian fighters from the stream of propaganda imagery by repeatedly pointing out that, while the filmmakers speak and the images are spoken about, the Palestinians are either silent or when they do speak it is about their own plans or even their deaths. This allows the Palestinians to appear as bodies that are then related textually to the moment of their deaths and, crucially, to the French filmmakers' failure to have filmed or even really accounted for this death. This produces a complex montage-image in which the bodies of the Palestinians imply the countershot of their absence, both in the film and in France. Godard thus uses montage to undo the common meaning of images within a chain of signification, to unmake the surface "propaganda" of the original footage, and to block the function of montage as the organization of isolated images into a coherent whole, since it always references a missing term. In "Fors," Derrida writes:

> Anasemia reverses the meaning and the meaning of meaning. . . . What has to be found out here is what happens when, beneath the paleonymy of inherited concepts, beneath the same old words, the 'radical semantic change that psychoanalysis introduced into language' comes about. That change is never clear-cut, unequivocal, homogenous. It has to work with all sorts of remnants, precisely because of the identity of old names, . . . It is a kind of theory of errata.[19]

Here and Elsewhere is a film composed of errata, of images that Godard and Gorin had to discard when they could not turn them into a proper document of the Palestinian struggle and the loss of the still-living inherent in this historical oppression. As Miéville and Godard state throughout the film, one of the obstacles to finishing the original was that the filmmakers had not properly understood the nature of the resistance, both of the Palestinian people and of the images they had filmed. While they were able to frame the visual spectacle of resistance (young girls training in calisthenics, a woman reciting a political speech, a soldier giving a speech about the revolution), they had obscured the stubborn *silence* of the image, the silence that points to the deaths incorporated within the political struggle.[20] When this silence erupted into the film through the death of the "actors" during the September Massacre, Godard and Gorin did not have any footage that could express the real loss encrypted within the spectacle of revolution. Returning to this footage to assemble *Ici et ailleurs*, Godard and Miéville use a topographic montage—the relationship between here and elsewhere—to insert a visible gap, a temporal and spatial interval or dissociation, between spaces and temporalities. Like the linguistic anasemia proper to psychoanalysis, Miéville and Godard's anasemic montage undoes the referential and semantic clarity of the images by ripping them from their customary usage and isolating them within an editing structure that foregrounds the image's nonrelation to other images that surround it.[21] Understood in this way, "isolation" is not the absence of relations but the decryption of the image that brings it into a new relation, outside the text, with the obscurity of the unseen. The necessity of placing the footage from the failed film of the Palestinian resistance within the unseeing interiority of the French home reveals the image in its function of erasure, in its visible blockage of the invisible and unfilmed precinematic content, that is, the bodies of the dead revolution(aries).[22]

The Broken Symbol and the Countershot

Godard's montage practice starting with *Ici et ailleurs* organizes three components of a broken symbol: a visible shot, a missing but "projected" countershot, and the interval. A broken symbol is, according to Abraham and Torok, an isolated fragment of a "presymbolic unity whose dissolution occasioned the formation of the Unconscious."[23] In other words, it is a part of speech that has been broken off from an earlier unity—a conversation, a complete thought, an overheard secret—and that is now missing its complement. Like a clay fragment from an archaeological dig, the broken symbol refers back to a lost and materially irretrievable object, and with it to an entire topography and social world buried in the past. Abraham and Torok compare this situation to a jigsaw puzzle where some of the pieces have been lost. "Confronted with such an enigma," they write, "we would have to reconstitute, one by one, most of the fragments as a first step before being able to put them together. Only then could we join these recovered partial components with their hypothetically missing half . . . which has itself been reconstructed in accordance with known rules."[24] There are three components that make up the broken symbol: a fragment of speech that originated in an earlier but now occluded situation, the missing complement or cosymbol that once belonged together with the given fragment but has since been relegated to a cryptic unconscious, and the hypothetical unity that contained the symbolic pair and necessitated their fracture. The shot, the countershot, and the interval similarly organize a relationship between the visual (but always incomplete) frame, the unseen situation from which the visual was broken off, and the principle of unity that relates the given image to its occluded origin.

Although Godard encountered the limits of the image that would lead him to develop a practice of anasemic montage in *Ici et ailleurs*, it was not until the 1990s that this practice reached its full fruition as a mode of historical thought. Dominated by the completion of the multipart *Histoire(s) du cinéma* in 1998, this period of Godard's work saw a marked turn to the past; the films of this period are frequently extended meditations on history, death (both personal and social), and the weight of the past. Douglas Morrey writes that "montage works by reviving the memory of the real, by bringing out the reserve of sense contained within an image in order to place it in relation with another image."[25] Montage, in the broad sense suggested here, is not simply one of cinema's formal parameters but a nascent and virtual complement to every filmic image. Like the semantic unruliness of the alloseme that the cryptophore exploits to speak without saying the taboo word, montage is the virtualization of all the "reserves of sense" contained in the image of the real but closed off by the text's organization of shots and the given order of images. Montage indicates the entire constellation of possible but unseen countershots that were passed over in the film.

It should be clear from this broad conception of montage that for Godard a countershot is not the traditional reverse shot that completes an exchange of looks (or of a look and an object) between two images. The countershot is, rather, an "elsewhere," a second scene, that is foreign to the original image but which in some ways complements or completes it. This is the role, in *Ici et ailleurs*, of the scene of circulation of images in France in relation to the original scene of revolutionary production. When Godard and Gorin traveled from France to film the Palestinian struggle but left out the situation of the fate of French revolutionary cinema from their images, they isolated the Palestinian struggle from the total situation. For the European filmmakers (though not for the Palestinian revolutionaries), the total situation of the anticolonial struggle in Palestine necessarily includes the new conditions of television as the mode of circulation of images and the concurrent internal-exclusion of political cinema outside the domestic interiors of Paris.[26] By leaving this situation out of account, the filmmakers saw only the spectacle of the Palestinian revolution and could not account for the demands that these images and words made on them as witnesses. *Here and Elsewhere* is an attempt to reconstruct the original situation by recreating the missing cosymbol of anticolonial struggle with images of the cryptic domestic interior of the metropole. Crucially, however, these two terms—here and elsewhere—are not given as coequal fragments of a dialogue. Their difference is emphasized through the unmourned bodies of the Palestinian revolutionaries whose death outside of the film can never be properly reconstructed within the text. Thus, although the film aims at recreating the original unity, Godard and Miéville are just as insistent on telling the history of an irreconcilable fracture figured by an interval or gap that cannot be incorporated into the regime of images. The three components of the image: the shot (the Palestinian revolutionary struggle), the countershot (the Parisian home and its domestication of the image of otherness), and the scene of original unity (Godard and Gorin's desire to make a film, as French filmmakers, of the Palestinian struggle, as well as the global conditions of capitalism and colonialism that enable and determine the shape of this desire) are all fractured by the death of the Palestinian fighters and by the failure of cinema to have borne witness to this death.

Like the anasemic process of ripping words from their common, everyday usage to return them to their occluded origins, anasemic montage rips an image out of its conventional place in a cinematic narrative, displacing it in relation to an absence. This is precisely what, in the voice-over of *Here and Elsewhere*, Miéville accuses Godard and Gorin of having failed to do in their original footage, where they (mis)took the *image* of revolution for the revolutionary struggle itself. Gilles Deleuze notes Godard's constant and active refusal of the cinematic cliché. This refusal, Deleuze shows, does not simply avoid clichés to construct images from nonimages. Instead, Godard sets himself the task of rediscovering, within the cliché, an original and powerful image. Deleuze writes: "if images have become clichés, internally as well as externally, how can an Image be extracted from all these clichés, 'just an image.' . . . An image *must* emerge from the set of clichés . . . with what politics and what consequences?"[27] Deleuze's capitalization of "Image" in the above passage is evocative of Abraham's capitalization of psychoanalytic terms that contain, in muted form, their anasemic opposite. While working from a different tradition, the ploy of capitalization denotes, in both cases, a term that includes its negation; Image in this case also indicates the nonimage or what can't be seen in the cliché. For Godard, at least, montage can be used to reveal an image within a cliché by breaking apart a preconceived shot/countershot order and putting the shot in relation to another countershot, further "up the chain" of meaning, that is not visible in the original film or seeable in the normal logic of the text.

In his films of the 1970s, Godard prefigures anasemic montage as a return to zero. Initially, this return was aimed specifically at exploring the clichés of dominant commercial films, and it is only later, beginning especially in the 1990s, that Godard started to see history as a set of images that had to be re-visioned anasemically. Starting in the 1970s, Godard takes an increasing distance from the popular styles that still served as the ground of an active critique in his New Wave films, betraying a sharpening distrust of the image(s) of classical cinema. This suspicion is born not so much from an Adornian critique of the popular as false consciousness, but rather from Godard's conviction that the clichés inherent in these images contain, albeit in a cryptic form, a lost cinematic object. Godard does not reject the popular dimensions of cinema but rather subjects it to a formal and, increasingly, material critique aimed at showing what is hidden and obscured within. This critical apparatus is formalized in *Le gai savoir* (1969), where the proposed "return to zero" of filmic expression starts with already existing news and commercial images that function as a kind of blackboard or working table. In the film, two students—Patricia Lumumba and Émile Rousseau—institute a didactic program by which they hope to discover the "original" point of visuality, the place from which they can begin to make images anew, unencumbered by the spectacle that has warped and enslaved cinema to commercial interests. "What we need to discover are words and sounds that are free," they agree during their first meeting. They proceed, however, not by simple subtraction but by linking the existing images to foreign elements, most notably words and phrases that are written over or inserted within the frame. The textual overlay is placed beside scenes in which Patricia and Émile discuss their project in a dark television studio. The effect is to break apart the pre-given messages of the found images, unmaking the popular, clichéd images into component elements that can then be manipulated independently of a unified scene. The blank slate or black screen, the degree zero of cinema, is discovered from within this existing visual regime. Their goal, as they set it out, is "to know ... mark off in time and space, the silent word that separates [images]." The film emphasizes the process of erasure—one that often paradoxically involves adding visual elements that unmake the univocality of the image-screen—over the mythic origin of cinema in a blank/black screen.[28] This process is designed to bring to light a silent word, an absent term that can be used to break apart the perceived unity of existing television and filmic discourse.

Godard continues to explore the possibilities of a montage form capable of breaking apart clichés in the television series *France/tour/détour/deux/enfants* (1977), made in collaboration with Miéville. Armed with the new powers of video, Godard-Miéville explore the full poetics of slow and stop motion, repetition and reverse action, and jarring shifts between the distance of a television news broadcast and the intense intimacy of the video camera inserted into (at times close to a violation of) children's domestic and pedagogic spaces. The cumulative effect of these strategies is to warp the clichés adopted by children, in both speech and bodily gestures, under the demands of the "monsters" of society: their parents, teachers, and the various producers of images of the "proper" child. Under the pressure of video manipulation, mundane situations of school, play, and family life dissolve as the child's body becomes an active agent of material resistance, even if only in small and local ways, to the visual clichés to which it is subjected.[29] This body as resistance functions as the lost object whose crypt-image, the disciplined body, Godard-Miéville unmake. Video allows Godard and Miéville to extend the formal possibilities of montage beyond the relation between shots and into a zone *within* the image that functions as an interval or gap. This internal composition still deserves the name of "montage," however, because it puts one image—visible and present in the frame—in direct and critical relation to a second image, this one unseen and absent, to produce a new meaning.

Notre musique and the Historical Interval

The rest of this chapter will focus on *Notre musique* because it is here that Godard explicitly presents an object lesson in his montage practice. In fact, the didactic center of the film is a lecture that Godard addresses to a group of film students on the relationship between word and image. The film is composed of three distinct sections: Hell, Purgatory, and Paradise. Hell and Paradise depict twinned (if seemingly contradictory) sets of images that are situated outside of time: the first a collage of decontextualized clips of war and violence and the second a pastoral Eden watched over by American marines. Purgatory, the lengthy middle section that makes up the bulk of the film, is set during a Literary Encounters conference that Godard attended in 2000 in Sarajevo at a time when the city still bore the physical wounds of war. The conference brings together a large number of characters—some wholly fictionalized and others real persons playing themselves—acting out various scenes of dialogue around the possibility of historical reconciliation. These somewhat fragmentary scenes are woven together by the presence of two young Jewish women: Judith Lerner, an Israeli journalist who has come to interview Palestinian poet Mahmoud Darwish, and Olga Brodsky, who attends Godard's lecture and meets with her uncle to discuss the philosophical significance of suicide. Godard exploits the visual similarity between the two actresses, Sara Adler and Nade Dieu, by filming and then editing the scenes together so as to generate some confusion between the roles. Indeed, on first viewing many spectators do not notice that they are separate characters. The effect is to interweave the scenes of linguistic and cultural dialogue with the meditation on suicide as a gesture of philosophical and political (self-)constitution, as if the cross-linguistic cultural translation were haunted by the specter of the unmournable dead.

Writ large, *Notre musique* presents history as a series of fragments, broken symbols and clipped scenes, while hinting at the possibility of reconstructing their unity through a mode of viewing analogous to what Abraham and Torok call psychoanalytic listening, a viewing whose aim "is to find the symbol's complement, recovering it from indeterminacy."[30] The film examines a number of historical conflicts ranging from the divisions in postwar Bosnia, the scars that World War II left on contemporary Europe, and the genocide of Native Americans. The thrust of the film, however, is an extended meditation on the state of the Israel-Palestine conflict, and it is thus a historical companion piece to *Here and Elsewhere*. Now, however, the central problem is not the reconciliation of two places but the difficulty of reconciling a past trauma of violence and slaughter encrypted within a present and future time. The film thus figures the historical death drive, the topographies of history built around the traumas of the past, and suggests a number of ways, each partial and unsatisfying, of overcoming these fissures. Michael Witt sums up what he considers to be the film's utopian tone as follows: "Imagining a future less catastrophic than the recent past, the film strikes an optimistic note. Godard is interested in the possibility of people approaching one another in a spirit of sincerity and openness, in anticipation of a dialogue that might allow a tentative step forwards into a less dreadful future."[31] Whereas the film does, indeed, stage dialogue as a path toward reconciliation (precisely the kind of dialogue that, in *Here and Elsewhere*, Godard-Miéville accuse the Dziga Vertov Group of having failed to engage with), the interplay of seeing and not-seeing that runs throughout complicates the film's utopian promise. While the film ultimately does not resolve this tension between the narrative of reconciliation and the figuration of historical trauma, it does, in typically Godardian fashion, suggest that the act of spectatorship has the potential of completing the unfinished task of historical redemption. The new importance of history for Godard also angles the meaning of the shot/countershot structure used as spatial terms in *Here and Elsewhere* toward temporality. Thus, the shot or visible image refers to a present situation, the countershot to a historically past moment that is nonetheless woven into the present, and the interval marks a fictive scene of "original unity" in which the two noncommunicating terms formed a whole and from which they were broken off.

The lecture scene in *Notre musique* begins by establishing two elements of a fragmented dialogue: the camera is placed at the back of a classroom, looking through rows of students seen out of focus, as Godard, in focus, walks to the center and prepares to speak. Holding up a picture of a ruined building, he asks the students to name what they see. After various wrong answers that span the history of modern bloody military conflicts—Sarajevo, Hiroshima, Stalingrad, Beirut—he announces that the photograph was taken in Richmond, Virginia, in 1865. The implication is clear, and it is one that Godard has explored often since at least *Letter to Jane* of 1972: unless it is named by an external referent, a clear image will often include (and, in its clarity, disavow) an element of obscurity as to its origin and intent. Sometimes, Godard calls this external referent the "text" and treats it as a second scene that provides the image with its hidden meaning. Just as frequently, however, this second scene is posited as radically other to the image and a threat to its powers.[32] This obscurity proper to the scene of the image is both a source of potential misunderstanding and one of cinema's most important ways of understanding and reflecting on the world. While it opens images up to the danger of being manipulated to show something that they don't say, this same horizon of obscurity also allows for the figural rhymes, the mode of imagistic punning, central to Godard's montage practice in his post–New Wave films. Due to this structural indeterminacy, each image contains a secret history based on its ability to evoke words, names, and other images belonging to a radically different social and historical situation. This series of visual rhymes is not, for Godard, only a set of false images or the errata of interpretation, though it can be that. More importantly, the series of rhymes gives the cinematic image the power to evoke a secret, figural history that leaps across linear historical narratives.

As the lecture proceeds, Godard holds up a series of image-couplets organized in an implied shot/countershot relation. Far from an innocent exchange of views, each of these image-couplets contains a social imbalance in the order of the look. This social imbalance has been built into almost every one of the film's dialogic scenes, as the differences between young and old, man and woman, colonizer and colonized necessarily insinuate history into any attempt to reconcile the present. In making this imbalance explicit, Godard asks us to (re)watch the film as one in which every shot/countershot sequence contains a history of its own historical impasse. Godard continues the lecture with a seemingly straightforward example from Howard Hawks's *His Girl Friday* (1940): a shot of Cary Grant looking off screen frame right is followed by one of Rosalind Russell looking off frame left. "Look closely," Godard enjoins the students, "you'll see that it's the same thing twice. That's because the director is incapable of seeing the difference between a man and a woman." The point is not simply to implicate Hawks in a critique of gender politics but, more fundamentally, to mark the fact that, in classical editing, montage is often used to create a unified visual and narrative order that erases the gaps and antagonisms inherent in the social world from which the images are drawn. If the two images can be made to simply mirror each other in the film, it is because the difference between the gendered looks—the fact that they, in fact, don't see the same thing or in the same way—has been forgotten. The cut, the fragmentation of the dual symbol of the exchange of looks, has been phantasmatically erased by a classical editing structure that henceforth incorporates this radical difference as the internal exclusion of Hollywood cinema. This is not to say that differences between men and women are not fundamental to Hollywood films, but only that the difference is constructed as a function of narrative and can thus be resolved within the film. Hollywood places all of its bets on cinema's ability to repair the broken fragments of social difference through a gesture of narrative integration that excludes the fundamentally fractured nature of the gaze.[33]

Moving from this basic nature of cinematic "grammar," Godard expands it to encompass a gap in cinema's power of thinking through history. In the next set of images, he shows an image of an emaciated body lying on the ground with eyes wide open in horror—labeled "Jew"—followed by an image of a corpse slumped over, eyes closed, labeled "muselman." In this reference to the Nazi extermination camps, Godard evokes a dualism that Giorgio Agamben explores in *Remnants of Auschwitz*. Agamben uses testimony writing from camp survivors to argue for the importance of the figure of *der Muselmann*, literally the Muslim: the name given to those prisoners who have lost all recourse to subjectivity and fully succumbed and submitted to the condition of the lost object—the living corpse—that is the founding and final logic of institutionalized mass extermination. Unlike the survivor's testimony that Agamben reads, the muselmann have no story to tell or be told; they are "the untestifiable, that to which no one has borne witness."[34] The muselmann stands in contrast to the survivor who, in spite of the horrors of the camps, maintained the power of testimony or truth-telling speech, maintained, in other words, a relation to the text of history. Having established this difference, Agamben meditates on the nature of the witness and testimony as textuality. On the one hand, he argues, the witness occupies the position of one who speaks in the place of those who cannot. Thus, the witness is the one who was able to emerge from the camps to testify to the presence of the muselmann. Noting that few such testimonies exist, however, Agamben posits an aporia within this logic of witnessing: the figure of the living dead is the figure of a body that cannot be gazed on, and thus the muselmann constitutes an absence incorporated within the camps that resists every promise of full testimony. The muselmann is a nonimage that makes any full textual recounting of the camps impossible. This absence marks a limit internal to and constitutive of testimony: unseen, there seems to be nothing to be said about the muselmann except to pass over its mute nonbeing. "A heap of dead bodies is an ancient spectacle," writes Agamben, "one which has often satisfied the powerful. But the sight of *Muselmänner* is an absolutely new phenomenon, unbearable to human eyes."[35] The division between Jew and muselmann subtends a series of other divisions between testimony and the unspeakable, spectacle and the unbearable image, even history and forgetting.

In the camps, however, this difference is only ever contingent and phantasmatic, as each of the terms is in constant danger of slipping into the other. What unites them, at least potentially, is their copresence within the body of the prisoner. At any moment, the prisoner was prone to succumb to the muselmann rising up within him or her, and thus to slip out of history and into the realm of the untestifiable. "This is why the prisoner's most pressing concern was to hide his sickness and his exhaustion, to constantly cover over the *Muselmann* who at every moment was emerging in him."[36] The prisoner's body in the camps is the ground or unity of an unbearable knowledge: that between speech and its mute failure, mourning and its impossibility, there is only the ghost of a difference. Producing and reproducing the terms as if they occupied different positions in a historical shot/countershot of testimony, as if they were two opposites ends of a death-bearing look, erases the essential incommensurability of the broken symbol (since the truthful witness can never bear witness to the muselmann, the final horror and crime of the camps) and its original unity in the body of the camp prisoner. The production of this difference, Godard claims, is what makes history possible, since the muselmann stands at the ruin of history, and its internal presence within life would produce a truly monstrous time. The erasure of the muselmann is also, however, the forgetting of the trauma of the camps by incorporating its unbearable scene into a history "fit for human eyes."

The resonance between Agamben's (and Godard's) language of the camps and the language of Abraham and Torok's necro-analysis reminds us that the analyst's work, as much as that of the philosopher and the filmmaker, was born of a desire to bear witness to this unspeakable and unfigurable scene of history. Themselves touched by the history of Nazi genocide, having lost family members in the camps, Abraham and Torok treated Holocaust survivors whose stories are the unmistakable origin of the theory of the internal crypt and the transgenerational phantom. It is remarkable that this history is only ever tangentially present in their writing (which in other ways frequently evokes the biographical and the writers' desire), as when Abraham recounts the case of a child who mimicked the death of his mother's lover in a gas chamber by collecting butterflies that he killed in a can of cyanide. While the history of the Holocaust and their personal relationship to it is excised from cryptonymy, this silence itself *is* the crypt of history lodged within the psychoanalytic discourse. The historical scene returns not through a retelling of a missing scene but by grounding the entire verbarium of crypt-words to describe the psyche. These metapsychological words construct a memorial to the taboo scene of history. The gothic language of their analysis—the dramatis personae of crypts, specters, premature burials, and silent witnesses—is not simply a metaphoric lure. This language is the crypt of cryptonymy, an encryption of history within the generic narrative forms of the novel. It allows them to speak of the trauma in their own lives without saying its proper name, or perhaps even fully recognizing themselves as its spectral sentries. The power of Godard's images is to invent an anasemic practice *without* (that is, as the cryptic form of) the analytic session.

Although it is rooted in the trauma of the camps, cryptonymy's contribution as "heard" by Godard (a silent witness, since he is likely unaware of their writing) lies in *not* returning to the camps as an original or primal scene. Instead, cryptonymy uncovers, in the mute language of the camps, the terms for the conditions of the present.[37] In the survivor testimonies Agamben analyzed, we can hear echoes of the concepts that Abraham and Torok used to listen to their patients after the war: concepts such as incorporation, in which a subject encrypts the lost object within the self, and failed mourning, where the lost object "identifies" with the still-living self. This is most pronounced, however, in the case of the muselmann, where it is as if the self becomes, for itself, the lost object of impossible mourning incorporated in the deepest recess of a radically divided psyche. What makes the muselmann unspeakable, in this case, is that it is a pure (non)being without testimony, a mute corpse. For Agamben, however, the muselmann is not just a historical figure but also one instance of a condition he calls bare life, life stripped of all properties of the subject. While fully visible in the camps, and without reducing the specific conditions of institutionalized genocide undertaken by the Nazis, bare life is the condition of a growing number of the human population *after* liberation.[38] The camps are not a singular historical moment but the inauguration of a new situation that will expand under the "liberation" of capital into the spectacle of global circulation in the postwar era.[39] Unlike Agamben, however, Abraham and Torok suggest that just as much as the muselmann resides within, and threatens to emerge from, the body of the camp prisoner, so too is every muselmann a potential witness, if only we could learn to listen to their cryptic speech.

The potential for anasemia as a historical method resides in the possibility it offers of giving language, and thus subjectivity, to the living dead by returning them to a scene before the loss of self and language condemned them to silence. Godard explores this historical retracing in the following series of images during *Notre musique*'s lecture sequence. Following the shots of Jew and muselmann already discussed, he holds up a color image of what he calls the "Israelites" wading through water to reach the "Holy Land" and, after it, a black-and-white image of Palestinians "walking into the water to drown." Here, the shot/countershot that gave rise to the internal fracture, within the camps and within the body of the prisoner, of Jew and muselmann is extended into a historical shot reverse shot showing the founding of the Jewish state on one side of the cut and the expulsion and drowning of the Palestinians (the "drowned" was another name for the muselmann in certain camps) from their land on the other.[40] Whereas the settling of the Israeli state produced a "clear" image of Israel, an image structured by the exclusion of the Palestinians, it also absented the Palestinians into a phantasmatic historical "reverse shot." The violence of the camps is repeated in the violence of colonialism and, in the process, as Godard says in voice-over, the Israeli Jews were made a subject of history while the Palestinians became the subject of documentary. These terms must be understood in the specific sense Godard intends: *history* implies a readable and ordered narrative akin to traditional linear editing, *documentary* connotes a reality that is captured "cinematically" but does not have a corresponding image. In this sense a "documentary" captures Abraham and Torok's condition of Reality (the capitalization indicates a psychoanalytic term) as a secret that is avoided by consciousness. The condition of statelessness to which the Palestinian refugees have been condemned ever since Israel's founding abandons them to a Reality outside of history and also outside of the cinematic frame. Israel's founding encrypts the secret history of the muselmann and the broken symbol of the camp prisoner as an absent reverse shot within the map of world history. Mahmoud Darwish, during his interview with Judith in the film, is explicit about the importance of not only the historical violence at Israel's founding but also the violence that this founding had for the ability to give a full account of history: "Do you know why we Palestinians are famous?" he asks, "because you are our enemy. The interest is in you . . . not in me." This articulates the image of the broken symbol as a historical figure, for the historical violence is not only the violence performed on bodies or land, but it is also the transformation of this material violence into a historical discourse that is robbed of its ability to speak the *proper name* of the victim. What is at stake is neither the use of past horrors to justify the present (such that the Nazi genocide is the historical signatory of the state) nor the conflation or identity of two historical moments, the Holocaust and the expulsion of the Palestinians. Rather, what Godard highlights are the ways in which the presence of an unmournable body, a body expelled from and incorporated within an experience of impossible mourning, is often at the heart of a history that cannot *see* the countershot of the visible.

A number of observations can help clarify the uniqueness of Godard's practice, in this lecture sequence and in his description of montage more broadly. First, anasemic montage demonstrates the path by which an internal condition born of a shameful impossibility to mourn is externalized as a historical situation. This type of anasemic history involves a movement "up" from the present as Godard traces a fractured history, an antagonism, to an earlier moment of perceived unity (within the camps, within a single body) and to the site of its original division in the land. However, this "original" is not a key or primal scene that holds the secrets of a present moment, nor does this method of historical research replace other types of investigations. The argument is not that the division of language was the original cause of the historical antagonism, but rather that the historical antagonism is built on the cryptic foundation of a broken symbol. Psychoanalytic listening is attuned to the history of repression, the return of the repressed word in various guises and forms, born at the moment of the production of the unconscious. Psychoanalytic listening can only hope to recover the original cause of the unconscious split as a phantasy or specter of the analytic situation. Hence, Freud famously concluded his search for a primal scene in the Wolf Man case with the status of a *non liquet*, a structural undecidability as to the scene's true origin in the parents' bedroom or the couplings of animals. Likewise, Godard's anasemic montage recounts the history of broken images, charting their path through cryptic figural rhymes without ever necessarily arriving at a moment of true historical origin.

Second, akin to Freud's positing of an unknowable scene (the primal scene) at the origin of the history of the subject, so too does Godard propose that an unseeable image, a phantom, lies at the origin of the history of modern cinema. This phantom marks the place of a real image of bodies that cannot be mourned. This unseeable image, according to Godard, is an image taken from *within* the gas chambers, an image that would serve as a full and truthful witness to the crime of historical erasure. The absence of such an image is at the heart of Godard's conception of film as historiographic machine, and it appears as a failure of cinema to fulfill its role as historical witness. As Jacques Rancière writes, "it's not a matter of calling into question what cinema would still like to do after the horror of the camps. Godard's thesis is the opposite: if cinema has become 'impossible' after Auschwitz, this is not because the horror is unfilmable, it's because it hasn't been filmed."[41] The sources of this untimely claim in Godard are twofold. Michael Witt traces it to the *Histoire(s)*, when he writes that "for Godard, World War II was the central cataclysmic event of the twentieth century, and it was cinema's failure to testify to the unbearable horrors of the Holocaust that resulted in the most damaging reduction yet of its powers."[42] The second source is a phantasmatic debate, staged in separate interviews and statements but never face to face, between Godard and Claude Lanzmann about Lanzmann's *Shoah* (1985). Godard accuses Lanzmann of repeating cinema's modern sin: that of refusing to show images of the Holocaust. This refusal, suggests Godard, is an abandonment of cinema's documentary promise to bear witness to the horrors of history. As Libby Saxton has argued, however, Godard goes further than simply stating a hypothetical case for the redemptive power of showing horror and insists on the existence of a missing film or reel of history: "Strangely, but tellingly," recounts Saxton,

> The non-encounter between the two directors has centered around the disputed existence of a tiny fragment of film which Jean-Jacques Delfour has aptly named 'la pellicule maudite' ('the accursed reel'). Ever since 1985, not insignificantly the release date of *Shoah*, Godard, citing the Nazis' bureaucratic mania for recording every last detail, has been repeating his conviction that this hypothetical footage allegedly shot by the Nazis inside a gas chamber to record the very heart of the process of extermination is merely buried in an archive somewhere.[43]

For Saxton, Godard's insistence on the archival, if buried, presence of such an image betrays his "insecurity with regard to the imaged real" and ultimately forces him into a logic of simple visibility (even if only in potential) as the defining marker of cinematic evidence.[44]

While noting that "such a position would appear disconcertingly to contradict much of the oeuvre of a director notorious for his claims to present *'pas une image juste, juste an image,'*" Saxton does not attempt to reconcile Godard's claims with his work as a whole, asking how this claim operates within the overall poetics of montage that Godard uses.[45] As I have been arguing, however, Godard considers the image not as the framed visual field but instead as the phantom effect of the shot/counter-shot structure: the image is not the shot, but the relation between the shot and an absent countershot. This should be understood in historical as well as cinematic terms. If the fate of the shot it to incorporate and erase its countershot across the interval, this is because history itself is based on the incorporation of what has been written out of history by being made unmournable. Like Freud, Godard does not reject the relevance of historical evidence; however, he posits that in each case this evidence must be grasped in relation to what is left unsaid and unseen, and that it is the particular power of the cinematic image to actualize this relation through both internal and external montage. Thus, Godard lays claim, in the name of cinema, to the task of charting the nonlinear path of symbolic formations that arise from the relation between visual testimony and the unfilmed, the document(ed) and the off screen. It is between the "shot" of the meticulous documentation of the gaze (the Nazis' "bureaucratic mania for recording every last detail") and the shot of the muselmann as the internal limit of testimony that an image that "record[s] the very heart of the process of extermination" comes into being. This missing reel is buried not because the archive was destroyed, but because cinema forgot how to see the difference between shot and countershot and thus proceeded to erase the unmourned images (and the images of the unmourned) that it was tasked, historically, with documenting. The footage of historical trauma was erased by the cinematic apparatus itself, and thus Godard's insistence that its absence is not merely a contingent historical failure to film but the death of cinema qua cinema.

A third point that emerges from this lecture scene has to do with the relationship between fiction and reality within anasemic montage. These terms have, in various incarnations, been central to Godard's thought since his time as a film critic and then a New Wave director. Crucially, they appear from the start not as aesthetic categories (fantasy vs. realism) or as modes of production (fiction vs. documentary), but as the major powers or attitudes of the cinema.

Fiction, for Godard, is the power to organize images of the world (images taken directly from the world) into an order by which the world appears as itself. In this sense, fiction is always that which is overcome from within fiction, allowing the bodies of the actors or the streets of the city to resonate with the power of the universe. Reality, which Godard sometimes cavalierly calls documentary, appears in cinema only within a didactic practice of commentary that extracts the truth of the world from its image. Cinema does not arrive at an image but always begins with an image that it must analyze in order to uncover its internal logic and order. Reality is what exists but is missing a "proper image" and can only be extracted from other images.[46] These two gestures—the overcoming of fiction from within and by way of fiction, and the uncovering of an image's "reality" by marking the surface of its visual appearance—constitute the singular expression of cinema as a modern art. The different roles given by Godard to these two potentialities can be seen in the different treatments of the human body in his films. In the New Wave films in particular (though Godard never fully abandons this practice), the actors' bodies appear as the convergence of all the characters' possible gestures. The body is not a tool used by the craft of acting; rather, acting is valued only to the extent that it allows for a program that investigates the movements and gestures proper to the actor. The Dziga Vertov films, however, display a more programmatic use of the body. In these films, bodies do not refer to actors or even to the space of action but are instead treated as screens for analysis. Here, the body is crossed over by a series of annotations and markings etched on its surface, either through text or voice. At other times, the body is analyzed using the material properties of the medium—still frames, slow and fast motion, and such—so that its gestures can be isolated and investigated. This recalls not so much the distanciation effects Brecht championed as it does Franju's filming of the transformation of animal bodies into part objects in *Blood of the Beasts* or even Bava's interest in the passage, through special effects, of the body from one state to another (from youth to old age, from the dead to the living). In each case, the body is realized as a material fragment within the image that has to be "worked on" outside of cinema proper: in the abattoir, in the special effects laboratory, or in the classroom of political action.

Although I have thus far been emphasizing the different powers of fiction and reality, Godard has always treated them as two aspects of a single cinematic project. While a specific film or image may rely on one or the other, it is in the interplay between the two that cinema discovers its most inventive and transformative powers. Daniel Morgan argues that for Godard the nouvelle vague was "neither simply fiction nor reality, but both together," and quotes Godard in claiming that "the New Wave ... may be defined in part by this new relationship between fiction and reality."[47] This is true not only for the New Wave's explicit theatricalization of reality, but also for every major period of Godard's career. Thus, *Numéro deux* (1975), which announced the phase of "investigative" collaboration with Miéville, focuses on applying the force of documentary-like truth to fiction. The film subjects images of an extended family to an external critique by isolating and fragmenting its fictions (the multiple framings of televisions, for example, frequently break up the space of the family home into individual units of parents, grandparents, and children) and organizes this disassembly into a loose narrative (complete with a primal scene of rape witnessed by the young girl) that reveals the family as the generational production and reproduction not only of bodies, labor, and care, but also of trauma. In *Notre musique*, and in the period of "Late Godard" in general, the relationship between fiction and documentary is given a historical weight through the increasingly central role of anasemic montage in which history is read through the lens of an original but fictive unity. The image, for Godard, often splinters precisely along the fault line of fiction and documentary, and the absent image is then the unfilmable moment that combines the two or, more precisely, in which the one emerges from within the image of the other.

A final point has to do with the affective powers of anasemic montage, which speaks to the pervasive melancholia of *Notre musique* as noted by many of its critics. If anasemic montage works to decrypt history by revealing its origin in a scene of blocked mourning, and thus to let the dead speak, wouldn't it—like the successful therapeutic session—generate an affect of life-affirming Eros? We can sense this in the optimism that seems to underlie Godard's funerary mode, or when Michael Witt calls *Notre musique* "remarkably light in tone and forward-looking," in spite of its long excursions into scenes of death, violence, and destruction.[48] However, this forward-looking nature is only present fleetingly in the lengthy middle section of the film, and even here it is set within a mise-en-scène of ruin and hopelessness. The bookend sections, Hell and Paradise, encrypt this hopefulness within images of eternal war and permanent occupation. Rather than seeing a contradiction between these two affective tones of the film, I want to suggest that they are in fact parts of the same process of decryption. No matter how painful the contents of the original, absent scene may be, it is, for the subject who incorporated it, a truly utopian image. The missing or absent scene is the guarantor that something did take place (and thus that the subject's testimony is truthful) and also the image of a whole or unified symbol before the cryptic fractures of language forced the subject into shameful silence. It is only through the incorporation of loss that the subject can maintain the role of a truthful witness and refuse to acknowledge that a real loss has taken place. In this sense, even the body of the prisoner in the camps is "utopian," if by utopia we understand not a projection of desire but the mark of a successful incorporation of loss. Utopia, in this sense, is the jouissance born of the erasure of history and the phantasmatic annulment of trauma. At the same time, retrieving this "lost object" by recognizing its historical place involves not its resurrection but a successful work of mourning. Writing in a different register, Judith Butler describes the effects of a prohibition on mourning:

> What follows . . . from prohibitions on avowing grief in public is an effective mandate in favor of a generalized melancholia (and a derealization of loss) when it comes to consider *as dead* those the United States and its allies killed. . . . It seems important to consider that the prohibition on certain forms of public grieving itself constitutes the public sphere on the basis of such a prohibition.[49]

As I have been arguing, for Godard this social prohibition on mourning is inseparable from cinema's failure to bear witness to the dead of history and from the shot/countershot structure when it is used to erase the interval of nonseeing in which the image is buried. Anasemic montage cannot recreate the original image, but it aims to make the gap, the place of the unseen image, visible in a utopian gesture that removes the prohibition against seeing the unfigurable.[50] Thus it is, in its very nature, a forward-looking but haunted and mournful discourse.

The Graveyard of Stones and the Lost Utopian Object

In a scene following shortly after Godard's lecture, Judith Lerner travels to the site of the Mostar bridge. Built by Ottomans in the sixteenth century across the Neretva River, this bridge symbolized the spanning of heterogeneous cultures and communities. This material and infrastructural staging of a symbolic unity has a temporal as well as spatial connotation. Susan Forde notes that "socially and transgenerationally, the bridge became a source of topophilia (love of place) for Mostarians, with Mostari meaning 'the bridge keepers' in Bosnian; in this respect, the Ottoman institutional staging of the bridge was transgenerationally scripted into social identity."[51] The destruction of the bridge in 1993, during the Bosnian war, was an act of symbolic social violence aimed primarily at Mostar's Muslim population. The struggle over the bridge instantiates the psychoanalytic concept of the broken symbol as a transgenerational and topographic reality as it not only unites and divides a social whole but also takes aim directly at the ties between social identity and an original event of perceived unity. The words of some of the planners responsible for the reconstruction project taken up by the World Bank and other institutions of the European order reveal the deep imbrication of the bridge's destruction with the shattering of the symbolic fabric of Bosnia and Herzegovina, and by metonymy of the very idea of a unified postwar Europe:

> The bridge withstood 427 years of natural disasters, earthquakes and war. But on 9 November 1993, the Old Bridge in Mostar collapsed into the waters of the Neretva River after being subjected to three days of heavy shelling. The bridge was deliberately destroyed for its symbolic significance rather than its military value, which made its loss even more devastating. Mostar was defined by the bridge and with its loss the identity of the city was literally broken apart.[52]

The peace that ended the Bosnian war did not, of course, return a state of social unity, but rather implemented the social and geographic divisions as a more permanent state. The desire to rebuild the bridge was the geopolitical encryption of an internal fissure within the highly charged symbolic image of unity. Like the words of the cryptophore that deny the presence of a trauma through the invocation of cryptonyms that continually speak of its nonexistence, the bridge's reconstruction is a crypt-image memorializing the wish that a violence had never taken place and the subsequent refusal to mourn (at least on the part of European institutions if not of the locals of Mostar) the loss of the object of a unified Europe.[53]

Judith has come to the conference in Sarajevo with the goal of creating dialogues that could bridge historical divisions. In addition to interviewing Mahmoud Darwish, she goes to the home of the French ambassador, who hid her grandfather from the Vichy police in 1943, to ask him to take part in a conversation on the topic of atonement. When she goes to photograph the bridge's reconstruction, it represents for her an image of historical reconciliation. Capturing it with her camera would allow her to remember and reframe the symbolic ruins of the past. At the bridge, she encounters the French architect Gilles Péqueux, who at the time of filming was in charge of the reconstruction project. Péqueux shows her the stones of the original bridge that had been retrieved from the waters, arrayed like a broken jigsaw puzzle on the riverbank, each marked and tagged. He explains the goals and methods of reconstruction in a way that emphasizes its historical and symbolic aspirations. "The stones were salvaged in two stages. . . . Each stone was identified on a card on which each detail was noted. Its position in the water, its position in the structure, and a description of each face. It was like rediscovering the origin of language. . . . We must at once restore the past and make the future possible. Combine the pain . . . and the guilt." Philip Rosen distinguishes between two methods of reconstructing past monuments: restoration and preservation. Restoration entails remaking old buildings according to their original architectural style, modernizing them with the signature of the past. Preservation, which is the mode Péqueux describes here, aims to prolong the existence of the old material—the stones and other fragments of the past—by incorporating it into a new structure, rebuilding the past as a cryptic monument in the present. This is an architecture of the living dead, and Rosen emphasizes this gothic aspect: "The dead cannot be brought back to life, but reverence for their remains can be kept alive in memory. Restoration cannot replicate the historical actuality of a building . . . but preservation can provide an encounter with that actuality by refusing to interrupt its passage through time."[54]

What Péqueux's explanation makes explicit is the complex historical aporia at the heart of preservation. Rebuilding on the cryptic ground of old structures, preservation gestures toward a "future possible" that will preserve the pain and the guilt of the past, entombing them in the crypt of a world to come. Like the incorporated guest, the preservation of the past facilitates the repetition of the original trauma in the topography of the present and memorializes it as the lost object of an unfulfilled desire. As Péqueux's comment about rediscovering the origin of language shows, however, preservation is not aimed only at the present, but also at salvaging the original moment of historical loss (the destruction of the bridge) beyond which lies an even earlier scene of unity. Preservation preserves not only the broken fragments of the building but also the desire symbolized by the original structure and, moreover, the utopian wish that it had never come to harm. It is not enough to simply place the stones of the past back in their "proper" place. The lines of fracture have to be traced along the symbolic resonance of history so that the story of trauma and its effects on the past can be preserved along with the original, fictive image of pretraumatic unity. This is what combining the pain and the guilt means: to preserve the fractures of a silent and impossible mourning alongside a utopian image of the original body resurrected.

Here, the full historical weight of the anasemic *moving up* through the linguistic chain to the origin of speech comes into focus. Taking literally the "bridging" of history across a violent wound, for Péqueux restoring the bridge promises a full-fledged de-metaphorization of history. This involves a leap from the destruction of concrete and the loss of life to reparations at the scene of language through which old conflicts may be phantasmatically bridged, but only at the cost of taking the word *bridging* literally, and in so doing transferring the work of mourning into a singular, and thus magical and phantasmatic, act of restoration. This is therefore a truly cryptic discourse of the erasure of historical destruction and the preservation of a historical trauma as an internal exclusion.[55] In an interview, Godard reminds Michael Witt that these aspirations were greater than the historical possibility, and that the project quickly became a more straightforward restoration:

> Gilles Péqueux was fired and replaced by a Croat who made a bridge like any other, constructed out of new stone clad to make it look authentic. It's what they do on DVDs: a restoration. All the stones I filmed, which were retrieved from the river and individually numbered, weren't used—though watching the film the viewer thinks they're going to be. They're now in a spot the inhabitants of Mostar call "the cemetery of stones."[56]

Coming shortly after Godard's lecture on shot and countershot, the Mostar bridge episode serves two key functions in the film. First, it establishes anasemic montage as a historical construct. For Godard, montage is a mode of thinking proper to the cinematic age while not belonging to cinema alone. Thinking of history as a montage is not a metaphor or even an extension of a cinematic concept beyond itself; instead, it points to the importance of history as one of the facets of cinematic thought. In the historical ensemble of the reconstruction of the Mostar bridge, we can see anasemic montage brought to life as a historical procedure. On one side, there is the "shot" of the bridge's destruction shown in saturated but low-fidelity video images. On the other, there is the act of preservation that de-metaphorizes the word "bridge," turning history into a text or linguistic miracle ("like rediscovering the origin of language") in order to create an image of a future utopian reconstruction, social as much as architectural. For Godard, it is not a question of choosing the image over the text, the past over the future, but of making the difference, even nonrelation, between these two shots visible. This site of nonrelation—the interval as it takes on the properties of a full image and not a grammatical mark—is the marker of the lost object of history, the dead that resist and refuse any simple (cryptophoric) reconciliation.

Godard emphasizes the importance of this interval by including the figures of three Native Americans within the sequence. As she is photographing the bridge, Judith turns back toward the shore and raises her small camera, only to notice three Native Americans on the riverbank. Wearing the full historical regalia with which the image of Native Americans has been entombed in the genocidal museums of US colonial history, these figures (who have appeared at other points in the film, though always as misfit images, slightly decentered from the European narrative) are, as Burlin Barr states, "a narrative disturbance." They stand for the historical remainder that must not be forgotten and yet cannot simply be entombed within the shot/countershot structure of past and future, pain and guilt. "The scene before the journalist is not what she actually sees," writes Barr. "Her efforts at documentation result in another moment of erasure as the native-Americans are cast according to her preconceptions and not by their on-going self-definition."[57] For Barr, the cliché of the Native American dress is a sign of the ready-made images that Judith seeks in her search for reconciliation. Appearing as phantoms in the interval between the destruction of the past and the image of the future, they emphasize the function of the cinematic interval as the site of an embodied, corporeal resistance to the erasures of montage. When Michael Witt asks Godard about the relationship between image and text, which Godard associates with the relationship between shot and countershot, Godard replies that the "rapprochement" between the two does not produce a third image, as in Eisensteinian dialectical montage, but simply "provokes a question or introduces another response in the form of a question, so that we don't say the same things over and over again."[58] The Native Americans embody the "interval" of historical narratives, that is, the encrypted erasures of history, and offer, precisely by highlighting the ready-made image that allows us to recognize them, the possibility of resistance to the suturing of two historical moments.

A second function of the Mostar bridge sequence is to return the film to the theme of utopia that has been touched on obliquely in Godard's lecture. While we see that for Judith the utopia of reconciliation is still ensnared in clichés of the past, this sequence recenters the problem of utopia around the character of Olga Brodsky. Olga was first introduced, without being named, in Godard's lecture. As the camera pans across the group of distracted students, we see a young woman with her eyes closed, listening intently. When Godard introduces the theme of shot/countershot, the camera pauses again to frame her face as she opens her eyes. This leads immediately to a cut showing two images being held up next to each other. This sequence introduces the theme of the black screen as the unseen or unseeing interval between shot and countershot and alerts us to Olga's body as an avatar of this interval. It also begins a series of images in which Olga's look or nonlook is emphasized. Later, she meets with her uncle to discuss the philosophical meaning of suicide, and it becomes clear that she sees it as a personal gesture capable of reconciling solitude with social action. Olga attempts to realize this philosophical idea in a final, utopian gesture. After the conference, Godard receives a phone call from Olga's uncle telling him that Olga went into a movie theater in Jerusalem, threatening to detonate explosives in her backpack and asking for one Israeli to die with her in the name of peace rather than of war. After she was shot by the Israeli police without anyone coming to her side, her backpack was found to contain only books.

Before examining the significance of Olga's act, I want to briefly return to the Mostar bridge sequence and to the utopian implications of its reconstruction. It is, quite literally, against the failed utopia of the graveyard of stones that Olga's figure comes into focus. As I argued, for Péqueux what was utopian about the project of reconstruction was not so much the bridging of social divisions shattered during the war, nor the production of a unified landscape broken by bombs, but the unification of historical time. The past would first be retrieved as the literal fragments of the missing scene, all those stones coming from but never adding up to the entombed scene of prewar unity. This past would then become the foundation of a possible future but only at the expense of having lost its singular value as testimony to be overcome by a future possible. There are two ways in which this historical reconstruction may be understood. From the position of history, the incorporated past could potentially function as a grave marker of the missing scene of trauma. In *Utopics*, Louis Marin argues that if utopia is to be understood as a historical—rather than merely aesthetic or literary—idea, it must be thought in terms of the absences present in any historical situation. "Utopic discourse occupies the empty—historically empty—place of the historical resolution of a contradiction."[59] In this sense, utopia is a gap that appears within the contradictions of the present and into which their future resolution can be projected, like the becoming visible of the interval cut in Godard's anasemic montage. The missing scene built into the architecture of the future—that is, the image of reconstructed unity—would then stand in for an achieved utopia, a historical resolution of the contradictions of war and, more importantly, of the contradictions of history by which past antagonisms return in times of conflict. It is this possibility that Godard seems to be mourning when he reminds us that Péqueux's project was never completed and left in its place only a "cemetery of stones."

Seen, however, from the perspective of Olga (a cryptophore who seeks to bring about through suicide a magical-symbolic act that would free her of the burdens of history) the bridge symbolizes a very different type of utopia. Abraham and Torok argue that for the cryptophore, incorporation is a utopian gesture. By internalizing the external (missing) scene of trauma, the cryptophore saves the object from the already suffered loss and resolves the contradiction between the still-living desire and the living-dead absence. They write:

> The primary aim of the fantasy life born of incorporation is to repair—in the realm of the imaginary, of course—the injury that

really occurred and really affected the ideal object. The fantasy of incorporation reveals a utopian wish that the memory of the affliction had never existed or, on a deeper level, that the affliction had had nothing to inflict.[60]

Utopian introjection is always a contradictory and phantasmatic resolution to a real, though irreconcilable, difference: to at one and the same time repair a loss, thus keeping alive the future pleasure embedded in it (by keeping the lost object alive within the self), and to deny that the loss ever took place and thus free oneself of the shame of its desire (by erasing all traces of its ever having existed). The planned reconstruction of the Mostar bridge, when treated as a gesture of historical restoration, buries the traumatic wound within the architecture of the future and reveals a desire to return the landscape to its condition before the trauma took place.

Olga's haunting presence in the Mostar bridge sequence is asserted by a curious shot that aligns her both as the "negative" image of Judith and shifts the film's narrative focus to her story. This shot takes place immediately after the sequence where Judith sees the Native Americans standing on the riverbank with the half-built structure of the bridge filling the background. An additional cut, seemingly unmotivated by Judith's look, shifts the angle to a closer framing of the figures, who now occupy most of the foreground. Godard next cuts to an out-of-focus image of a street in Sarajevo where, from the background, Olga appears—almost spectral in her insubstantiality—and begins to walk toward the camera. On the soundtrack, we hear: "It is . . . like . . . an image . . . but a distant one. There are two people side by side. I'm next to her. I never saw her before. I recognize myself. But I have no memory of all that. It must be far from here. Or later on." As Olga approaches the camera, she comes into focus against the blurry background and, blinking rapidly, as if to clear a darkness from her eyes, looks up toward the sky before turning to stare directly at the camera. This is the second in the series of images that emphasize Godard's alignment of Olga's look with the presence of a clear or unclear image. She says something that is not heard on the soundtrack, or perhaps she merely mouths words silently, and then Godard frames her head from behind as she looks around and walks down the street, fading back into an out-of-focus shot. Over the soundtrack we hear an intonation of ruin and destruction: "The lucky ones are the defeated." This statement, which echoes with Mahmoud Darwish's assertion that he would always be the poet of the defeated people, emphasizes Olga's identification with historical loss, though here it is framed as an act of despair rather than a poetic calling into being. As with the lecture scene, Olga's vision is aligned directly with Godard's, as her act of blinking her eyes and then seeing clearly is rhymed with her coming in and out of focus in the film. The phantom-POV I discussed in the previous chapter here includes not only a character's look that sees an absent (out of focus) self, but also by extension Godard's seeing himself not looking.

This sequence organizes Judith's curious gaze, the gaze that sought to find the possibility of reconciliation within the image of historical ruin, across a vector of loss. Attempting to capture an image of the present, Judith is confronted first with the haunting presence of the untimely image of the Native Americans. Throughout the film, these same characters have entered the scene to insist on the claims made on the present by the past and to emphasize the violence of forgetting that follows quickly on the heels of physical violence and mass murder. While they stand for the persistence of an image through history, it is, however, at the cost of a de-figuration that writes them out of the narrative frame and turns them into images for Judith's searching gaze. This shift in narrative registers, this shift into the realm of the phantasmatic, is highlighted by the cut that reframes the Native Americans from the explicit countershot of Judith's look to a closer, more iconic or pictorial framing. It is as part of this series of historical de-framing (and we recall that a similar fate befell the Palestinians who, as they were driven out of their homes in Palestine by the Israeli settlers, became subjects of documentary rather than of fiction) that Olga, whom the narrative places as Judith's obscure double, comes into focus. Olga's spectrality in relation to the narrative is emphasized by the vagueness of her situation, "far from here or later on," as well as by her slow movement in and then back out of focus. I have argued throughout this book that a taboo image is not an image of horror, but rather that it is the horror of the nonimage, the frame that contains the visual signifiers of what it cannot show. In this sense, Olga appears as the taboo image of Judith, the marker of what Judith's camera, and by extension Godard's, cannot properly frame. If, however, Olga is a key to the film's taboo image, this is not due to her contemplation (and eventual fictional enactment) of the "taboo" act of suicide.

Instead, what is taboo in Olga's story is its evocation of a utopian image that erases the memory of historical trauma.

Godard further associates Olga with an unseen image that implicates him in his own failure to see properly, a failure that aligns him, in the final analysis, with cinema's failure to bear witness to history. In the airport, as he is about to leave Sarajevo, Godard is approached by a group of students who give him a DVD of a film shot by Olga that she hopes he will watch. Godard absentmindedly opens and closes the DVD case (on the inside is Olga's face, deformed by the hole of the spindle), but quickly forgets about it. When, back in Switzerland, he receives a call about Olga's death, his difficulty in remembering her name implies that he never watched her film. Erin Schlumpf wonders if seeing the film would have allowed Godard to save Olga, suggesting that the film could have been a way for them to be able to talk to each other.[61] In this sense, Godard's decision to not look would be a kind of rejoinder to the possibility of dialogue with which the characters experiment throughout the conference in Sarajevo. This is supported by Godard's earlier refusal to answer the question about digital cameras as potential saviors of cinema, a silence on which the camera lingers extensively. Godard would thus appear as an obstacle or barrier to communication, unseeing and unspeaking, that would color the more utopian aspects of the film. In relation to Olga, however, the unseen film associates her with the unseen image as an interval, a bit of material reality incorporated between two looks that radically disassociate the two poles of the look and the image. That is, she occupies, here as elsewhere, the unseen image that inscribes a difference between looks or a difference between looking and not looking.

The final section of the film, Paradise, further explores this theme. The short sequence is of a seemingly Edenic scene on the banks of a river (a utopian vision of the Nevetna, perhaps) where young people are occupied in idyllic activities: playing volleyball, reading on the banks of the river, or simply sitting quietly and eating an apple. The river, however, is being watched over by US Marines in military uniforms. Although they seem to be play-acting their roles, at times miming stamping the back of Olga's hand or unsure about what it is that they are guarding, their presence situates this utopian space as a pyrrhic Paradise earned at the cost of permanent military occupation. According to Godard, he wanted to demonstrate the reality of a song sung by US Marines that includes the lyrics "If the army and the navy ever look on Heaven's scene, they will find the streets are guarded by United States marines." Paradise is thus achieved only through the erasure of history, the perpetuation of the eternal present in which any need for dialogue has been eliminated because all conflicts have been resolved into an image of perpetual occupation. Perpetual occupation, Godard suggests, marks the desire to undo history and erase trauma through an incorporation of loss.

This is the sense in which the cryptophore's utopia is a world in which the wound had never taken place, and it thus presents an image not of the resolution of difference through dialogue but of an original unity in which military power exists peacefully and naturally in a place where historical trauma has been permanently erased. Olga haunts this cryptic space of nondifference, walking through it like a specter as she passes by the groups of teenagers at play or rest without speaking to them or joining in. Finally, at the bank of the river, she looks up and closes her eyes; Godard cuts to black, signaling the end. The film thus ends with a truly cryptophoric gesture that refuses the very possibility of a countershot. The black screen here is not the interval between two looks that inserts a difference or question, but the marker of the limits of montage to make a difference. Associating this black screen with Olga's "unseen film"— and perhaps here we can speculate that paradise is a version of her film that Godard never watched—thus suggests that in *Notre musique*, rediscovering the origin of montage means returning to a place before the image (that is, before Olga opened her eyes during Godard's lecture), a place of nonlooking analogous to the moment of nonknowledge to which Abraham and Torok's anasemia returns everyday speech. What remains an open question is whether this suggests a truly cryptic scene from which no true image can emerge, or whether the image of nonseeing can lead to a new poetics of the cinema.

Re-Visions

Naomi Uman and Cinematic Decryption

> Installed in place of the lost object, the
> incorporated object continues to recall the fact that
> something else was lost: the desires quelled by repression.
> —Maria Torok, "The Illness of Mourning and
> the Fantasy of the Exquisite Corpse"

> I focus on customs that are about to disappear I live with people who
> continue to milk cows by hand; who plant, harvest, and preserve their
> own food. I, too, engage in these practices. . . . Seeing the past before it
> vanishes prolongs the present and makes it more profound.
> —Naomi Uman

Border Zones

The previous chapters have traced various figurations of cinematic crypts buried within images of European postwar cinema. These crypts emerged as both spatial and temporal responses to failed mourning. Built into the modern architecture of rezoned European cities, the crypts functioned as spaces of internal exclusion that appeared, cinematically, as displacements between interior and exterior spaces. The crypts did not contain, however, the bodies of the dead and the forgotten. Instead, they enclosed and expelled the absence of an image, the designifying mark of what hasn't been filmed or seen. Cinematic crypts produced narrative and historiographic temporalities of secrets: fragments of the past inherited across generations that remain invisible and unknowable across time, a condition of nescience shared by characters, filmmakers, spectators, and critics. In this chapter, I return to focus on the spatial character of the crypt to consider Naomi Uman's ethnographic practice as one of spatial decryption. This takes the history of cinematic cryptonymies beyond postwar Europe and outside the boundaries of European art and genre filmmaking to reveal the power of cinema to decrypt the image and break the walls of cinematic incorporation, allowing the phantoms of the missing bodies to speak.

Transient and temporary in regard to its circuits of production and circulation, at least when compared to the edifices of national and commercial filmmaking, Uman's artisanal avant-garde practice aims to actively interrupt and reframe the spaces and images in which she intervenes. It is in this sense a critical (or reparative) rather than a cryptophoric cinema. And it is this reparative function that gives the general form to the cinematographic figure that I call the internal off-screen, the incorporation of the invisible within the visible as a new, visual figure. Uman invents and reinvents the internal off-screen in each of the films I discuss in this chapter, but in each case, it functions as a visible erasure that reveals a previously hidden absence, a heretofore erased occlusion of a missing or marginalized body. This body under erasure is the internal law of each of Uman's images and also its unframed exteriority. Thus, while the body is retrieved from within its nonvisibility, this is only through a radical act of nonfilming and nondocumentation that remains at the heart of Uman's artisanal and ethnographic practice. Uman's experimental cinema is defined by her attempt to give form to bodies that, no longer able to appear in their own image or speak their own name, have passed into the grave of signification. Calling forth the dead or socially vanished into the world of the living demands the invention of a critical, embodied historical practice that transforms the power of visual negation into a manifestation of real absence. This entails a series of methodological practices that situate the dislocations of bodies within images, creating a unique cinematic structure: the internal off-screen. In contrast with the off-screen that skirts, bounds, and extends the image, the internal off-screen is a foreign body lodged in the scene of the visible. While designating an out-of-placeness and a disruption of the image, it remains a visual and figurative element: a readable trace of what is not seen. As such, it unframes the image, incorporating a foreign presence of an origin elsewhere. The internal off-screen articulates the very boundary of the seen and the unseen, presence and absence, the proper and the taboo.

The internal off-screen takes a different form in each of the two great modes in which Uman has worked to date: found footage and experimental ethnography. The two forms are united by a commitment to artisanal production and an exploration of spatial and temporal boundaries and passages. "I focus on customs that are about to disappear," she says. "I live with people who continue to milk cows by hand; who plant, harvest, and preserve their own food. I, too, engage in these practices. . . . Seeing the past before it vanishes prolongs the present and makes it more profound."[1] This search for horizons of disappearance, and for a method that can preserve them in the present, has led Uman to create a unique cinema of borders, passages, and temporary zones. Where Georges Franju mapped a spectral topography of the internal exclusions of the dead within a landscape undergoing modernization but still organized by center and periphery, Uman traces the boundary spaces at the far ends of the geographic dispersal of economic activity that has characterized the global economic system since the 1980s. In her book *The Global City*, Saskia Sassen argues that the decentralization of economic activity in the postindustrial era has led to an increased centralization of management and profit in a small handful of global cities that link and organize the peripheral zones.[2] It is in these externalized territories that older modes of subsistence are being rezoned in the interests of a capitalist order located *elsewhere*, in places of economic management that are no longer in any real sense the *center* or interiority of the periphery. Uman's camera follows the line of a boundary that has lost its coordinates. In the found-footage films, she refashions the cinema screen into an interstice across which diverse elements are animated around an absent center. Her ethnographic films are documents of, and direct lived interventions in, a series of disappearing acts performed on and by the raced and sexed bodies that haunt the border zones. Both function according to a logic that Abraham and Torok call incorporation: the inclusion of a lost object within the self as a way of isolating it beyond the "proper zone" of psychic life. The interior off-screen figures incorporation within visual technologies.

The Disembodied Hand

Uman's films return frequently to the site of an absent figure incorporated within an image. The incorporated figure transgresses the borders between the visible and the nonvisible, the framed and the unframed, by creating a unique zone of in-visibility: the internal off-screen. Abraham and Torok stress the difference between incorporation and the process of introjection as defined by Sándor Ferenczi. Whereas introjection describes the expansion of the ego by way of its symbolic apprehension of the outside world, incorporation is the inclusion of an object in the self as an isolated fragment, absent the symbolic connections that enrich our inner lives. Incorporation reduces the lost object to a literal, material remainder, a *thing* lodged within the psyche. Like psychoanalytic incorporation, the internal off-screen signifies the inclusion of a foreign body within a topographic frame. While appearing as a textual gap, the incorporated figure produces, and is produced by, interstices within a social order, invoking a subject incorporated *within* and *against* an already determined image of social reality. Giving these incorporated bodies shape reclaims them from their erasure within the visual. This process can be understood as taking up, in a different register, Walter Benjamin's call for history to be used as a mode of political critique that reanimates past forms and bodies within the present. In "Surrealism: The Last Snapshot of the European Intelligentsia," Benjamin posits that surrealism substitutes a political for a historical view of the past, and he credits André Breton with having been the first to perceive the revolutionary energies of the outmoded, those dead forms with the potential to rupture the self-presence of the present.[3] Uman's invention of an internal off-screen figures this historical process cinematographically.

By focusing her camera on those customs and ways of life that are about to disappear, Uman incorporates the absence of old forms into the acts of re-vision that define her found-footage and ethnographic practices. Reading the resulting internal off-screen as a place of cinematographic incorporation emphasizes several commonalities between the psychoanalytic and cinematographic techniques of corporeal inclusion. In both situations, a process of figuration includes what is outside of itself as an active and signifying material element that hollows out the figure's expressive unity. Understanding loss, in its broadest sense, as denoting that which cannot be assimilated or signified, we can see that in both cases incorporation interiorizes loss as a figure of designification or nonmeaning within a symbolic structure. Additionally, in both cases the incorporated figure is isolated from the other characters in the scene, preserved in toto but cut off from its associations with the ideas or figures that surround it. The result is a spatial dislocation and a temporal desynchronization: the past as a pause of the present, the outside as a zone of the inside. As such, incorporation produces the film as a spectral body marked by the presence of a revenant, the figural "mark of the untimeliness and disadjustment of the contemporary," as Jacques Derrida describes the condition of haunting.[4] This situation blurs temporal and spatial boundaries by bringing a number of incommensurate states into direct relation across a gap in signification. Likewise, in Uman's work, the internal off-screen is the site of an intimate linkage of past and present, observer and observed, filmmaker and film body, across a visual gap, producing a haunted field of vision.

Uman's early found-footage film, *Hand Eye Coordination* (2002), is a playful meditation on the screen as a spectral field without clear boundaries. Following a black-and-white shot of an eye that fills the frame, opening suddenly, we see an animated collage of found footage and newly filmed shots of Uman's hands. The hands move through a series of signifying gestures: opening, clenching, caressing, pointing, writing, and tattooing. As the hands explore the tactile boundaries of the screen, the eye is displaced from the center and origin of the image and the frame is, in turn, decentered and transformed into a field of free-floating signifiers. This also produces a shift from a detached and passive relation with the image to an embodied one. "Shooting and editing [on actual film]," says Uman, "implies a physical contact and a rote repetitive action of cutting and splicing as well as winding the camera that is all very manual, very tactile."[5] By inserting her own hands into the series of symbolic gestures, Uman inscribes this manual activity of filmmaking within the image, asserting the primacy of the filmmaker's body as the precondition for any act of cinematic seeing. In-visioning its manual origins, and integrated into the series of images, filmmaking is incorporated into the signifying practices being documented. The formula of the film may be stated as: *Where the eye was, the hand comes to be*.[6]

As the terminal point of the gaze, the cinematic image has been theorized as the locus of a reflective depth at which the spectators grasp themselves at the other side of a look of no return. In this theorization, the look precedes the image, since it is the condition of its existence, and constitutes (genders, races) bodies within an imaginary field of difference that can be mastered by the spectator's free-floating eye. Crucial to this formulation is the constitution of the image as an already complete and unified reality. It is the necessary exclusion of the spectator from the framed image that guarantees the mastery of the image, the ability to see everything that it has to offer, and thus the sense that it shows the fullness of vision.[7] By including her hands within the frame, Uman uncompletes this full image, incorporating the time of production within the future tense of the spectator's look while preserving her own (past) labor as a visual figure within the present. Perpetually unfinished, the image shows not a complete visual totality, but the figuration of the process of symbolic creation.

Two shots emphasize the experience of watching a film caught in the pleasure of its own (un)making. In the first, Uman's hands write out the film's title, "Hand Eye Coordination," in white on a black surface. This shot plays on the metaphor contained in the title and its reference to the eye's function in guiding the hand as it grasps and manipulates objects in the world. As the spectator's eye follows Uman's hands in titling the movie, it forms a compound body: the looker's eye coordinated with the filmmaker's hand in the production of an embodied dialogic text. This compound viewer-maker body uncouples the filmmaker from the origin of the image, relating this origin back to another's look. This is the sense of incorporation borrowed from Abraham and Torok in which an absent body is included within the cinematic crypt-image. At the same time as this shot reassembles the filmic body, subverting the active-passive binary that so often structures the relation between filmmaker and spectator, it also highlights the spectators' absence, having necessarily arrived too late for the making of the film.

Later, in one of the film's final shots, Uman's hands are shown directly in close-up as she scrapes the emulsion from a strip of footage, etching and scratching the material. Unlike the earlier scene of writing, this shot of removal generates a field of unreadable marks as Uman's hands unmake the found image. The presence of visual errata is a feature of many of Uman's films, often denoting a printing "error" preserved in the chemical compound. Scratches, stains, dust, and seams: entire poems of the impressions left by the touching intimacy between film, body, and world transform the image into a corporeal translucence. This process shot envisions the resonance, central to many of Uman's films, between the maker's body and the unmade image. In the films, an image often comes about through the unframing or unmaking of a previous one, a gesture that she frequently visually associates with writing. The filmmaker's hand is a boundary relating the spectator's eye to the screen and connecting the image to its erasure in translucent light. Cutting out the hands from the original film footage, detaching them from a whole body, and animating them within delicate calligraphies of cracked and scraped emulsion, Uman transforms touch into a cryptic absence designating the host of missing bodies that populate the film's internal world: spectator, filmmaker, and figure.

Writing Erasure: *Removed*

Uman's touch also *creates* absent bodies in the found-footage ghost-comedy *Removed* (1999). The procedure for the invention of bodies is as straightforward as it is exacting: working directly on the emulsion with nail polish remover and household bleach, she strips two fragments of a German porn film—frame by frame—of its most obvious visual lure: the women's naked bodies. In so doing she manifests a second, haunting body that hovers within the still intact but now vacant seedy hotel rooms and moves among the male performers left to their own devices. This spectral elsewhere within the frame testifies to a scene of incorporation. Abraham and Torok write that the only visible evidence of the Wolf Man's incorporations were two complementary images,

> each incomplete in its manifest state: the first the erogenous image of a woman in the position of a scrubwoman, then the second one, a complement to the first, of a phobia-producing erect wolf. We understand now that the Wolf Man could expose only his various modes of not being himself to analysis.[8]

Having buried loss—and with it any possibility of its mourning—within himself, the Wolf Man was left only with these two complementary images by which to represent the shameful and anxiety-producing desire that he had locked away and preserved in the corporeal crypt. *Removed* also confronts us with two complementary but incomplete images. Through the partial and unfinished marks of erasure, the original image continues to flicker around a loss that it (and the male characters within it) cannot acknowledge. But the spectral image itself seems to have arrived from another time to announce the still unfinished project of a critical feminist history. Read as the space of multiple incorporations, the absent body transforms *Removed* into a crypt-film on (the surface of) which Uman's visible and embodied marks are inscribed as the writing of a critical historical dialectic.

In each of *Removed*'s two scenes, a banal and generic pornographic encounter is revealed as a playful scene of textual, and erotic, misrecognition. Each scene stages not the sexual act itself but the circulation of its signifiers (language and the image) and the signifiers of its circulation (money and the look). In the first, a woman lies on a bed spread with piles of loose cash as a man, bored almost to the point of indifference, looks on. The visual metonymy of the woman's excessively desirous body and the overflowing excesses of loose cash figure commercial pornography in its most naked guise. As originally screened, the woman's body anchors the frame, guaranteeing the gaze's mastery of a visual depth without lack or absence. The woman's removal, however, decenters and surfaces the image, allowing the spectator's eyes to wander across the cheap mise-en-scène and to notice the man's indifference to his partner's presence, the flatness of lighting and decor, and, most prominently, the surface of representation itself; in short, the spectator is invited to see everything that the woman's body had previously seduced the viewer into overlooking. In the second scene, a man and woman spy on a young couple in an adjoining hotel room through a two-way mirror. As the man describes what he sees—the shape of the woman's breasts, the flatness of her stomach, her way of undressing—his partner compares his words to her own body, breathlessly demanding to hear more. The insertion of a hint of lesbian desire, mediated by the man's look, flickers a second scene into view: that of the erotics of Uman's hands stripping the women's bodies frame by frame from the visual center of masculine desire. While in the first scene the association of the woman's naked pleasure with money provided a shorthand for the pornographic scenario as commoditized fetish, this second scene queers the image, turning speech into a lure of vision and a substitute for women's bodies. In their absence, language misses its target, describing precisely what is not there in the image and thus reflecting the deferral of desire. It is into this erotic theater of mirrors and reflections, into this mise en abyme of the pornographic scene, that Uman inserts an abyssal gap on the surface of the film.

Most discussions of *Removed* focus on the resulting absences, reading in their place a critical revision through which the expectations of industrial, heteronormative pornography—centered on the absolute visibility of the woman's body—are subverted.⁹ Undoubtedly one of the pleasures of viewing the film is the reversal of the photochemical reaction—dissolving rather than binding the image—and the pulsations of the pornographic fetish as it emerges from and is again obscured by this mark of its dissolution. The result, however, is not principally subtractive. Rather, Uman's act reifies, in place of the women's images, a new figure of desire: a flickering body composed of light passing through clear celluloid. This phantom body reverses the logic of the original film: where the women's bodies appeared as reflections of male desire, the phantom is the terminus of a nonreflective logic of touch, light, and intimacy that interrupts the narrative and figural circulation of looks. Akira Mizuta Lippit posits that a corporeal double vision, the duplication of a body and its erasure, is constitutive of cinema as a whole. The cinema, he says, images an ecstatic body, a body beside itself, because of the act of photographic duplication that "produces at once an extension of the body indexically from world to cinema, and which also generates an absent body, a phantom body that appears in the film under erasure."¹⁰ The originality of *Removed* is that Uman incorporates this absent body, the figure and its erasure, as a visual component within the frame. Like the complementary images treasured by the Wolf Man as the expressions of his cryptic desire, the visual complement of the phantom-body speaks of a transgressive erotic scene. "I wanted to see what would happen if you remove the women [from the pornographic film]," explains Uman of her motivations for making the film. "Would it still be pornography? In an odd way the resulting film is far more erotic than the original."¹¹ This erotic supplement arises from the destruction of the possibility of the simple screening of a sex film.¹² Created by stripping the chemical emulsion, the erotic specter appears where the original image is violated by a touching look that has had to reach across time (across the temporality of revision) to complete the discarded image in a film to come. In so doing we—filmmaker and spectators, worker and seer—reanimate the women's bodies, reclaiming them from their burial in the banal scenarios of industrial pornography. How should we read these erotic and still-living phantoms that return from the present? "[Eroticism's] function on the level of discourse is the same as on the level of bodies," argues Denis Hollier in his book on the writings of Georges Bataille. "It weakens the discontinuities that create individuals, ruptures limits and frontiers (both psychological and epistemological), and adds incompletion to completion."¹³

Far from a simple gap, the phantom in *Removed* is the erotic incompletion of the original finished film, a rupture of the frontier of both frame and time that responds to Uman's promise of filmmaking as the preservative vision of things and practices at the moment of their vanishing.

And yet it is the body's clear opacity, its transparent visibility, that haunts us in turn across the temporal breach. Insofar as the gesture of erasure inscribes a new eroticism of ruptured and collaged bodies, it does so by envisioning the withdrawal of the woman's look from the represented scene, rewriting it in the register of a second scene of filmmaking. It leaves the original film in abandon, hollowed out, not unlike the crypt that, in a vastly different time and place but in a similar register, was abandoned by Christiane in *Eyes without a Face* to become the burial place of an entire series of nameless women. What this unsettling rhyme between the cryptic scenes in *Eyes* and *Removed* suggests is that the phantom appears not (only) in the place of the women's presence, but as the crypt-image of women's original absence from the cinematic scene. And, moreover, that it (does not) speak(s) to a buried substitution of violence against and erasure of women's presence across the history of images.

An important tradition of feminist film theory has focused on precisely this figural and epistemological violence of woman's erasure in the screen image—a violence that is anchored by an embodied and structural violence in the social realm. Claire Johnston has shown that the woman's filmed body is at once the locus of visual pleasure and the sign of her nonbeing, since it answers to the law of verisimilitude in which the image of woman is also the "celebration of her non-existence."[14] Turned into spectacle and become the mere object of the gaze, the woman's image anchors the spectator's mastery of the frame because it offers no reverse shot from which the looking subject can be challenged. Kaja Silverman builds on this contention to argue that the visibility of the women's bodies—that is, their spectacular absence—not only signifies a nonbeing but also absorbs the male subject's lack. The image of woman stands in for that which can't be mastered, but it does so only by becoming a fetish or screen blocking the various gaps constitutive of the framed image. Staged as the object *for* the circulation of the male look, as the lure for the play of desire and vision that structures the classical cinema, the female body incorporates "the various losses which haunt cinema, from the foreclosed real to the invisible agency of enunciation."[15] The classical narrative film—and here the pornographic image and its demand for the absolute visibility of the female body is merely the nude expression of this more general principle—*begins* by removing the woman from the film, placing her, phantasmatically, beyond the frame and outside the symbolic order. As Linda Williams has shown, this is a nonplace that women share not only with the Real and the spectatorial Subject, but also with the monster of the horror film.[16] Crucially, in each of these cases it is not absence alone that gives rise to the twinned affects of desire and terror—in pornography as much as in the horror film—but the ability of woman and monster to appear *in their absence*, to occupy the place of their nonbeing and in so doing to deframe the image and mark the subject's blind spot and lack of mastery over the completed whole. These now classic studies have been properly criticized for their generalizations from a limited corpus of privileged examples, and undoubtedly this condition of absence does not describe the cinema (or pornography) as a whole, yet we should not lose sight of the fact that this absence figures not only in the Hollywood dream factory or its shadows in the art cinemas of Europe, but also continues to describe the dominant mode of the cinematic image.[17] In any case, it is along this trench of representation within which the woman's image is already a crypt-image, in and of itself the figural displacement of women's social nonbeing, that the erasures in *Removed* ironically mimic the female body as an image of nonpresence and lack.

Seen in this light, Uman's work *returns* the women's bodies to the film by removing their absence while at the same time incorporating their loss as figures of erasure. By giving corporeal form to the nonpresence that has been screened by the body, Uman enframes this absence at the center, and as the very condition, of the screened visuality. Where the pornographic image had used the crypt-image of the naked body to preserve the woman's absence, *Removed* erases this invisibility. The spectral body appears *in place and as a substitute of* the crypt-image. To the extent that the original film had already incorporated the woman—already transformed her into the substitute image of her specular form in order to repress her repression, erase her erasure—*Removed* is the incorporation of incorporation; it is the parodic-critical gesture by which an incorporation in the pornographic film (and the social field that it images) is transformed into a joyful eroticism in an act of cinematic transference.[18] *Removed* is, in this light, a kind of contact sheet onto which the found footage has been impressed and onto which both the original image *and* the unconscious wish of absence contained therein have been transferred. Secreted from the pornographic surface of the original, the women's absence is actualized in the chemical body of *Removed* and can appear within a second scene of desire: Uman's desire, our desire, for the still living but encrypted—the revivified—filmed body.[19]

The consequences of the irruption of this second scene in the internal off-screen are twofold, encompassing an institutional-discursive transvaluation along with a textual and social decryption. Where the original film would most probably have been screened in the solitude of a darkened porn theater or in the secret privacy of the home, the experimental film is far more likely to find life in the social gatherings of film festivals and pedagogic viewings in the classroom. And, where the original was aimed at the corporeal frisson of the body genres Carol Clover and Linda Williams describe, *Removed* is at least equally destined for the realms of a (discursive) critical analysis.[20] Of course the film's power, even its eroticism, can largely be traced to its ability to occupy both registers simultaneously, but its frame has shifted, and this shift can in part be understood as arising from the *blockage* of the circulation of embodied desire. This is a symbolic blockage that short-circuits the pornographic spectacle and inserts in its place a new figure: linguistic, discursive, and, in any case, graphemic. Like the aporias of Franju's taboo images, the phantom creates a readable body that interrupts the self-evident unity of the represented scene. This discursive phantom in turn makes the artisanal labor of Uman's intervention into a form of handwriting that signs the surface of the film. Writing about the painted and scratched film surface in Carolee Schneeman's *Fuses* (1967), Akira Mizuta Lippit argues that it "transforms the act from a spectacle to a sign, a tactile proximity to an optical distance; the entire event is moved to the surface of the film."[21] What is unique to *Removed* is that, in taking on the very form of the spectacular body whose signature it is, the marked surface designifies the original, inserting a real absence (the scratch where the emulsion has been stripped) in place of its sign (the woman's body as signatory of her absence, the words and bills that put it into circulation). Abraham and Torok propose that incorporation involves two interrelated procedures: "*demetaphorization* (taking literally what is meant figuratively) and *objectivation* (pretending that the suffering is not an injury to the subject but instead a loss sustained by the love object)."[22] By incorporating the marks of production within the original found footage, *Removed* literalizes the "metaphor" of erasure of the woman's body by commercial cinema (which is itself always more than a metaphor) and inscribes a loss directly within the cinematic love object.

For Uman, however, it is not enough, as it was for Franju, to map the cryptic topographies of incorporated bodies. Instead, *Removed* opens the figural crypt to the haunting demand of those buried in its original fabrication. This decryption demands the creation of bodies capable of envisioning their own images, signing their own names. This, according to Walter Benjamin, is the promise of the image to come *after* the assault on the social body practiced by surrealism:

> In all cases where an action puts forth its own image and exists, absorbing and consuming it, where nearness looks with its own eyes, the long-sought image sphere is opened, the world of universal and integral actualities, where the 'best room' is missing—the sphere, in a word, in which political materialism and physical nature share the inner man, the psyche, the individual, or whatever else we wish to throw to them, with dialectical justice, so that no limb remains unrent. Nevertheless—indeed, precisely after such dialectical annihilation—this will still be a sphere of images and, more concretely, of bodies.[23]

Uman's mark is precisely the type of action that, following the paths of demetaphorization and incorporation, absorb and consume bodies—her own (absorbed in the labor and signed on the image of the found footage) as well as those she discovers in the crypts of the past.

Because it reveals the materiality of erasure, because it is readable as the white script through which the women's disembodied and rent images continue to flicker in the twilight of their dialectical annihilation, the figural phantom suspends the body within its concealment. Brought to visibility as a missing figure, the image under the sign of visible erasure produces an extratextual scene. Uman's intervention in *Removed* is to materialize women's social invisibility as the ground of the visible, written on the emulsion, such that what remains of the hypervisibility of the body in the pornographic look is only the material disappearance of its nonbeing. This absence, the gap through which the male subject organizes his own fictive unity, makes visible the very figural origin that the dominant cinema places beyond representation. In so doing, Uman also isolates the women's images from the original scene, allowing them to appear, instead, as love objects personified for a second scene, the scene of handmade production and Uman's acts of tactile revision. She thus reclaims its erotics, removing it from the economy of pornographic production and preserving it whole for the pleasure of our own desire. In the act of incorporation, the encrypted and silent object becomes the testimony of a missing exteriority for which the language of desire is written.

Ethnographies of the Internal Off-Screen

Uman's twin dairy films document the condition of raced and gendered bodies in the cryptic peripheral spaces of labor set against the horizon of the US-Mexico border. *Leche* (1998) was filmed at the Rancho la Primavera in the central Mexican state of Aguascalientes. The film was shot on black-and-white 16mm stock, and Uman processed it by hand on the ranch using the same tools that the farmers used in their daily work. *Leche* explores the rhythms of a relatively traditional way of life deeply connected to the land and to the social community that develops among family members and the daily activities of work, food, and play. *Mala Leche* (2003) shifts the setting to Pixley, California, where men from the same family as in the earlier film work twelve-hour shifts in an industrial dairy farm. Shot in color and punctuated by long intertitles of text printed against a black screen, the film emphasizes the isolation of the immigrant community, who live among the many signs of their internal exclusion within the social, political, and economic topography of the United States. To make these films, Uman lived with the families, working among and with them on the films while letting her camera capture their daily lives. Each of the films is also about her own place as an outsider within the spaces that she documents. Whereas *Leche* shows Uman participating in the artisanal labor of the dairy ranch, in *Mala Leche* we witness several scenes that, in various ways, elude and escape her camera, creating a visual absence, an unfilmed or unfilmable image. In one seemingly minor example, Diana, a young girl, deliberately ducks away from the camera, slipping behind the brick column of the house where Uman is shooting. Only her ponytail remains visible as the shot holds briefly, framing the haunted space of the girl's figural refusal. An intertitle reveals that Diana did not want to be filmed without her makeup. Although the scene demonstrates a small, and playful, game of hide and seek between filmmaker and subject, it is part of a larger pattern of figural absence that runs throughout the work, culminating in a reported but unfilmed scene of violence. Taken together, the two dairy films present a lived ethnography that tries to capture the border space of a body's vanishing within the crypts of social incorporation.

The films return throughout to two related themes. The first is the theme of affective domestic labor performed primarily by women. Uman's interest is in the embodied character of this work as she investigates what women's bodies do as they cook, cut hair, care for children, and so on. A second, related theme is that of the role of the camera within the spaces it films and, moreover, the role of Uman's filmmaking as part of the larger experience of women's labor. "I think of myself as an ethnographer," says Uman in describing her practice of lived documentaries, "and I have a particular way of observing and interacting with my world and my subjects."[24] This inhabited ethnography can be understood as an act of framing (observing) and as one of acting (participating in the family, filming and developing the film, and such). Uman's ethnographies require a coordination of eye and hand, observer and participant. Understood thus, these films belong to the practices marked out by the intersection of feminism and experimental ethnography as outlined by Catherine Russell in *Experimental Ethnography: The Work of Film in the Age of Video*.

> Autobiography can . . . be an important form of experimental ethnography and points to another intersection of feminism and ethnographic representation. The interest in "everyday life," the representation of detail, and the routines of daily life are also crucial ways in which feminist concerns have combined with ethnographic forms in the renewal of an alternative film culture.[25]

While clarifying the experience of cohabitation so central to Uman's work, this evocation of experimental ethnography also suggests the potentials and dangers that Hal Foster points to in "The Artist as Ethnographer?" For Foster, the promise of a collaborative investigation contained in the (self-)fashioning of the artist as ethnographer too often leads to a fetishization of the other as the privileged image of a politics of alterity producing an "ethnographic self-fashioning in which the artist is not decentered so much as the other is fashioned in artistic guise."[26] Culture here becomes the site of the political, but, Foster warns, it thus runs the risk of an enculturation of politics as aesthetic practice.

How does Uman inhabit the space of the ethnographic artist? She begins, she says, with a long period of waiting that allows her to transform the ethnographic space into one of her own experience. All her nonfiction films draw from personal experience: "I live with my subjects for long periods of time, often waiting to film or record sound until I have become integrated into a community or a family."[27] This is precisely the point of intersection between autobiography and ethnography touched on by Russell above. The artist is decentered from the center *elsewhere* of ethnographic knowledge to the middle of the everyday and the social whose image she wants to capture. Next, Uman remains attentive in these films to the ways in which the coordination between (ethnographic) eye and (autobiographical) hand—this connection between a certain way of seeing and touching that is also the connection between self and other, artist and ethnographic subject—is disturbed and haunted by a body under erasure, a body incorporated within or between these two privileged organs of filmmaking and the two bodies of ethnography, the self and the other. The possibility offered by this figure of erasure is not, of course, that it magically solves the problem of alterity discussed by Foster. There is no secret incantation with which to wish away the asymmetrical nature of an encounter between filmmaker and "subject." Rather, the power of the incorporated body under erasure is its ability to figure the social and private spaces of ethnography as already cryptic, already incorporating an exteriority that they (fail to) erase.

In *Removed*, Uman made her own acts of erasure visible as the manifestation of an erotic body placed within the specular and linguistic circulation of desire. Bringing this specter into the visible demanded both retracing an absence whose origin was outside the image (women's social nonbeing as the reverse side of the image of desire) and figuring the ways in which this external absence was itself subject to an encryption within the image. This is why I called this internal off-screen in *Removed* a crypt-image: like the psychoanalytic crypt, it is an erasure of an erasure, the repression of a repression. It created a new body, a figural taboo incorporated as a gap in the circulation of looks and words and cast outside of the proper textual scene to the material emulsion and the second scene of production. The result was a contradiction in the spectatorial experience. The women's bodies, while partially displaced from the mise-en-scène of the visible, remained *readable* as revenants of another time, and the spectator was tasked with looking through the original in order to see the material trace of the women's bodies outside of the pornographic look.

In the dairy films, however, absence more often demarcates the film's visual limit, inscribing the *unfilmable* within the frame. In the shot described above of Diana's refusal to be filmed, as in the dairy films more generally, Uman's camera marks a boundary or zone of visibility from which the subject removes herself, leaving behind an incomplete visual field. This act of unframing is performed from within the original scene and not from its revision; that is to say, it belongs to the documented scene, the original interplay between camera and world. In one sense, we can understand this action as it relates to the concept of *objectivation* mentioned earlier, the process by which an injury suffered by the subject is treated as a loss sustained by the love object. The internal off-screen left vacant by an act of refusal before the camera "injures" the film in the sense that it objectifies what the film cannot witness. This zone of nonwitnessing, however, is not only a gap in the visual field but also the visual testimony of the subject's exclusion from the social field. This is why the internal off-screen is also an act of *deframing*, haunting the framed image with an absence in the world. The frame of the visual thus becomes the periphery of the unfilmed figure, and the haunted spaces become border zones registering various acts of figural exclusion through the internal off-screen space left vacant by the evasive bodies at their center. Being unable or refusing to film here figures the search for a way of seeing and being as an ethnographer of crypts whose subjects embody a temporality of disappearance and erasure.

Leche, filmed between 1996 and 1998 when Uman was living at Rancho la Primavera, is composed of several series of fragmentary images and sounds: portraits of family members at work, school, or play; shots of animals loose or in pens; intertitles describing events or listing the names of children and cattle and written by Uman's hand on a blackboard in English and Spanish; and an asynchronous soundtrack weaving together Uman's voice, a woman's song, and animal noises. Its organizing rhyme is the repeated but varied gestures of hands that appear, often in close-up and performing different activities. In contrast with the hand's isolated symbolic and signifying function in *Hand Eye Coordination*, in *Leche* the hands are engaged in social activities of labor and care: pressing cheese, flipping tortillas over a wood fire, branding livestock, feeding a calf from its mother's udders, knitting, cutting hair, and many other actions small and large. As the film passes from hand to hand across rhyming but distinct gestures, the seriality of images evokes the polyrhythmic temporality of everyday life. Henri Lefebvre discovered a similar temporality in the gardens and courtyards outside his Paris apartment:

> Continue and you will see this garden and the *objects* (which are in no way things) polyrhythmically, or if you prefer symphonically. In place of a collection of fixed things, you will follow each *being*, each *body*, as having its own time above the whole. Each one therefore having its place, its rhythm, with its recent past, a foreseeable and distant future.[28]

While evoking a place abandoned or lost to time, a place *before* industrial mass production, the rhythm created by the shots of manual labor in *Leche* contains the promise of a time to come, a foreseeable and distant future grasped in the intimacy of hands. This is because the temporality of the acts is inscribed within a rhythmic future time based on the repetition of singular gestures. Rhythm, says Nicolas Abraham in a tacit agreement with Lefebvre, contains its own future as the continuity of past forms.

Although Uman doesn't include images of her filmmaking practice in *Leche*, filmmaking frames and is incorporated as a virtual image within the series of hands. Filmmaking is visually registered by the splotches, scratches, and other "imperfections" that mark the surface of the black-and-white 16mm film. Working with the tools available on the ranch, Uman left her film to dry on a clothesline outside. The contact between the unfinished film and the sun, wind, and dust on the ranch created the visual imperfections, and these imperfections are ghosts in time, figuring the history of the image's coming into being, the adventure of its exposure to the rhythms of the natural environment. As such, these "imperfect" images preserve not only another, vanished, time but also the fugitive presence of the filmmaker whose manual labor process—that physical contact and rote repetitive action of cutting and splicing as well as winding the camera—is denoted on the emulsion (inside the image's outside). In short, these phantoms, like every incorporated guest, figure the lost object within a dialectic of history that calls forth the past into the present as it embodies, at the other side of vision, "the past before it vanishes" in order to "prolong the present and mak[e] it more profound."[29]

Writing about found footage films, Catherine Russell has developed the allegory of experimental ethnography as time travel, an allegory echoed by *Leche*'s invocation of a passing way of life. In archival film, writes Russell, "the appropriated image points back to the profilmic past as if it were a parallel universe of science fiction."[30] In this *untimely* quality of found footage, we discover the critical history called for by Benjamin, a history in which the refuse of past forms, rather than being located in a distant past, is used as the haunting negation of the present in order to imagine, from within a historical horizon, the figure of a future to come, a future loosened from the inevitability of our tomorrow. What is discovered by the use of the found footage time machine is that this surrealist historical dialectic is not merely a reversal of time by which the past becomes a possible future but is more profoundly an assault on the very conditions of historicity as temporal progression. As archival cinema incorporates a new image *into* a salvaged original, it twists and spirals the teleological edge of origin and finality, blurs the distinct temporalities of past and future, scrambles the magnetic poles of original and revision, and—perhaps most crucially for my purposes—displaces the acts of spectatorship and filmmaking. Akira Lippit calls this the politics of revision. In a discussion of what he terms recycled cinema, including not only *Removed* but also Bruce Conner's *Crossroads*, Harun Farocki and Andrei Ujică's *Videograms of a Revolution*, and Peter Forgács's *The Maelstrom*, among others, Lippit unfolds their strange temporal enfoldings:

> Found-footage works define the conflict between fact and figure, archive and invention, by inscribing an aesthetics and politics of revision. They undermine the originality of the original, as well as its immutability, drawing into question the singularity of any text. . . . Like the temporal logic of the unconscious, past and present appear simultaneously in found-footage films.[31]

In both Russell's conception of found footage as time travel and Lippit's exploration of recycled cinema as the temporal logic of the unconscious, the present is inscribed into the past in order to preserve this past *as presence* within the future. What Abraham and Torok's incorporation adds to this dialogue, as we saw in the incorporated bodies found in *Removed*, is the insistence that such a presence always appears in its absence, as a gap or silence that blocks and disrupts (historical) signification as it testifies to the encrypted scene: the scene of (impossible) desire that led to the construction of the substitutional archive.

Although *Leche* is not an archival or found film in the sense used by Russell and Lippit, its images evoke the mournful experience of leafing through an old family album discovered in the attic. As the children arrange themselves to be photographed in the doorway of the house, as Hilberto walks out in his full charro gear ready to show off his fancy lasso moves, or as Altagracia demonstrates her technique for cooking tortillas on a wood fire ("they were so delicious we sometimes ate them with just salt" says Uman in voice-over), the frontal framing, the isolation of the figures in space, and the clear intimacy between Uman and her subjects give the impression of images captured in private so as to remember the fleeting experiences of everyday family life. There is a twofold sense of the found image deployed here. First, for the spectators, it is like coming upon images meant for another: another time, another eye. Marked by their own decay on the emulsion and structured through a familiarity from which we are excluded, these portraits point back to a past that we, travelers from an incompossible future, can only haunt. Second, Uman's filmmaking—dependent on extended cohabitation, the open temporality of waiting, and her own integration into the spaces she documents—is a posture of the filmmaker through which she can find images within the chronotopes she occupies. Living and working alongside the family for an extended period of time, Uman discovers their poses, gestures, and bodies in the passing moments that she spends with them, just as much as they, playing to and with the camera eye, discover their own image in her mediated look. Where found footage is defined as the salvage of old film remainders that are then revised and worked over, here the process of discovery is that of the image as it gives itself to the camera to be found within the frame. While we normally think of the time travel of found footage as the itinerary of a return—from the present to the past (hence its confusion with the archive)—Uman's ethnographic films originate with a reverse journey, one much more suited to the cinematic time machine: the past projected into a future to come. In *Leche*, the past *vanishes into* the future, "prolonging the present and making it more profound," while the future appears as the archive of the past, the preservation of its virtualities, and the promise of its finding, as if in a home movie.[32]

While *Leche* projects a vanishing way of life into a possible future, it nonetheless preserves this past within the horizon of its disappearance. In this way it recalls the magical act of incorporation aimed at preserving the object in its loss. The names given to this act of preservative repression—the crypt, encryption, incorporation, haunting—point, as I have been arguing throughout, to the funereal and cannibalistic nature of this repression. This is why Abraham and Torok call incorporation a *failed* introjection; instead of acknowledging and working through loss, it incorporates it within a still-living body. Can we say that the film-body of *Leche* incorporates Rancho la Primavera as a (vanishing) chronotope within a still-living future, the projected future of the film screening? The sense of a repressed loss, of an absent object of pleasure encrypted within the rhythms of everyday life, is palpable in a series of shots that are interwoven with that of hands at work and play. When the camera wanders away from the immediate family, Uman often focuses on the small, incidental details found around the ranch: a butterfly with death's-head wings, crickets copulating on the dry earth, a coyote carcass cured and hung up as a remedy for cancer, bottles and debris left behind in the dying grass. These images conjure the same twinning of future and past, ephemerality and finality, symbol and accident that structure the family portraits as found or archival images. However, it is in their excessive but silent symbolic relation to death that they cast a shadow over the living and inscribe a living death within the temporality of a critical and projected future. The loss that is present here in a series of mute signs will haunt Uman's future work as she figures filmmaking as a reparative intervention at the site of historical erasure. For now, however, I want to emphasize that the fantasy of an "animated space" as the "extension of the space of bodies" shared by filmmaker and subject in *Leche* encrypts a host of slippages at the formal level, slips that mark an absent body.[33]

These slippages occur at those places where the body appears in its absence—namely, in those places where Uman's presence, never shown directly in the film, speaks and writes itself into the frame. While visually absent, her body is materially present in the grain and gesture of her voice and handwriting. She tells stories in both English and Spanish, often ones centered on bodily threats both small and large: recalling how one day a donkey, the gentlest creature on the ranch, twice threw her off ("my ribs and feelings were hurt"); or how during the revolution Altagracia twice saw her father lynched ("he survived both times"); or reporting Blanca's story of the first time she ever went to the movies ("She ran out of the theater, terrified that she would be trampled by the onscreen horses"). In handwritten intertitles, Uman catalogs the names of the more than one hundred cows that live on the ranch and those of the children who were born there. She narrates events, charts the geography, and describes the roles played by different members of the family, a narration that is all the while split along a number of fissures and cracks. Rarely appearing in sync, the images constantly run ahead or fall behind the narration, and the narration is itself divided between registers (writing and voice) and languages (English and Spanish) so that the traditional power of the documentarian to stitch together the fragments of the world captured on film is haunted by the signs of a foreign voice, a second discourse.[34] The result is the incorporation of a figure of embodied foreignness through the asynchronous stutters that uncouple language from image, narration from found footage, present from past.

This is similar to the broken symbol that I analyzed as characteristic of Godard's work. However, whereas for Godard the broken symbol—a symbol that is missing an undetermined part—was found in the fissures of a historical dialogue, in Uman's work it is her body that fractures the scene. Through her bilingual narration, the asynchronicity structuring sound-image relations, and the persistence of violence in a minor key characterizing many of the stories being told in the titles, Uman's embodied presence appears as a foreignness within the rhythms (that is, the temporalized histories) of the ranch. By fracturing the signs of cinematic signification across the boundary of her own embodied expression, Uman forces her ethnographic images into a direct confrontation with their partial and incomplete temporality, with the indeterminacy of any reading that fails to account for their lost dimension. This lost dimension has to be grasped in multiple registers: spatial, temporal, social, and their complex imbrications. Most of all, the notion of a lost dimension, as developed by Paul Virilio, is the loss of the independence of bounded zones.[35] Understood merely in the terms of the local and the pastoral, the inherent foreignness of the space being documented is displaced from the border *between* languages and bodies (the US-Mexico border across which both filmmaker and film travel) to another time (a time other to the making of the film, the time of found footage) characterized by the disappearance of artisanal labor. Uman's intense interest in the space of the pasture and the dairy ranch can be understood as the insistence of a topographical reading as a resistance to the temporal flattening of history—history's reduction to a series of completed events, modalities, or ways of life. The lost dimension, however, also registers the strange topography of the crypt as the place of internal exclusion, a subterranean invisibility at the heart of the ethnographic image. By emphasizing the impossible place of her own body—a foreign body, a body included as an elsewhere—Uman manifests the specter of the undocumented body within the document, a body unseen and yet subject, excluded and yet accounted for, a body always located in the *between* that characterizes any act of translation, any crossing over of cinematic bands.

What happens, however, when this reparative gesture of cosymbolization fails, when the absent body eludes (and for good reason!) any attempt to be documented, envisaged, or translated? What happens, in sum, when the filmmaker is confronted with a refusal of visibility and with the subject's own fading from and of the image? The internal off-screen, assuming the cryptic function of the space of an *already completed repression*, deforms the image by indicating the presence of what cannot be seen within the visual. By displacing the unseen from the outskirts of traditional off-screen space to the interiority of the screen, the internal off-screen plunges the frame into the visual, erasing its boundaries and flattening its dimensionality. The internal off-screen objectivizes off-screen space, reifying it and figuring it within a definite form. This reification made visible the extent to which off-screen space was complicit with the erasure of marginal bodies and envisioned Uman's cinematographic practice as the critical objectivation of the allegory of the off-screen in the pornographic, experimental, and ethnographic practices that she revises.[36] So far, however, my analyses have encountered the internal off-screen as a supplementary body that came into being in the absence or even erasure of an enigma.[37] In *Removed*, to the extent that it still communicated with the original footage, the phantom off-screen of the woman's body appeared in the place of her already existing nonbeing and thus posed no barrier to the pornographic scene, which continues to function *as pornography* for the original footage. It is true that this new body surfaced an erotic surplus for a second scene, but this surplus was precisely an erotic supplement that translated an original enigma—sexual pleasure in the woman's absence—into a readable text of sexual pleasure in the absence of women. The logic is one of superimposition and the displacement of the enigma of gendered lack.

Leche, for its part, embodied the gaps and slippages that appear within dialogic encounters: between languages, between actions, between bodies. To the extent that translation, in its typical function of making the foreign readable or knowable, erases the gap or silence of dialogue, Uman's gesture was to give this gap a form: that of her own body as it crossed over from an exteriority (a series of borders both global and local) into an interiority. But in so doing, she added a readable figure of *foreignness* into the space of the dairy ranch, an invisible visual supplement into the series of bodies in action. The internal off-screen again appears as a critical revision that implies the splitting of the film along the fracture of its bilingual speech and then adds to it a superimposition of the two registers of cohabitation.[38] As with early cinema's use of superimposition, here too it registers a manifestation of the spectral within the material world.

In *Mala Leche*, Uman's second dairy film, the internal off-screen appears as a refusal or failure to film, document, and see. It results in a cryptic image at whose center is a figure "shrouded by an enigma too dense to be deciphered by known forms" of looking.[39] For Godard, the missing reel of the Nazi Holocaust situated the failure of cinema as a historical witness. In *Mala Leche*, however, the refusal to film and document must be understood within a tropography of undocumented bodies.[40] The kind of vanishing act by which Diana absents herself from the image is suggestive of the larger questions of the filmmaker's responsibility in choosing what bodies to show and which to leave outside the frame—the social cost of visibility. Uman pauses on this act, or rather on the enigmatic gap left in the image after the girl escapes off screen, suggesting her own anxiety about what she cannot show, document, and screen as part of her ethnographic filmmaking practice.

As a twin film to *Leche*, *Mala Leche* inscribes the US-Mexico border as a site of invisibility, the inclusion of bodies within a social off-screen. Unseen in either film, the national border figures powerfully *between* the dairy films and returns us in a new way to the question of the documented and undocumented body, giving it a fully political and social dimension. An early title card introduces the border as the specter of debt and the organizing form of social and communal life for those who have crossed over:

> Chivo helps many new immigrants by paying their coyotes, picking them up at the drop-off points and offering them a place to live until they can get on their own two feet and return the money they owe him. . . . Due to the nature of immigration and the high cost of crossing over, many immigrants form communities made up entirely of people from their hometowns in Mexico. In Pixley, most people are from the state of Aguascalientes in Central Mexico.

In *Leche*, a coyote carcass was cured and hung as a ward against a woman's cancer. Here, the figure of the coyote metastasizes a foreignness within the social order, an otherness within bodies, and a silence within language. The border is not only a social or topographic boundary in the films. It is also tropographic in the sense that it displaces language. The word "coyote" extends a spatial locus of language that, in each case, signifies the presence of a foreign body within one that is taken to be proper or clean. The border also organizes the spatial dimensions of silence and invisibility, marking the bodies that cross over with the lacerations of becoming unseen, undocumented.

Fredric Jameson uses the idea of cognitive mapping to argue that one of the most important tasks of contemporary art is to provide a graspable image of the relationship between lived experience and the abstract flows that determine its character. Specifically, cognitive mapping plots the positions of actual lived spaces within the abstract flows of circulation and exchange that characterize global capital.[41] The national border, especially as it divides countries with tremendous inequality in their position within global capital as the border between the United States and Mexico does, is a particularly resonant mark on a cognitive map; it is at once resolutely material and spatially located *and* a signifier for the abstractions of circulation. In *The Militarization of the U.S.-Mexico* border, Timothy Dunn shows that one of the primary functions of the border as an apparatus of police and military control has been the regulation of labor power. Border patrols enforced the illegal status of undocumented labor crossing into the United States as a mechanism for keeping this labor force outside of visibility, in the internal off-screen of the American image, just as demand for cheap labor was increasing. Thus, the border created and maintained populations of precarious flexible labor that served as a check on labor demands in the United States.[42] By including a foreignness as a nonlegal entity within the social body, the border transforms the global center into a crypt, or rather, the border encrypts the living dead form of labor within the topography of the capitalist center.

Mala Leche maps the border as an absent site and as a site of absence, as the cryptic boundary that creates the undocumented body as the phantom of an impossible tropography: a periphery within the interior, the global within the local, and the invisible within the visible. The signs of the border are seen throughout the film, for example in the makeshift billboards that encircle the small community of Pixley and dot the highways between it and the main employer, California Dairies. Roadside signs urge drivers to report illegal aliens or warn of a stark choice: US or UN.[43] Formally, however, the experience of this satellite community as a cryptic space of unmournable bodies is already inscribed in the film's enigmatic opening sequence, a small back-and-forth pan across three shots. As birds sing quietly on the soundtrack, the camera begins by panning left across a muddy field, revealing the carcasses of cow and calf half sunk in the wet earth. Only much later in the film do we learn the reason for these discarded carcasses: so many cows die in childbirth, explains Uman in a stark intertitle, that their bodies are left by the side of the road to be picked up by special garbage trucks. In the opening sequence, however, the image of mass death strikes the viewer with its mute corporeality, a dark echo of the enumeration of the names of the one hundred cows living at Rancho la Primavera and the excretory after-image of the animals being prepared for consumption in the abattoirs of Paris as the butcher sings his noontime song. Half buried in the open grave of the muddy field, these animal corpses open up a cryptic, nameless space, the absent return gaze of the dead staring back at Uman's camera. Another cryptic rhyme is condensed in this image that draws from across Uman's oeuvre. In the opening shot of *Hand Eye Coordination*, a seeing eye was displaced from the centrality of the image by the acting body and by Uman's proper name (that is, by her handwriting). Here, however, the film begins with a dead eye, an eye belonging to no one and unable to elicit even the phantasmatic gaze of the specter present in Bava's films. Thus, whereas *Hand Eye Coordination* connected the eye to an experience of embodied, personal filmmaking, here the eye marks the distance between the act of documentation and the unseeing look.

Uman next cuts to a shot of the film's title, *Mala Leche*, one of the few times that Spanish appears and, by contrast with the unclaimed body that opens the film, names the images to come. Like all of the text screens in this film, the title is shown in a white typewritten font set against a black screen, contrasting formally with the handwritten titles of *Leche*. Also, unlike *Leche*'s bilingual speech, *Mala Leche*'s remaining titles are written in English and tend toward a descriptive and objective address: giving information on the costs of border crossing ("The fee for a coyote (border crossing guide) is usually somewhere between $1000 and $3000 U.S. Dollars"), relating the shape of a pig's penis ("like a corkscrew"), or describing Pixley's fluid economy ("A car belonging to one person belongs to someone else in any moment when the other person might need it more. The same is true for watching other's children and eating each other's food"). When they do narrate events, these are often stories of things that are not shown. Thus, the titles *interrupt* and *screen* the image track, repressing the foreignness of language and body so central to the use of writing in *Leche*, where writing, handwritten or spoken, was connected to a body. In *Mala Leche*, the typed and impersonal intertitles block the film's visual operations by creating formal breaks in the image where the camera's nonseeing internalizes an off-screen space. Concurrently, the image track displaces the textual narration, relegating the information to an off-screen space without any precise relation to the bounded space of the image. To the extent that they appear as blocks of words dissociated from the images, the intertitles loosen their descriptive function and take on the autonomy of textual objects, word things.

The word thing has two functions in relation to the undocumented bodies of the living dead: a disavowal and a spacing. The word thing erases their absence within the image by speaking of their experiences (filling the image with words like language fills an empty mouth), and it manifests their absences as border images that appear as a gap between images. This dual relation to the lost object is the hallmark of a cryptonym, and the intertitles take the place of an unseen image by figuring the body's absence. Covering up an ellipsis in the scene, the intertitle produces, in another register, a (seeming) fullness of meaning within the visual gap. Whereas in *Removed* writing entered the text through a metaphorical operation that related Uman's physical acts of filmmaking, and in *Leche* writing entered by way of Uman's absent body that was made visible, in *Mala Leche* writing appears as blocks of text that are increasingly isolated from the image and whose force is that of demetaphorization, the arrest of signification that arises from taking literally what is meant figuratively.[44] I use this term to indicate the shift in registers from the visual image to the text screen and the way that this shift works partially to contain and block the figurative nexus linking the body to desire, labor, and violence. This containment takes place as a material interruption within the figurative chain—either by marking on the emulsion (in *Removed*), by highlighting the hand-processed nature of the film (in *Leche*), or through the blocks of text interleaved with images of confinement, birth, and death (in *Mala Leche*). This is the fetishistic function of writing, where it disavows, spaces, and mimics the loss of the image. What Uman marks is a split in the text between image and word but also between body and language, across which writing spectralizes the incorporated object that produces the image as a cryptic space.

Following this textual crypt-image of the film's opening shots (the pan across the field of dead cattle and the title card), Uman cuts to a figuratively empty shot: train tracks converge in the depth of a people-less space as a truck rumbles overhead on a highway bisecting the frame horizontally. A left to right pan, retracing the movement of the opening shot, reveals just out of frame a squat, nondescript building on whose side is emblazoned the yellow starburst of California Dairies' corporate logo. In these dairies, the film will uncover masses of huddled cows with feet bound for milking by pneumatic machines and cows being washed with sprays of water from below while men who work twelve-hour shifts alternate the use of a narrow bed on the premises. The tracks and the road exemplify the nonplaces—places of pure transit, circulation, and consumption—described by Marc Augé as the unseen and peripheral foreign interiorities at the heart of the global city.[45] Although Augé focuses most of his work on the ephemeral nonplaces of supermodernity such as airports, toll booths, and roads, Uman shows that the space surrounding and occupied by California Dairies has many of the attributes of a nonplace.

The experience of nonplace, writes Augé, is that of a simultaneous distancing from the spectator and the spectacle, a kind of long shot that, erasing spatial discontinuity, removes people from the place they occupy and from themselves. In *Mala Leche* this distance is manifest in the relative distance that Uman takes from her subjects—in contrast to *Leche*'s close-ups of hands, *Mala Leche* stages many shots with figures in the middle or even background of the image—and by her distance from the material; gone are the many marks of handmade production or the personal touch of handwriting. Whereas *Leche*'s mode of portraiture placed the filmmaker at the external border of the image, an embodied vision at the source and limit of the scene, *Mala Leche* dramatizes the growing distance and increased absence of the film subjects. Second, nonplaces are defined by a certain invasion of space by text. These nonplaces "have the peculiarity that they are defined partly by the words and texts they offer us—prescriptive, prohibitive, or informative—the airport, the roadway, or the supermarket is organized through a language degraded of its symbolic function and reduced to 'instructions' for use."[46] I have shown how this sequence incorporates the title screen, a rare instance of a Spanish text in the film, into its opening pan as both a prescription of how to read the film and a prohibition against the dairies and their "bad milk." However, it is again as a contrast to the handwritten and intimate language of *Leche* that the descriptive opening intertitles of *Mala Leche* become "informatic" rather than symbolic texts. Finally, Augé posits that nonplaces should be understood through their opposition to utopian spaces. Unlike utopias, nonspaces are actually existing places that do not contain any organic society.[47] By opening the film with this series of crypt-images, Uman contrasts the topography of *Mala Leche* with the lived rhythms found in *Leche*. In the earlier film, the ranch constituted a horizon of the social. In *Mala Leche*, the displacement of the community under the sign of an unpayable debt transforms Pixley into the place of pure existence severed from its organic social life, a place without a utopian image because it is a place without horizon—a nonplace defined by its *crossing* and the costs associated with it.

Augé relates nonplaces to the condition of borders and frontiers characteristic of globalization.

> In the global world, the global occupies the same relationship to the local as the inside to the outside. This means that the local is intrinsically unstable: either it is a simple reduplication of the global ... and the notion of frontier is indeed being erased; or the local disrupts the system and may become the object, in political terms, of an exercise in the right to interfere.[48]

Abraham and Torok's work, however, recognizes that within this interiority there is another hidden space internal to the inside and external to the outside: the cryptic space of incorporation where bodies that are defined by their globalized exteriority—their foreignness, their crossing, their undocumented status—are erased from view. The evocative pan that opens the film neatly encrypts a (dead) body within a constellation of astral, noncentered space, folding loss into the nondimensionality of capital circulation by way of the smallest (camera) movement. This opening sequence maps the tropography of the border—(bad) milk, the (un)documented body, the (open) grave—within a topography of globalization and its nonplaces.

Jacques Derrida highlights the nature of the psychic crypt as a foreign body included within the self. By blocking all lines of symbolic exchange between the cryptic body and the rest of the psyche, the crypt preserves the foreign character of its contents. "The more the self keeps the foreign element as a foreigner inside itself, the more it excludes it," notes Derrida.[49] In *Leche* and *Mala Leche*, this psychic metaphor is transformed into a topographic condition involving real bodies. The national border, understood as a cryptic space of global capital, writes a foreign body into the circulation of labor. This is what the visual and typographic strategies of *Mala Leche* indicate when read in their tropographic displacement from *Leche*: the attempt to film a beyond-place, a place in place of another, a border crossing. "But no typocryptography can exist in the absence of the determination of this singular 'beyond-place' or 'no-place' [*non-lieu*]," continues Derrida. "The topography ... requires us to think ... about a no-place or non-place within space, a place as no-place."[50] The border crossing bounds the spaces of the film, de-signifying them in relation to a beyond-place that is never simply outside but runs like a wound through the land, fracturing and isolating bodies from their social function: an external inclusion. In so doing, it transforms Pixley into a no-place situated within space, transforming a place into a nonplace, like the peripheries of global cities Sassen analyzed. The border crossing that inscribes a nonplace in place of another image (in place, that is, of the images of *Leche*), is both the fracture and complement of *Mala Leche*'s crypt-images since it rejoins them with the earlier dairy film. Without the images' reference to this instigating force, the film's *documentary* images remain unreadable. The importance of Uman's contribution to cinematic cryptonymy appears here in the relationship between film and the social milieu it frames. The crypt-image in this case acts directly on the body, and the violence of the zero hour during which the crypt first comes into being is a violence that leaves physical marks.

If the border as the nonplace of circulation and displacement is the external wall of the crypt in *Mala Leche*, its internal support is the home and the accumulation of debt. For example, Chivo, though he doesn't speak or write English, buys homes in Pixley that he rents out to other immigrant families that arrive in the United States already deeply in debt to their coyote. Like the border, the home registers an undocumented scene of bodily violence whose meaning is the exclusion of a missing body. This internal scene of domestic erasure stages a scene whose repetition at the zero hour is the very foundation of incorporation: that of a silent witness. The Wolf Man's drama centers on the child's position as a witness: having seen an unspeakable crime, his sister's abuse at the father's hands, he is torn between his desire to cry out and denounce the father (his desire to bear witness) and his desire to save the father through his silence (a silence supported through his mother's terrifying insistence that his words have the power to bring down the entire family). In *Mala Leche* the monetary debt is also a linguistic and visual debt. Linguistically, the border crossing strips Spanish of its power to signify beyond the self or the encrypted community of immigrants, and thus is devalued. Spanish words become word things as they pass across the internal borders of Pixley, standing as mute foreign bodies within the circulation of language. This condition is highlighted by Chivo's silence and by the absence of Spanish in Uman's intertitles, which, by contrast with the multilingual *Leche*, makes the film largely unreadable for non-English speakers. The silence thus stands for the unpaid debt of signification exacted at the site of social incorporation across national borders.

The silent debt of language further emphasizes Uman's role as a partial witness since she cannot access the unsaid words—a situation that is again highlighted by the absence of Spanish in the subtitles. For Uman, the condition of the witness is one that she takes up as soon as she crosses the threshold into the community or the home with her camera. It is the fundamental question she enacts as a documentary filmmaker, especially as she works within undocumented communities. *Mala Leche* ends with a haunting description of domestic violence, a scene to which Uman was witness but that she did not film. The absence of the camera at the scene should be understood not as a failure on Uman's part but as a refusal to film and to show. Not simply unseen, this missing scene is constructed by two strategies of visual displacement: it is transformed into writing, and it is repressed by a series of crypt-images of a foal being born in confinement. Understood as cryptonyms, both the words and the screen images encrypt a second drama at the origin of the film: Uman's act of (not) filming, a nondocumentation that demands the visual reconstruction of this scene of the zero hour of incorporation. In the discussion of *Blood of the Beasts* in the first chapter, I argued that the displacement of historically vanished bodies by the crypt-images of animal slaughter functioned not as a screening of horror but as the incorporation of the refusal to see within the visual economy of postwar France. This earlier displacement was structured around an aesthetic ornament that breathed life into the abattoir by making it a condition of the absence of human slaughter. In *Mala Leche*, however, the animal shots that appear in place of images of domestic violence dramatize Uman's decision to not film and thus to refuse the incorporation of the unfilmed image as a foreigner within a visual body:

The same night, as I was sleeping on the floor next to Diana's bed, I was awakened by Esther. It was midnight. She was hysterical. "Dónde está Diana?" she asked me.

In my sleepy delirium I responded that she was probably with Juan, her boyfriend, who lived on the other side of the driveway.

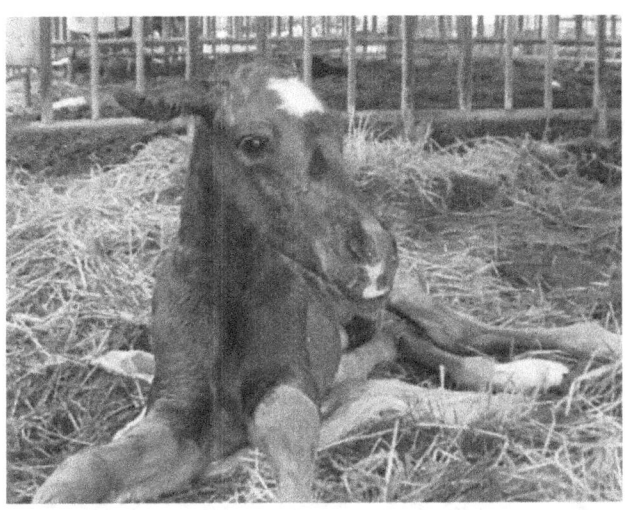

Esther grabbed the telephone and called her neighbor. "Dónde está Diana?" she could barely speak the words. As we waited, Joana impossibly feigned sleep. Esther clutched the telephone, waiting for someone to locate her daughter, Diana.

Suddenly, while Esther was still holding onto the telephone, Diana came running into the room wearing her little-girl pajamas with short sleeves and legs.

Chivo followed immediately behind her, wielding with great skill his "cuarta," a four-pronged leather horsewhip. He hit her over and over again.

She used to be Chivo's favorite child. She had her own room, new clothes, name-brand beauty products, and many stuffed animals.

Diana refused to cry a single tear.

The next day Juan's parents called from Mexico, requesting Diana's hand in marriage. Chivo refused to speak to her. There were tears in his eyes. She had just turned sixteen.

Border Crossing

Toward the end of their analysis of the Wolf Man case, Abraham and Torok pose a straightforward but heretofore unasked question. Their work up to that point has consisted in describing the Wolf Man's cryptic language and the ways this language blocked all analytic attempts to listen to his speech, to hear what he has been saying for his entire life in a series of secret internal dialogues. But, beyond describing his cryptophoric machinations, wonder the analysts, could the Wolf Man be analyzed and cured? Would it have been possible to break through the walls of the intrapsychic crypt and to penetrate the enigmas of speech in order to return his words to a scene free of the silences of failed mourning?

> To overcome this obstacle to analysis and succeed in making the Wolf Man accept his status as witness without any aggressivity or despair, it would have been necessary . . . to challenge the juridical code that permitted the nurse's blackmail in the first place. . . . But this would have been an analysis in quite a different style.[51]

To succeed, the analysis would have had to extend beyond the sphere of individual symptom formation, would have had to include an analysis of the extended family and of the legal and social codes that govern the inheritance of (and in) silence. When he woke up screaming from the "dream" of his sister's rape by their father, the Wolf Man's nurse made use of this knowledge to blackmail the family. They would pay their debt to her, and to the father's crime, in silence. And, though he was just a child, the burden of this debt fell on the Wolf Man's tongue, and he paid it in silence for the rest of his life. Opening a crypt, Abraham and Torok show, is not *simply* a psychoanalytic task. The crypt is constructed with the materials of a juridical and social code as much as that of psychic processes. Or, more to the point, a crypt is the imbrication of the psyche and the juridical as forms of nonknowledge and silence.

Uman's films invent one mode of this analysis in a different style, an analysis that opens visual crypts. The other works discussed in this book have, each in their own ways, mapped the unique figures of absence embedded in European film and visual culture. By contrast, Uman's filmmaking—the artisanal practice of cohabitation and handcrafting as it is made visible by the films—crosses over (and, to some extent, crosses out) the "proper" boundaries of the (social) image: the border between the image and its surface emulsion in *Removed*, between filmmaking and domestic labor in *Leche*, between national borders in the dairy films, and between the act of witnessing and the refusal to film in *Mala Leche*. This style of filmmaking as critical analysis is situated on the unruly border between bodies, screened images, and the social economy of vision and speech. Uman's films capture this uncertain border zone directly, her images constantly flickering between its registers, marking the absences constituent of each, figuring her own absence and giving voice to visual erasures as practices of political and social resistance. In her films, invisibility is rescreened and revised *as* speech or symbolic action.

"But one thing must be clear," insists Derrida in relation to Abraham and Torok's work, "If it is true that nothing in this cryptonymy is purely verbal, it is nevertheless also true that nothing appears as a thing given directly to perception. Perception itself, like all mute pictures, falls under the law of the cipher."[52] In my analysis, I have shown how Uman invented a number of figures by which to speak this law of the visual cipher, to make it appear in its place as the incorporated margin of social visibility. In each of the films discussed in this chapter, this has meant returning perception to its de-signified origin in an absent image that precedes and grounds a fictional and reconstructed act of filming: a piece of found footage, a vanishing way of life, a scene of unmournable domestic violence, or even Uman's ethnographic practice of historical displacement. What is at work is not simply the missing term—the woman's body, the labor of production, the border and the interiority of the home—but the acts of their erasure: scratching, nonfilming, and screen images. It is these acts that reconfigure the location of the off-screen space from that which bounds the image to its most essential interiority in order to reveal an internal off-screen. Spatially, this gap appears as a new spectral absence. When apprehended temporally, however, it takes on a double life: first as a hesitation or blockage (the text screens of *Mala Leche*) and, second, through a historical dialectic that *returns the future into the past* in order to preserve a vanishing time as a form of internal historical critique. By making this secret off-screen of the image visible, Uman opens the cryptic structure whose function was to cover over the absence of the figure from the other scene.

In *Removed*, the internal off-screen was made visible through a material rendering of the already-absent bodies, the bodies absented by their very visibility, as the cipher through which a series of radically incommensurate bodies, languages, and looks were joined. In *Leche*, the body appeared, in its absence, as the incorporated figure of a foreignness within speech, the visual inscription of the incompletion of the ethnographic image. In *Mala Leche*, it is the unfilmed event that displaces the visual track, interrupting its representational and figural drive through an evocation of a refusal to produce an image at the sight of violence. Like Abraham and Torok's notion of cryptic incorporation, this erasure reveals the place of a crypt scene visible only in its reconstruction at another (verbal) register. Interred in this crypt is the body of a young girl, become unfilmable behind the pillar of the family home, located in the nonplace at the intersection of desire, labor, and violence, or escaping her father's house along an uncertain line of flight. It is thus that the interruption or obstruction of the image in the temporal register incorporates the unseen into the frame.

An off-screen internal to the image: this is not simply a potential image (to come) but a blockage of the symbolic operation of the image track, a hole within the reciprocity of identification and desire whose pivot, in the dominant cinema as well as in the dominant modes of social relations that it supports, is the woman's body. It is this missing image—not just an image but an image and the forces of production and encryption that cross over it and cross it over—that finds expression in Uman's work. In each case, what is at stake is the raising to the level of filmic material a fantasy (of) incorporation. The woman's absence at the pornographic scene, her alienation at the site of labor, and her violent expulsion (from) within the home are each made manifest as properties of the cinematic material. By linking the filmic material to her own body as the origin and end of the circuit of production, Uman inserts herself—an absent and organizing hand—as a force of critical transvaluation that traces erasure. She robs the cinematic image of its phantasmatic ability to maintain the figure of the woman's body as a substitute for her nonbeing. And what is true of the internal off-screen of the image finds its reflection in the off-screen or peripheral topographies of global capital, these places without images to which Uman gives a haunting form.

Conclusion

The Body under Erasure

> To overcome this obstacle to analysis and succeed in making the Wolf Man accept his status as witness without any aggressivity or despair, it would have been necessary . . . to challenge the juridical code that permitted the nurse's blackmail in the first place. . . . But this would have been an analysis in quite a different style.
>
> —Abraham and Torok, *The Wolf Man's Magic Word*

This book has staged a conversation between the psychoanalytic practice of cryptonymy and the cinematic image. It is my hope that such a dialogue will contribute to a renewed attention to psychoanalytic film theory and to film theory more broadly. Turning first to history and to the archive and then to the realm of the post- or extracinematic, film studies has, in Francesco Casetti's words, "acquired knowledge but lost its referential framework."[1] Increasingly, in film studies, it is as if the task of theorizing the cinema is over, its questions (what precisely we mean when we say "image," "spectatorship," "production," "analysis," and so on) either answered or no longer relevant in a world in which films are but a small share of the images in circulation. There are, of course, many theories of the cinema that continue to be published and debated, but, more often than not, these theories aim to contribute local and partial knowledge and explicitly abandon the global horizon of the cinematic. But the task of film theory has never been to define its object. Rather, each theory of film must invent the cinema anew in relation to changing demands and changing forms, aligning it with those forces that will bring a new cinema into being. This entails discovering, within the image or the discourse of film, a foreign interiority, a new world or body from beyond the frame, and reorienting cinema toward this figure. If there is, then, something of the perverse in a return to psychoanalytic theory after the ascendancy of "Post-Theory," I have tried to mark this untimeliness in my use of a largely neglected version of psychoanalysis, one whose project has always been the "renewal of psychoanalysis," as

Abraham and Torok's collected works, *The Shell and the Kernel*, is subtitled. For Abraham and Torok, too, a true metapsychology answers to the demand that the psychoanalytic institution be reinvented to allow new forms of the self to speak, even from beyond the grave. This reinvention puts psychoanalysis into a dialogue with other modes of speech: poetics, translation, phenomenology, and history. Recognizing this, it should be clear that cinema opens the way to a new theory of psychoanalysis, one based on the social and historical figuration of the death drive, as much as cryptonymy reorients cinema toward all that remains unseen. Today, increasingly, cinema has no more profound aspiration than to bear witness to the invisible and to bring into being a spectator who answers to the demand of staging the phantoms of social death, just as psychoanalysis must be reoriented toward a beyond of the family plot and the banalities of eroticism. I call this phantom, this beyond, the *body under erasure* to designate its marginal position in relation to the visible and the sayable, as well as to emphasize its dynamic character as a gesture or act of in-visibility rather than a stable visible form.

Gilles Deleuze has called the modern cinema a cinema of bodies and argued that in postwar films, the attitudes of the body disclose states of becoming, revealing life as that which is concealed from thought.[2] But after the war a new problem arose: the inclusion of the body as a lost object—a real but socially and historically invisible body—within an economy of images that spread out in all directions (and into every crevice of the psyche), occupying the territory of the real. The body had to be filmed not only in its attitudes of becoming but also in its gestures of erasure and disappearance. The problem was to invent ways to mark the presence of nonbeing in the very heart of a new social, economic, and corporeal realism. In each case, whether it took the form of a reflective surface or a black abyss, a spectral camera or an embodied emulsion, the gestures of erasure inserted a visible gap as an act of defiguration.[3] The body under erasure is not a visible form but a disturbance or deframing that blocks sight and diverts the look. In this way, it aims to preserve the singularity of loss while making it invisible. The image then becomes a crypt for the still living, the burial ground for "those who are already dead; or rather . . . those who *have already been dead*, who 'have lived' death."[4] Confronted with the still living—who are haunted by those who died without a proper burial and bear the dead within the self—cryptonymy aims to give voice to bodies that have been transformed into open graves. Cryptonymy, in other words, responds to an analytic desire to give speech to the cryptic body. Ian Baucom argues, in the context of a cryptonymic history of the slave ship *Zong*, that traumatic texts are "devoted both to preserving the singularity of loss and to listening to the voices speaking from the wound of this loss over and over and over again."[5] He argues that taken together, the traces of an unacknowledged loss constitute a history of silence, a history of a gap in the archive of knowledge. The body under erasure is the figure of this history in cinema, the form that it takes when the camera bears witness to undocumentable bodies. Abraham and Torok's practice redefines psychoanalysis in relation to the historical proliferation of the living dead.

Psychoanalysis in the contemporary world, writes Catherine Malabou in *The New Wounded*, encounters its limits in its inability to figure or give form to what lies beyond the pleasure principle: the death drive, the compulsion to repeat, and the indifference to pain and loss of symbolic reference that arises out of traumatic suffering.[6] Although she challenges the morbidity of psychoanalysis, she does not dispute its gains. Rather, she wants to imagine its beyond, reminding us that this search was already integral to Freud's thinking in his frequent but haphazard returns to somatic principles and in his faltering investigations of the death drive as the force that unbinds the psychic order. "What destructive plasticity invites us to consider," she writes in *The Ontology of the Accident*, "is the suffering caused by an absence of suffering, in the emergence of a new form of being, a stranger to the one before. Pain manifests as indifference to pain, impassivity, forgetting, the loss of symbolic reference points."[7] For Malabou, neurology acknowledges the force of destructive plasticity but leaves it unthought. Like cryptonymy, she recognizes mental processes of demetaphorization, processes of forgetting and indifference, and seeks ways of giving them form so they can be thought. I have been arguing that cryptonymy is also an attempt to think the beyond of psychoanalysis. Abraham and Torok seek an understanding of the body, what they call the somatic shell, as that which internalizes a kernel of nonbeing: "Yet the shell itself is marked by what it shelters; what it encloses is disclosed within it."[8] The psychic kernel, when it has been overtaken by the destructive forces of nonmeaning that define the death drive, is in turn disclosed by a somatic shell—a body—deprived of any power of signification. This is the emergence of a stranger that is not a different other but an indifferent self, an indifference within the self. Cryptonymy follows the paths of this new form of being to retrieve an original, though fictitious, scene of trauma from which the stranger emerged.

Cryptonymy, however, is not only a procedure of analysis or a psychoanalytic orientation. It is also a verbarium or a catalog of words and figures in which each of the terms of analysis appear as cryptonyms of all the others. Cryptonymy's characteristic nature as a rhyming dictionary of the names of the taboo word allows it to enter into dynamic relations with what it is not: neurology, literature, cinema, and history. The body under erasure enters this verbarium at the place where the other figures encounter a social and historical limit. The body under erasure translates the crypt, the phantom, and anasemia into cinematic subjects. In a unique article on psychoanalytic aesthetics, Abraham positions a textual or "wild" psychoanalysis as having to do not with the reconstruction of the past—Freud's search for a real primal or infantile scene that would unravel the mysteries of the subject—but with the unraveling of the unconscious of an ego that inhabits a work of art. This ego is not the unconscious of an author or reader, but the recognition of the autonomy of the work of art insofar as it includes a "bipolar unconscious (the wish and the superego) [which] denotes its own genesis as part of the fictional fabric of the work itself."[9] The wish, claims Abraham, is not defined by infantile desire but as a temporal fact: it brings a future into being by inserting a dynamic of protension—what he calls an eternal hope—within reality. The superego, a necessary complement to the wish, is nothing but its rhythmic modulation, the sum total of blockages, pauses, and interruptions that cause the wish to "pulsate" in relation to its future fulfillment. The ego, tasked with creating the temporal connections between the wish and its fulfillment, is thus a series of detours, "differals," and displacements of the wish in relation to the superego. The ego, claims Abraham, "possesses a correlate in the outside world, the reality referred to by psychoanalysts: the sum total of the paths and obstacles the ego has acquired as its own knowledge."[10] This implies, in turn, that the ego that inhabits the work of art is not a biographical personage but a specific relationship between the work's wish—that is, what the work aims to express or reveal—and the obstacles to that wish.

In cinema these obstacles are constituted by the entire structure of the expressive apparatus: the means and materials of production, the seeable and unseeable at any particular historical moment, the legal frameworks of censorship and distribution, and the relationship between the projection of images and the vision of spectators. The body under erasure thus accounts for the missing scenes of production, spectatorship, and history. It emerges *from them* to become a character in the image, and the marks of erasure incorporate them as internal off-screens that haunt the frame. This is especially evident when the work in question aims to shatter the taboos that hold a particular wish from being realized—when, that is, the films confront what is unseeable or nonsymbolized in reality as it haunts the cinematic frame. In these cases, the film is tasked with making the acts of social erasure visible *as* lost objects, and the entire text becomes a constellation of detours or displacements that lead the viewer into the cryptic heart of mourning. Confronted with a cryptophoric film, the analyst is tasked with *seeing* the phantom object rather than reading its returns, *inventing* a pretextual scene rather than uncovering its past, and *translating* its figural instances rather than interpreting a hidden meaning. Or, as Abraham and Torok's work suggests, the critic or spectator must supply the complementary image that, absent in the film, would return it from the dead-end of symbolic loss to the dynamics of speech. In each of the chapters I have presented such scenes: Dr. Génessier's death-dealing desire for his daughter in *Eyes without a Face*, the unborn child who died in Asa's womb in *Black Sunday*, the utopian film shot by Olga in *Notre musique*, and the scenes of border crossing in Uman's dairy films. The purpose of these invented scenes was not to unveil the textual secret, the hidden reality, or the true past of the films. Instead, these scenes put the figures of the text into circulation, allowing them to communicate with one another across the gap of a truly dead figure: a missing or scarred body characterized by the blankness of expression, the absence of suffering, or the loss of symbolic reference. The pretextual scene stages the relations among the film's cryptic images in relation to the body's erasure.

The importance of the body under erasure lies in the critical difference between the cinematic and psychoanalytic taboo. Whereas the psychic crypt contains a taboo word, the cinematic image comprehends and enframes real bodies. In this sense, cinema demetaphorizes cryptonymy's notion of the burial of the dead from the past within the self. The film image is, from the first, the crypt-image of a real body. Even in films that do not contain the human figure, the filmmaker's and spectator's bodies constitute a real field of vision encrypted within the scene, as we saw in relation to Naomi Uman's and Mario Bava's work, respectively. Abraham and Torok write of their astonishing recognition in the Wolf Man case that "someone could be driven to take on the same attitude toward words as toward things, namely, objects of love, and that such word-objects could upset a topography to the point where incorporation would seem a self-therapeutic measure."[11] In the cinema we have seen that bodies can sometimes be treated as love objects rather than as representations or shadows from the past. This occurs when the body in question has so upset a sociogeographic topography that it must be excluded in order to preserve the fantasy of a proper, whole, unified space and also included within this space in order to preserve its reality and to answer to the function of cinema as a truthful historical witness. The body under erasure then becomes a material fragment of the image: a white luminosity, a camera position that doubles over on itself, a black interval, or a writing surface. These figures of erasure inscribe the body as a love object that has been incorporated within the film due to its previous absence from the world. They figure the "new wounded" of Malabou's work as well as those haunted by trauma in Abraham and Torok's writings, staging the body under erasure within a social context that challenges the very juridical order of the visible and nonvisible.

Notes

Notes to Introduction

1. Gilles Deleuze, *Cinema 2: The Time-Image*, trans. Hugh Tomlinson and Robert Galeta (Minneapolis: University of Minnesota Press, 1985), xi.
2. Guy Debord, *The Society of the Spectacle*, trans. Donald Nicholson-Smith, rev. ed. (New York: Zone Books, 1995), 14.
3. Mark Fisher, *Capitalist Realism: Is There No Alternative?* (Ropley, UK: John Hunt Publishing, 2009). In a recent volume dedicated to the topic, Alison Shonkwiler and Leigh Claire La Berge write that "capitalist realism denotes the site upon which the limit of the imaginary is constructed. It insists on the circulation between imagination and reality, the ways in which this relationship is produced and disavowed." "Introduction: A Theory of Capitalist Realism," in *Reading Capitalist Realism*, ed. Alison Shonkwiler and Leigh Claire La Berge (Iowa City: University of Iowa Press, 2014), 6. In the same volume Joshua Clover reminds us that, as a concept, capitalist realism describes not an aesthetic mode or representational strategy, but "the ideological closure of possibilities beyond those already ratified by the imperatives of capital accumulation." It is thus the limit or displacement, rather than a mode of, cultural production. "Communist Realism," in *Reading Capitalist Realism*, ed. Alison Shonkwiler and Leigh Claire La Berge (Iowa City: University of Iowa Press, 2014), 242–47.
4. An early and still foundational discussion of off-screen space as a narrative paradigm is the section on "Two Kinds of Space" in Noël Burch, *Theory of Film Practice*, trans. Helen R. Lane (Princeton, NJ: Princeton University Press, 1981). The importance of censorship in the context of postwar national cinemas has been well documented, especially by scholars examining the cinemas of eastern Europe. For a discussion of eroticism, desire, and withholding, see André Bazin, "Marginal Notes on Eroticism in the Cinema," in *What Is Cinema*, ed. and trans. Hugh Gray, vol. 2 (Berkeley: University of California Press, 1971), 169–75. This work, while not written in a psychoanalytic vein, remains crucial to (though usually left out of) the history of psychoanalytic film criticism.
5. Nicolas Abraham and Maria Torok, *The Wolf Man's Magic Word: A Cryptonymy*, trans. Nicholas Rand (Minneapolis: University of Minnesota Press, 1986), 79.

6   This problem is not unique to the forms of wild analysis in which psychoanalytic ideas are applied outside of the analytic session. Indeed, it is a problem haunting the psychoanalytic institution since Freud's work in the *Interpretation of Dreams*. In *Questions for Freud*, Maria Torok and Nicholas Rand pose it thus: "The Freudian theory of dream interpretation combines an attempt to hear personal meanings with the use of universal symbolism. The search for the unique poetics of individual dreams collides with the restrictions that predetermined interpretations place upon their meaning." Maria Torok and Nicholas Rand, *Questions for Freud: The Secret History of Psychoanalysis* (Cambridge, MA: Harvard University Press, 1997), 9.

7   Abraham and Torok, *Wolf Man's Magic Word*, lxxii. Introjection refers to the process through which the ego expands its power by investing external objects with symbolic value for the self. Using the writings of Sándor Ferenczi, Abraham and Torok contrast introjection with incorporation, in which the ego "consumes" an unassimilable object, placing it whole within the self while blocking it from symbolic relations with the rest of the psyche.

8   A concise biographical sketch of Abraham and Torok and their relationship to French psychoanalytic institutions can be found in Elisabeth Roudinesco, *Jacques Lacan and Co.: A History of Psychoanalysis in France, 1925–1985*, trans. Jeffrey Mehlman (Chicago: University of Chicago Press, 1990), 598–601.

9   Jacques Derrida, "Fors: The Anglish Words of Nicolas Abraham and Maria Torok," in *The Wolf Man's Magic Word: A Cryptonymy*, trans. Barbara Johnson (Minneapolis: University of Minnesota Press, 1986), xlviii.

10 Ian Baucom, *Specters of the Atlantic: Finance Capital, Slavery, and the Philosophy of History* (Durham, NC: Duke University Press, 2005), 21.

11 Gabriele Schwab, *Haunting Legacies: Violent Histories and Transgenerational Trauma* (New York: Columbia University Press, 2010), 11.

12 Abraham and Torok, *Wolf Man's Magic Word*, 19. "The verbs *tieret* and *natieret* had to be entirely banished from the active vocabulary and not only in the sense of rubbing, but also in the sense of waxing and scraping. What if these parallel meanings, these allosemes, had to be stated? Each time they were, by means of synonyms, they obviously implied a constant reference, even if a negative one, to the *taboo word*. It was, we thought, because a given word was unutterable that the obligation arose to introduce synonyms even for its lateral meanings, and that the synonyms acquired the status of substitutes. Thus they became *cryptonyms*, apparently not having any phonetic or semantic relationship to the prohibited word."

13 John Foot, *Italy's Divided Memory* (New York: Palgrave Macmillan, 2009), 11.

14 Nicolas Abraham, "Notes on the Phantom: A Complement to Freud's

Metapsychology," in *The Shell and the Kernel*, vol. 1, *Renewals of Psychoanalysis*, ed. and trans. Nicholas Rand (Chicago: University of Chicago Press, 1994), 171.

15 Esther Rashkin, *Family Secrets and the Psychoanalysis of Narrative* (Princeton, NJ: Princeton University Press, 1992), 28.

16 Michael Witt, *Jean-Luc Godard: Cinema Historian* (Bloomington: Indiana University Press, 2013), 128. Emphasis mine. The embedded quotation is from an interview with Godard published in *CinéAction* no. 52.

17 Witt, *Jean-Luc Godard: Cinema Historian*, 128.

18 The term *chronotope* is M. M. Bakhtin's, which he borrows ("almost [as a metaphor] but not entirely") from mathematics. It names "the intrinsic connectedness of temporal and spatial relationships that are artistically expressed in literature" and designates an inseparable block or unity of space and time. See M. M. Bakhtin, *The Dialogic Imagination*, ed. Michael Holquist, trans. Caryl Emerson and Michael Holquist, University of Texas Press Slavic Series 1 (Austin: University of Texas Press, 1981), 84.

19 Nicolas Abraham and Maria Torok, "Mourning or Melancholia: Introjection versus Incorporation," in *The Shell and the Kernel*, vol. 1, *Renewals of Psychoanalysis*, ed. and trans. Nicholas Rand (Chicago: University of Chicago Press, 1994), 127.

20 Sigmund Freud, "'Wild' Psycho-Analysis," in *The Standard Edition of the Complete Psychological Works of Sigmund Freud*, ed. and trans. James Strachey, vol. 11 (London: Hogarth Press, 1957), 225.

21 To preserve the object means to erase its loss, to keep it suspended before the knowledge of its loss. Thus, film theory reduplicates the cinematic object while expelling it from the scene of knowledge: "Discourse about the cinema then becomes a dream: an uninterrupted dream. This is what constitutes its symptomatic value; it has already said everything. But it is also what makes it obligatory to turn it inside out like a glove, to return it like the gauntlet on accepting a challenge; it does not know what it is saying. Knowledge of the cinema is obtained via a *reprise* of the native discourse, in two senses of the word: taking it into consideration and re-establishing it." Christian Metz, "The Imaginary Signifier," trans. Ben Brewster, *Screen* 16, no. 2 (1975): 25.

22 Abraham, "Notes on the Phantom," 176.

23 Abraham and Torok, *Wolf Man's Magic Word*, 79. "It does happen . . . that [psychoanalytic] listening runs up against a form of speech that resists the search for a cosymbol and defeats every attempt at completion. In these cases it is as if the sense of the words were shrouded by an enigma too dense to be deciphered by known forms of listening. Or, at other times it is as if speech did not refer to any enigma at all."

24 This danger is often brought up in relation to Abraham and Torok's work.

Herman Rapaport, for example, after unpacking the ways in which cryptonyms are constructed, notes: "According to Abraham and Torok all this occurs not on the level of one thing representing another (signified for signified) nor on the level of one word representing another (by this they mean entire morphemes) but on the level of a 'lexical continuity of diverse meanings of the same word, that is to say, *allosemes*, such as those found in a dictionary. . . .' The hazards of such a theory when put into practice are only too clear: one can construct almost anything one wants." Herman Rapaport, *Between the Sign and the Gaze* (Ithaca, NY: Cornell University Press, 1994), 114.

25 Abraham and Torok, *Wolf Man's Magic Word*, lxx.

Notes to Chapter 1

1 Quoted in Raymond Durgnat, *Franju* (Berkeley: University of California Press, 1968), 91–92. This quotation is repeated by Lowenstein in "Films without a Face: Shock Horror in the Cinema of Georges Franju," *Cinema Journal* 37, no. 4 (1998): 37–58.
2 Kate Ince, *Georges Franju*, French Film Directors (Manchester: Manchester University Press, 2005), 7. "Franju's place in film history has been unjustly neglected [because] his relationship to it is displaced, or 'out of sync.'"
3 Henry Rousso, *The Vichy Syndrome: History and Memory in France since 1944*, trans. Arthur Goldhammer (Cambridge, MA: Harvard University Press, 1991), 22. My emphasis. An analysis of cinema's role in the Vichy Syndrome, the denials and silences that followed the fractures of Vichy, the occupation and the liberation is given in Naomi Greene, *Landscapes of Loss: The National Past in Postwar French Cinema* (Princeton, NJ: Princeton University Press, 1999).
4 Nicolas Abraham and Maria Torok, "'The Lost Object—Me': Notes on Endocryptic Identification," in *The Shell and the Kernel*, vol. 1, *Renewals of Psychoanalysis*, ed. and trans. Nicholas Rand (Chicago: University of Chicago Press, 1994), 141.
5 Introjection is the psychoanalytic process of assimilating an external reality into the ego. Mourning is the process of working through a loss and recognizing it as such; it is the introjection of loss. See Sigmund Freud, "Mourning and Melancholia," in *The Standard Edition of the Complete Psychological Works of Sigmund Freud*, ed. and trans. James Strachey, vol. 14 (London: Hogarth Press, 1957), 237–60.
6 Ince, *Georges Franju*, 25.
7 Gilles Deleuze, "Postscript on the Societies of Control," *October* 59 (1992): 3–7, at 3–4.

8   Abraham and Torok, "Mourning or Melancholia," 134.

9   *Le petit soldat*, was denied exhibition when it was completed in 1960 and was not shown publicly in France until 1963. Among the objections were its depictions of torture (chiefly by the FLN), its association of French special forces with acts of political terror, and the claim that it was an incitement to desertion. Leslie Hill notes that "from 1954 until 1962 . . . it was impossible to make public statements on film which were hostile to the conduct of the war in Algeria. . . . Commercial films that aimed to comment critically on the war, either explicitly or implicitly, risked being banned." Leslie Hill, "Filming Ghosts: French Cinema and the Algerian War," *MFS: Modern Fiction Studies* 38, no. 3 (1992): 795.

10   Durgnat, *Franju*, 78. The quotation is unattributed in Durgnat's text.

11   The best discussion of the reception of *Les yeux sans visage* in both the French and American contexts is given in Joan Hawkins, *Cutting Edge: Art-Horror and the Horrific Avant-Garde* (Minneapolis: University of Minnesota Press, 2000), 65–85. "When the film came to the United States as *The Horror Chamber of Doctor Faustus*, the horrific operating-room sequence . . . had been cut. Perhaps for this reason, the cultural and generic discourses surrounding the film and audience reception of the film appear even more mixed than they did in France, almost confused," 74. For a discussion of the domestic response to the growing recognition of French torture in Algeria, read as a "housekeeping" operation focused on consumption and cleanliness, see Kristin Ross, *Fast Cars, Clean Bodies: Decolonization and the Reordering of French Culture* (Cambridge, MA: MIT Press, 1996).

12   Adam Lowenstein, *Shocking Representation: Historical Trauma, National Cinema, and the Modern Horror Film* (New York: Columbia University Press, 2005), 37.

13   Ross, *Fast Cars, Clean Bodies*, 19. "Postwar French economic growth was a direct result of having modernized sectors of production that were seen to be vital—and the most vital of these was automobile production. In turn, the augmentation in French buying power after 1949 was used principally to buy cars." Ross also points out that in the 1960s, Paris was redesigned to accommodate the automobile.

14   The notion of temporalization is used here to suggest the experience of *rhythm* in psychoanalysis as explored by Nicolas Abraham. Abraham outlines five properties of what he calls a "rhythmizing consciousness." 1. It is apprehended as a semispontaneous activity of consciousness. It does not have an object (a meter, the movement of a train on the tracks, etc.) as its cause, but is rather the temporalizing activity by which consciousness experiences the object as an expectation. 2. The futurity of rhythm is an act of will by which consciousness

acts on the world, and thus "[it] creates itself in creating the world." Abraham compares this to the interplay between the pleasure principle and the reality principle, since once rhythmizing consciousness encounters too many obstacles in the world, it gives itself up and abolishes itself. 3. Rhythmizing consciousness is not a "perceived rhythm" but the rhythmizing of perception, "a creation within a consciousness of unreality." 4. Rhythm surpasses its object; it is the "intentional correlate of a specific effort of unification, of a truly creative act" that unites the corporeal experience of consciousness with the objective perception of an object. 5. It produces an effect of kinesthesia. Nicolas Abraham, *Rhythms: On the Work, Translation, and Psychoanalysis*, trans. Nicholas Rand and Benjamin Thigpen (Stanford, CA: Stanford University Press, 1995), 67–103.

15 Freud, "Mourning and Melancholia," 248. "So we find the key to the clinical picture [of melancholia]: we perceive that the self-reproaches are reproaches against a loved object which have been shifted away from it on to the patient's own ego."

16 Abraham and Torok, "The Lost Object—Me," 141–42.

17 Abraham and Torok, *Wolf Man's Magic Word*, 26. Of their rereading of Freud's Wolf Man case, Abraham and Torok write: "It should be clear that the preceding considerations relate to the Wolf Man only as a mythical person. Their wholly fictitious—though not gratuitous—nature illustrates an approach that can be of clinical use. What we termed *internal hysteria*, and considered the consequence of *incorporation*, often implies unconscious procedures motivated by a particular topographical structure involving the *cryptonymic displacement of a taboo word*. Rightly or wrongly, we discovered such a taboo word in the Wolf Man."

18 Esther Rashkin makes a similar point in relation to her usage of Abraham and Torok for a literary analysis of character: "The past dramas I reconstruct from short stories and to which I trace characters' behavior have the same fictional status as the characters themselves. Both the 'life' of the character as it is presented in the text and the past I conjecture are fictive, which is not to say fictitious. The familial dramas that can be reconstituted as motive forces in each story are not without textual basis but are inscribed and readable in the narrative." Rashkin, *Family Secrets*, 7. The difference in my approach is that I locate the reconstructed scene outside of the fiction, in history. Thus, the truth of any reconstruction is its ability to refer back to pretextual but historical determining image. In this case, though it is somewhat outside of my current concern, the postwar debates in France about abortion strengthen my reading.

19 The housing and treatment of the dead in Paris is itself an interesting question with its own history. Allan Mitchell, for example, considers the importance of the morgue as an institution in nineteenth-century Paris. A "place of detention for all those who were, so far as society was concerned, gone and forgotten," the

morgue was throughout that time a popular location for both tourists and those wishing to identify the unknown dead. Mitchell suggests that it is in part due to the history of two world wars that today the morgue is a less visible landmark of the city and that "very few are even aware of [the morgue's] present location." Allan Mitchell, "The Paris Morgue as a Social Institution in the Nineteenth Century," *Francia* 4 (1976): 595.

20 Rousso, *Vichy Syndrome*, 25–26.

21 M. Christine Boyer, *The City of Collective Memory: Its Historical Imagery and Architectural Entertainments* (Cambridge, MA: MIT Press, 1996), 53–54.

22 For a discussion of the nature of "incompossible narration" in postwar French cinema, see Deleuze, *Cinema 2: The Time-Image*, 130. Deleuze makes much of the concept of incompossible worlds, which he traces from Leibniz through Borges and finally to narration as the power of the false in the modern cinema. "Leibniz says that the naval battle may or may not take place, but that this is not in the same world: it takes place in one world and does not take place in a different world, and these two worlds are possible, but are not 'compossible' with each other." What I am suggesting here is that the crypt image, itself a product of the same forces that produced modern narration, operates as a *falsifying image* within the seeming inevitability of urban renewal and the modernization brought about by global capital.

23 Ross, *Fast Cars, Clean Bodies*, 22–23.

24 Douglas Morrey goes as far as claiming that the heart of the film is an "ethnographic document" of contemporary Paris. "Godard devotes considerable attention to the construction of 'grand ensembles,' large housing projects on the outskirts of the city. . . . The film opens with the images and sounds of these construction sites while Godard's voiceover gives precise details about the government legislation permitting these developments." Morrey, *Jean-Luc Godard*, 63–64. Jacques Tati's *Playtime* (1968) takes this theme to its logical conclusion in the alienation of the human subject within the technocratic city.

25 Nicolas Abraham and Maria Torok, "The Topography of Reality: Sketching a Metapsychology of Secrets," in *The Shell and the Kernel*, vol. 1, *Renewals of Psychoanalysis*, ed. and trans. Nicholas Rand (Chicago: University of Chicago Press, 1994), 159.

26 In his introduction to *The Wolf Man's Magic Word*, Jacques Derrida emphasizes this artificiality of the crypt, not to contrast it with a "natural" structure of the ego, but to highlight its noninclusion in the place where it is found and its status as the monument to a clandestine act of exclusion. "The crypt is thus not a natural place, but the striking history of an artifice, an *architecture*, an artifact: of a place *comprehended* within another but rigorously separate from it, isolated

from general space by partitions, an enclosure, an enclave. So as to purloin *the thing* from the rest." Derrida, "Fors: The Anglish Words of Nicolas Abraham and Maria Torok," xiv.

27 Quoted in Durgnat, *Franju*, 19.

28 Alain Schlockoff, "The Poetic Universe of Georges Franju," *Video Watchdog*, no. 108 (June 2004): 26.

29 Robin Wood, "Franju, Georges," in *The St. James Film Directors Encyclopedia*, ed. Andrew Sarris (Detroit: Visible Ink Press, 1998), 182.

30 Franju's visual vocabulary in this sequence draws heavily on F. W. Murnau's films.

31 Nicolas Abraham and Maria Torok, "The Topography of Reality: Sketching a Metapsychology of Secrets," in *The Shell and the Kernel*, vol. 1, *Renewals of Psychoanalysis*, ed. and trans. Nicholas Rand (Chicago: University of Chicago Press, 1994), 157. Italics in original. The capitalization is Abraham and Torok's way to indicate a metapsychological term that is used within that field, and not in its everyday usage.

32 Abraham and Torok, *Wolf Man's Magic Word*, 20. "The term 'seduction' might seem somewhat excessive to describe, as Freud did, sexual play among little children. For such games to take on the magnitude we know they can, an adult must be implicated." It may be that Freud was unable to hear this word properly because of his need to defend the seduction theory as a product of infantile fantasy.

33 Adam Lowenstein, "Films without a Face: Shock Horror in the Cinema of Georges Franju," *Cinema Journal* 37, no. 4 (1998): 40.

34 Maria Torok, "Fantasy: An Attempt to Define Its Structure and Operation," in *The Shell and the Kernel*, vol. 1, *Renewals of Psychoanalysis*, ed. and trans. Nicholas Rand (Chicago: University of Chicago Press, 1994), 30.

35 Torok, "Fantasy," 36.

36 Following common usage, and in distinction from Abraham and Torok's vocabulary, Kracauer calls this "incorporation." For the difference between the everyday cryptic use of the term "incorporation," and the confusion it causes in the psychoanalytic literature and the technical distinction between it and introjection, see "Mourning *or* Melancholia: Introjection *versus* Incorporation," in Nicolas Abraham and Maria Torok, *The Shell and the Kernel*, vol. 1, *Renewals of Psychoanalysis*, ed. and trans. Nicholas Rand (Chicago: University of Chicago Press, 1994), 125–38. In this essay, Abraham and Torok differentiate between the *fantasy* of incorporation and the *process* of introjection. In a perceptive metaphor, they place introjection on the side of metaphor and incorporation on the side of the photograph: "Introjection (= casting inside) is surely the same thing as incorporating, is it not? Certainly

the image is identical, but for reasons that will soon be apparent, it is important to distinguish between them, as we would distinguish between metaphoric and photographic images, between the acquisition of a language as opposed to buying a dictionary, between self-possession gained through psychoanalysis and the fantasy of 'incorporating' a 'penis,'" 127.

37 Siegfried Kracauer, *Theory of Film: The Redemption of Physical Reality* (New York: Oxford University Press, 1960), 305.

38 Lowenstein, "Films without a Face," 52.

39 Abraham and Torok, *Wolf Man's Magic Word*, 1986, 79.

40 Stefanos Geroulanos, "Postwar Facial Reconstruction: Georges Franju's Eyes without a Face," *French Politics, Culture, and Society* 31, no. 2 (2013): 27. "*Eyes without a Face* has been interpreted as an artistic response to the Holocaust or an assumption of traumatic national history. Such an interpretation is useful so long as it is taken far less than literally, for it relies more on metaphor and evocative detail than evidence, and it conversely expands and literalizes the scope and force of the film in a somewhat unsatisfying way—Dr. Génessier is hardly a Josef Mengele, the German shepherd he has used for skin grafting experiments cannot be seen as concentration camp guard-dogs, and so on." Note, however, that while Geroulanos cites Lowenstein on this point, Lowenstein's argument is actually far less "evocative" than he is credited for. It depends not on a simple metaphorical substitution (Génessier *for* Mengele), but on the artificial nature of Franju's images, which are said to create an estrangement by which the given meaning of the images is suspended.

41 Jeannette Sloniowski, "'It Was an Atrocious Film': Georges Franju's Blood of the Beasts," in *Documenting the Documentary: Close Readings of Documentary Film and Video*, ed. Barry Keith Grant and Jeannette Sloniowski (Detroit: Wayne State University, 1998), 185. Sloniowksi concludes that "in the Franju film death is necessary if people are going to eat meat. The film says no more and no less than this. . . . The film merely encourages an acceptance of life as it exists in the slaughterhouses," 186. This reading largely ignores the topographical structure of the film that locates the slaughterhouse as a taboo image within a surreal, or at least de-realized, space, suggesting anything but an acceptance of life as it exists. It is also belied by the presence of historical echoes in Sloniowski's own experience of the film ("The second sequence continues by showing the gates of an abattoir which are disturbingly similar to the gates of Auschwitz" 177).

42 Kracauer, *Theory of Film*, 305. My emphasis.

43 Abraham and Torok, *Wolf Man's Magic Word*, 79–80. "The idea of symbol implies a symbolizable entity and a basic presymbolic unity whose dissolution occasioned the formation of the Unconscious. But what happens if an additional

fracture fragments the already incomplete symbolic given and if, as a result, the patient on the couch carries a jigsaw puzzle whose pieces are as largely unknown as is their mode of assembly?"

44   Kracauer, *Theory of Film*, 306. My emphasis.
45   Lowenstein, "Films without a Face," 37. "When Georges Franju died in 1987, he felt bitterly dissatisfied with the spotty critical reception of his film career.... Franju's shadowy presence in film history probably has more to do with a remarkably multifaceted career that resists convenient categorization."

Notes to Chapter 2

1   Mario Bava, *Terror Fantastic* #3, interview by Ornella Volta, trans. Alwin Dewaele and Troy Howarth, December 1971. Reprinted in Troy Howarth, *The Haunted World of Mario Bava*, rev. and expanded ed. (Baltimore: Midnight Marquee Press, 2014), 175.
2   The story is almost certainly apocryphal. Bava first told this story of the letter in 1971, after the release of most of his best-known gothic horror films. The films thus appear to antedate the story, which Bava claims took place on the morning of the interview. However, even aside from the unlikely coincidence of the event's occurrence on the morning of an interview (Bava rarely granted interviews), we should also note that the date on which the letter was supposedly written ("ten years ago," that is, in 1961) roughly corresponds to the release of Bava's directorial debut, *Black Sunday*. The letter thus seems to indicate the return, for Bava, of the filmic text itself rather than providing a description of a "truthful" biographical event. It is as if the film took on the status of the dead letter whose message Bava burns in front of the inquisitive critic. This is another case of the obscurity of origins that is so central to Bava's work.
3   For Freud, disavowal is a defense mechanism in which the subject refuses the reality of a traumatic perception of lack (paradigmatically, of the absence of the woman's penis) by fixating on a fetish object. Disavowal played a particularly important role in the Wolf Man case. See Jean Laplanche and Jean-Bertrand Pontalis, *The Language of Psychoanalysis*, trans. Donald Nicholson-Smith (London: Hogarth Press, 1973), 118–21.
4   Mario Bava, *L'Espresso*, interview by Dante Matelli, trans. Roberto Curti, May 1979. Reprinted in Howarth, *Haunted World*, 184.
5   The Wolf Man, too, could be defined by the difference between his inner life of turmoil and external banality or placid typicality. It seems to be a trait of many cryptophores that they bury their cryptic life within the tomb of the most

mundane and typical of biographies. A similar "confusion" takes place in relation to Franju's rote genre film "exercises" and the surreal undercurrents of the encrypted dead.

6. Alain Silver and James Ursini, "Mario Bava: The Illusion of Reality" (1975), in *The Horror Film Reader*, ed. Alain Silver and James Ursini (New York: Limelight, 2000), 95–109, at 95, 109.

7. Abraham and Torok, "Mourning or Melancholia," 128. "The passage from food to language in the mouth presupposes the successful replacement of the object's presence with the self's cognizance of its absence. Since language acts and makes up for absence by representing, by giving *figurative shape* to presence, it can only be *comprehended* or *shared* in a 'community of empty mouths.'" Emphasis in original.

8. Abraham, "Notes on the Phantom," 171, 175.

9. Tim Lucas records that "Eugenio Bava was recruited by Mussolini to supervise the [Instituto Nationale LUCE]'s first major work, a documentary about the *Giovani Fascisti* ('Young Fascists'), which took him on an extended cruise to the Far East in the company of Mussolini's sons." Tim Lucas, *Mario Bava: All the Colors of the Dark* (Cincinnati: Video Watchdog, 2007), 52. Lucas also mentions Eugenio's mysterious absences from the family home, at least as recollected by his children and grandchildren: "There is a family legend that Eugenio once went out, ostensibly to get some tobacco, and did not return for three weeks." Another relevant story uncovered by Lucas involves the young Mario being slapped by his father for having dared to sign his name to a drawing he had made (50). It is the very piecemeal nature of these anecdotes that insinuate the presence of an unspoken trauma in Eugenio's past that is being transmitted to his adoring son.

10. Patricia MacCormack, "Barbara Steele's Ephemeral Skin: Feminism, Fetishism, and Film," *Senses of Cinema*, no. 22 (October 2002), http://sensesofcinema.com/2002/feature-articles/steele/.

11. Carol Jenks, "The Other Face of Death: Barbara Steele and *La Maschera del Demonio*," in *Popular European Cinema*, ed. Richard Dyer and Ginette Vincendeau (London: Routledge, 1992), 149–62. Jenks begins her study by quoting a number of critics and fans who place Steele's figure explicitly as the fetish object of their desire for the horror film. See also in this regard MacCormack, "Barbara Steele's Ephemeral Skin."

12. Jenks, "Other Face of Death," 161.

13. Lucas, *Mario Bava*, 298.

14. Andrea Bini, "Horror Cinema: The Emancipation of Women and Urban Anxiety," in *Popular Italian Cinema: Culture and Politics in a Postwar Society*, ed. Flavia Brizio-Skov (London: I. B. Tauris, 2011), 58. "When Asa returns from the

dead to seek revenge, the family she attacks is her own. From then on, Italian horror cinema often portrayed the female figure as subverter of the patriarchal social order by virtue of her irresistible provocative sexuality."

15 Linda Williams, "When the Woman Looks," in *The Dread of Difference: Gender and the Horror Film*, ed. Barry Keith Grant (Austin: University of Texas Press, 1996), 18.

16 Carol Jenks makes a similar observation about *Black Sunday*, reading the series of female looks as markers of both lesbian desire and the repetition of a mother-daughter relation.

17 It has been common, at least since Derrida's discussion of it in *The Post Card*, to recognize the halting and uncertain nature of Freud's speculation on the death drive, an uncertainty that Freud himself is not shy of discussing. *Beyond the Pleasure Principle* thus concludes not by asserting the truth of the newly discovered theory of the instincts, but with "a few words of critical reflection" in which Freud questions the validity of his hypotheses due to the lack of direct observation. It is striking, however, that for Freud this is primarily a problem of language and description: "We need not feel greatly disturbed in judging our speculation upon the life and death instincts by the fact that so many bewildering and obscure processes occur in it. . . . This is merely due to our being obliged to operate with the scientific terms, that is to say, with the figurative language, peculiar to psychology (or, more precisely, to depth psychology). We could not otherwise describe the processes in question at all, and indeed we could not have become aware of them." Sigmund Freud, *Beyond the Pleasure Principle*, trans. James Strachey, *The Standard Edition of the Complete Psychological Works of Sigmund Freud*, vol. 18 (London: Hogarth Press, 1920), 60.

18 Jenks, "Other Face of Death," 154. Italics mine.

19 See Mark Nash, "*Vampyr* and the Fantastic," *Screen* 17, no. 3 (1976): 29–67.

20 Nash, "*Vampyr* and the Fantastic," 60.

21 Nash, 66–67.

22 Pier Paolo Pasolini, "The 'Cinema of Poetry,'" in *Heretical Empiricism*, ed. Louise K. Barnett, trans. Ben Lawton and Louise K. Barnett (Bloomington: Indiana University Press, 1988), 167–86.

23 As an example of the first method, Pasolini singles out Godard (though this is also the mode Pasolini most commonly employed in his own films); for the second, his primary examples are the works of Antonioni.

24 Louis-Georges Schwartz, "Typewriter: Free Indirect Discourse in Deleuze's Cinema," *SubStance* 34, no. 3 (2005): 117. "True free indirect discourse must bear the inscription of the socio-economic difference between speakers in their

language and consciousness.... Pasolini interprets the existence of languages other than the dominant one as concrete forms of social resistance."

25 Pasolini, "The 'Cinema of Poetry,'" 177.
26 Laplanche and Pontalis, *Language*, 335. Laplanche and Pontalis define the primal scene as a "scene of sexual intercourse between the parents which the child observes, or infers on the basis of certain indications, and phantasies. It is generally interpreted by the child as an act of violence on the part of the father."
27 Silvia Federici, *Caliban and the Witch: Women, the Body, and Primitive Accumulation* (New York: Autonomedia, 2004), 11.
28 Paul Ginsborg, *A History of Contemporary Italy: Society and Politics, 1943–1988* (London: Penguin Books, 1990), 236.
29 Deborah Willis, "Reading the Early Modern Witch: Horror Films of the 1960s and 1970s," in *The English Renaissance in Popular Culture* (New York: Palgrave Macmillan, 2010), 104.
30 Undoubtedly, the witch as invoked in 1960 is not *simply* the witch of the era of the transition to capitalism. A few notes, however, are in order. First, the generational narrative structure of Bava's film already links the seventeenth century, the end of the transition to capitalism, with an open-ended futurity in a way that makes this kind of rhyming or echoing reading not only relevant but also necessary. Second, to the extent that the witch in 1960 represents the conditions of women's social roles in the postwar period, this is so *because* of the earlier history of the witch trials, and not in spite of it. This history makes the figure of the witch available for the kind of transgenerational inheritance that allows her to embody women's dispossession as a historical return or death drive. Thus Federici asks: "Why, after 500 years of capital's rule, at the beginning of the third millennium, are workers on a mass scale still defined as paupers, witches, and outlaws?" Federici, *Caliban and the Witch*, 11–12.
31 Nicolas Abraham, "The Phantom of Hamlet or the Sixth Act, *Preceded* by The Intermission of 'Truth,'" in *The Shell and the Kernel*, vol. 1, *Renewals of Psychoanalysis*, ed. and trans. Nicholas Rand (Chicago: University of Chicago Press, 1994), 188–89.
32 Martyn Conterio, *Black Sunday*, Devil's Advocates (Leighton Buzzard, UK: Auteur Publishing, 2015), 45. Scorsese also emphasizes the need for a *monograph* to serve as a verbal appendage to the films. Writing in the introduction to Tim Lucas's auteur study, *Mario Bava: All the Colors of the Dark*, he quickly corrects himself: "I take it back—I probably could *now* [tell you the plots of the films], after having read Tim Lucas' exhaustive, perceptive biography. But if this book didn't exist, I would find it difficult."
33 Lucas, *Mario Bava*, 297.
34 Lucas, 297.

35 Ken Gelder, for example, begins his book *Reading the Vampire* by analyzing Transylvania as a floating signifier of internalized (i.e., colonized) foreignness. He argues that as early as the publication of Stoker's *Dracula* in 1897, "'Transylvania' already operates as a transferable sign which carries its meaning to other places—places which, as yet, can only be imagined. In this case, it nominates a region which lies under the shadow of—but is still, for the moment, outside, colonization. . . . The place-name 'Transylvania,' with its evocative meaning, 'beyond (or, to the other side of) the forest', must have seemed highly appropriate as a designation for the last uncharted part of the island." Ken Gelder, *Reading the Vampire* (London: Routledge, 1994), 1.

36 Federici, *Caliban and the Witch*, 180, 184.

37 Aside from the enigmas of the crime and the figural enigma of the witch, a number of other factors spin the spider web of evidence that must be followed to conjecture the origin of a phantom. Among these are the subversive looks exchanged between Katia and her brother, the presence of Asa's naked portrait (holding a coiled snake) at the threshold of an inner passage leading from the familial hearth to the abandoned tomb, and the phantasmatic repetition of scenes of the dead witch being "birthed" as a corpse from her womb-like coffin.

38 Abraham, "Notes on the Phantom," 174.

39 Between the two films, Bava did make a number of supernatural horrors, including *Black Sabbath* in 1963. He also directed a series of murder mysteries—*The Whip and the Body* (1963) and *Blood and Black Lace* (1964)—that paved the way for the *giallo* film, as well as a number of minor works, including the science fiction *Planet of the Vampires* (1965) and the Viking-western *Knives of the Avenger* (1966).

40 Lucas, *Mario Bava*, 664 ("only in Italy").

41 Howarth, *Haunted World*, 84, 88.

42 Ewa Partyka, "The Influence of the Grand-Guignol on the Chiaroscuro and Giallo Horror Movies of Mario Bava," in *Redefining Kitsch and Camp in Literature and Culture*, ed. Justyna Stepien (Newcastle upon Tyne: Cambridge Scholars, 2014), 59.

43 Derrida, "Fors: The Anglish Words of Nicolas Abraham and Maria Torok," 1986, xiv.

44 Quoted in Carlo Testa, *Italian Cinema and Modern European Literatures, 1945–2000* (Westport, CT: Praeger, 2002), 7.

45 Angela Dalle Vacche, *The Body in the Mirror: Shapes of History in Italian Cinema* (Princeton, NJ: Princeton University Press, 1992), 53.

46 Dalle Vacche argues that "the style of silent and fascist cinema is operatic; neorealist cinema, instead, relies on the tradition of commedia dell'arte." Dalle Vacche, *Body in the Mirror*, 5. Her book traces the repetition of these two forms of the body—the opera and the commedia dell'arte—in Italian cinema as markers of

the tension between Fascist and realist tendencies. On Barbara Steele as part of the diva tradition, see Jenks, "Other Face of Death."

47. Rick Worland, "The Gothic Revival (1967–1974)," in *A Companion to the Horror Film*, ed. Harry M. Benshoff (Oxford: John Wiley and Sons, 2014), 286.
48. Angelo Restivo, *The Cinema of Economic Miracles: Visuality and Modernization in the Italian Art Film* (Durham, NC: Duke University Press, 2002), 9.
49. Restivo, *Cinema of Economic Miracles*, 9.
50. Abraham and Torok, *Wolf Man's Magic Word*, 82.
51. David Cook, *A History of Narrative Film*, 3rd ed. (New York: W. W. Norton, 1996), 429.
52. Cook, *History of Narrative Film*, 428.
53. Undoubtedly, Freda's conception of neorealism was limited and perhaps, as Carlo Testa argues, tinged with a Fascist nostalgia. For Bava, however, the rejection of neorealism is not rooted in a distaste for films focusing on "common people" but on a desire to capture the images from which the worlds of neorealism arose. In other words, it is not neorealism itself that Bava rejects, but the status of the visible world as the origin of truth.
54. Lucas, *Mario Bava*, 665.
55. Howarth, *Haunted World*, 85.
56. Lesley Caldwell, "What Do Mothers Want? Takes on Motherhood in *Bellisima*, *Il Grido*, and *Mamma Roma*," in *Women in Italy, 1945–1960: An Interdisciplinary Study*, ed. Penelope Morris (New York: Palgrave Macmillan, 2006), 226.
57. Félix Guattari, *The Three Ecologies*, trans. Ian Pindar and Paul Sutton (1989; repr., London: Bloomsbury Academic, 2008), 41.
58. Maggie Günsberg, *Italian Cinema: Gender and Genre* (New York: Palgrave Macmillan, 2004), 163.
59. Schwab, *Haunting Legacies*, 46.

Notes to Chapter 3

1. Nora Alter, "Mourning, Sound, and Vision: Jean-Luc Godard's *JLG/JLG*," *Camera Obscura* 15, no. 2 (2000): 76.
2. Daniel Morgan, *Late Godard and the Possibilities of Cinema* (Berkeley: University of California Press, 2013), xiii.
3. Michael Witt, "The Death(s) of Cinema According to Godard," *Screen* 40, no. 3 (1999): 334.
4. The talks that Godard gave at Concordia University in the late 1970s have been collected under the title *Introduction to a True History of Cinema and Television*.

These talks are sketches of the project that would, decades later, become the *Histoire(s) du cinema*. See Jean-Luc Godard, *Introduction to a True History of Cinema and Television*, trans. Timothy Barnard (Montreal: Caboose, 2012).

5   Christopher Pavsek, "What Has Come to Pass for Cinema in Late Godard," *Discourse* 28, no. 1 (2006): 177.

6   Sigmund Freud, "Analysis Terminable and Interminable," in *The Standard Edition of the Complete Psychological Works of Sigmund Freud*, ed. and trans. James Strachey, vol. 23 (London: Hogarth Press, 1964). In this well-known essay Freud lays much of the blame of the failed analysis at the Wolf Man's feet: "We made no progress in clearing up his childhood's neurosis, which was the basis of his later illness, and it was obvious that the patient found his present situation quite comfortable and did not intend to take any step which would bring him nearer to the end of his treatment. It was a case of the patient himself obstructing the cure: the analysis was in danger of failing as a result of its—partial—success."

7   Alter, "Mourning, Sound, and Vision," 75–76. "I want to suggest that, consistent with much of Godard's work, this sequence does not hierarchize the aural and the visual. On the contrary, it fuses the two together as a *sound image or rebus*."

8   Witt, "Death(s) of Cinema," 331. Italics mine.

9   Morgan, *Late Godard*, 1.

10 Abraham and Torok, *Wolf Man's Magic Word*, 19.

11 Pavsek, "What Has Come to Pass for Cinema in Late Godard," 177.

12 Derrida, "Fors: The Anglish Words of Nicolas Abraham and Maria Torok," 1986, xiii.

13 Nicolas Abraham, "The Shell and the Kernel: The Scope and Originality of Freudian Psychoanalysis," in *The Shell and the Kernel*, vol. 1, *Renewals of Psychoanalysis*, ed. and trans. Nicholas Rand (Chicago: University of Chicago Press, 1994), 79–98. Barbara Johnson, who translated Derrida's "Fors," provides a useful etymology of Abraham's neologism: "*Ana-* indicates: (1) upward, (2) according to, (3) back, (4) backward, reversed (5) again; *-semic* indicates 'pertaining to the sign as a unit of meaning.' 'Anasemia' is thus a process of problematizing the meaning of signs in an undetermined way. *Anasemia* is to be the general title of Nicolas Abraham's collected works." Translator's introduction to Derrida, "Fors: The Anglish Words of Nicolas Abraham and Maria Torok," 1986, 117n1.

14 Irmgard Emmelhainz, "From Third Worldism to Empire: Jean-Luc Godard and the Palestine Question," *Third Text* 23, no. 5 (2009): 650. "Artists, writers, journalists and film-makers produced works speaking for and about revolutionary struggles in the Third World. These accounts mixed the genres of documentary, travel diary, photojournalism and reportage. Political tourism came with its self-critique, as the self-reflexive examples of this body of works activated diverse

mechanisms in order to render an awareness of the speaker's position as external observer aware of his or her position as such."

15 Shai Ginsburg, "Between Documentary and Agit-Prop: Jean-Luc Godard's *Ici et Ailleurs*," *Tikkun* 22, no. 1 (2007): 76. This article goes on to criticize the final film for "presenting a one-dimensional portrait of the Palestinians caught between the guilty conscience of the European left and Israeli/American racial imperialism," 76. The film, however, is clear in presenting the Palestinian struggle as a struggle against colonialism and transgenerational genocide, and although Godard interrogates the role of the "actors" within the film, they are never presented as dupes of foreign powers.

16 "Corporium" modulates Abraham and Torok's creation of a "verbarium" of crypt-words in their analysis of the Wolf Man case. On one level, the verbarium is simply a catalog of the Wolf Man's cryptic language and the translations given to it by the analysts in the course of their work. The corporium would thus indicate the constellation of crypt-images produced by a particular film or historical situation. The "verbarium" also has the sense of the word game in which players must invent the maximum number of words from a limited set of letters, and thus it suggests that the words inscribed within it are elements of an open-ended combinatory play. Corporium translates this linguistic game into the exquisite corpse of cinematic cryptonymy.

17 Ross, *Fast Cars, Clean Bodies*, 77.

18 In a discussion of *Histoire(s) du cinema*, Richard Neer explains Godard's idea of a truthful image: "What matters in the scenario is not the putatively indexical nature of the photographic image. It is, rather, the fact of shared perception: 'Several people can see it together.' The experience is public by definition." This shared perception, according to Neer, depends not only on the material apparatus of film projection but also on the "rules of enumeration and montage [that] are the ligaments of a sort of community and the condition of being in a body." Richard Neer, "Godard Counts," *Critical Inquiry* 34, no. 1 (2007): 152, 137.

19 Derrida, "Fors: The Anglish Words of Nicolas Abraham and Maria Torok," xxxi.

20 For an insightful discussion of the relation between speech and silence, especially as it relates to translation in Godard's films about Palestine, see Rebecca Dyer and Francois Mulot, "Mahmoud Darwish in Film: Politics, Representation, and Translation in Jean-Luc Godard's *Ici et Ailleurs* and *Notre Musique*," *Cultural Politics* 10, no. 1 (2014): 70–91.

21 A related approach to anasemic montage is offered in James Leo Cahill, "Anacinema: Peter Tscherkassky's Cinematic Breakdowns," *Spectator—The University of Southern California Journal of Film and Television* 28, no. 2 (2008): 90–101. Cahill's use of anacinema draws on both Abraham's psychoanalytic writings and

Jean-François Lyotard's notion of *acinema* to argue that Tscherkassky rips images from their original context (and, literally, from the films in which they first appeared) in order to redeploy them as expressions of the inexpressible mourning exterior to any language. This involves recourse to a kind of supple supplementarity by which Tscherkassky's multilayered superimpositions turn the very material of the film strip *against* its representational content, using the apparatus to exclude or designify the representational image from within.

22 Pavsek, "What Has Come to Pass for Cinema in Late Godard," 178. "For Godard, an image is precisely this invisible moment that appears when two 'realities' are brought together in montage; pictures in and of themselves do not have this status of image."

23 Abraham and Torok, *Wolf Man's Magic Word*, 79.

24 Abraham and Torok, 80.

25 Morrey, *Jean-Luc Godard*, 223. Morrey is largely summarizing Jacques Aumont in this passage.

26 For a discussion of Godard's fraught relationship to television as a "second scene," see Michael Cramer, *Utopian Television: Rossellini, Watkins, and Godard beyond Cinema* (Minneapolis: University of Minnesota Press, 2017).

27 Gilles Deleuze, *Cinema 1: The Movement-Image*, trans. Hugh Tomlinson and Barbara Habberjam (Minneapolis: University of Minnesota Press, 1986), 214.

28 Gilles Deleuze positions Godard as one of the founders of a regime of images constituted by the importance given to the irrational cut, defined as a cut that belongs neither to the end of one series or the beginning of another, but in which the interstices are valid for themselves: "irrational cuts thus have a disjunctive, and no longer a conjunctive, value." The irrational cut can take a number of forms in Godard's films, but Deleuze highlights two of them: the black or white screen. "Now this limit, this irrational cut, may present itself in quite diverse visual forms: whether in the steady form of a sequence of unusual, 'anomalous' images, which come and interrupt the normal linkage of the two sequences; or in the enlarged form of the black screen, or the white screen, and their derivatives." Deleuze, *Cinema 2: The Time-Image*, 238–39. Contra Deleuze, I do not believe that the black screen functions as a mere irrational interstice, but rather that it marks the definitive place of an unfilmed image that must be retrieved from the history of cinema. However, Deleuze's recognition of the formal importance of the black screen and his recognition of its function as a narrative interruption hold true.

29 For Godard, only the girl's body revealed this potential for resistance, whereas the boy remained trapped in a fully socialized body. While a full discussion of this film is outside the scope of the present chapter, Michael Witt also

emphasizes the importance of the resistant and resisting body in *France/tour/détour*: "What we discover as we watch Miéville-Godard manipulating their material in the stop-motion sequences is that the body *resists*. Much of the irrepressible vitality and optimism that the series conveys derives from this conviction that the body—human and cinematic—can and does resist." Michael Witt, "Going through the Motions: Unconscious Optics and Corporal Resistance in Miéville and Godard's *France/Tour/Détour/Deux/Enfants*," in *Gender and French Cinema*, ed. Alex Hughes and James S. Williams (Oxford: Berg, 2001), 186.

30 Abraham and Torok, *Wolf Man's Magic Word*, 79.
31 Michael Witt and Jean-Luc Godard, "The Godard Interview: I, a Man of the Image," *Sight and Sound* 15, no. 6 (2005): 28–30.
32 Both of these possibilities are suggested by Godard in the interview with Michael Witt cited above. In the first case, Godard tells the story of Werner Heisenberg who arrives at Elsinore castle to visit Niels Bohr. He posits that we should understand this story as the shot of the castle and the "reverse shot," the description "Hamlet's castle." "In this case," Godard says, "the image is created by the text." Later in the interview, when Witt reminds Godard that he once called *Notre musique* a book, Godard responds: "It's not a book, it's a film. But that was a way of saying to the book people: 'See it as a book. But see it, don't read it.'" In this case, Godard emphasizes the need for a visual literacy that is different from a textual or readerly one. Witt and Godard, "Godard Interview."
33 This problematic is central to so-called apparatus theory; see especially Nick Browne, "The Spectator-in-the-Text: The Rhetoric of *Stagecoach*," *Film Quarterly* 29, no. 2 (1975): 26–38.
34 Giorgio Agamben, *Remnants of Auschwitz: The Witness and the Archive*, trans. Daniel Heller-Roazen (New York: Zone Books, 2002), 41.
35 Agamben, *Remnants of Auschwitz*, 51.
36 Agamben, 52. And further on: "That at the 'bottom' of the human being there is nothing other than an impossibility of seeing—this is the Gorgon, whose vision transforms the human being into a non-human. That precisely this inhuman impossibility of seeing is what calls and addresses the human, the apostrophe from which human beings cannot turn away—this and nothing else is testimony. The Gorgon and he who has seen her and the *Muselmann* and he who bears witness to him are one gaze; they are a single impossibility of seeing," 54. Compare this with the fable of the Medusa, which marks the unbearable taboo image in Kracauer's writings on cinema, as developed in chapter 1.
37 We may remember here that the paradigmatic case of cryptophoria, that of the Wolf Man, spans many of the great moments of contemporary history. Child of a Russian aristocrat who lost his family fortune due to the 1918 revolution,

Sergei Pankejeff lived in Austria during the Anschluss, and his wife gave herself to death by filling their apartment with gas as the annexation was announced. In later life, Pankejeff lived the mundane life of a salaried insurance salesman, an occupation central to the modern transformations of capital. For the Wolf Man's life, see Muriel Gardiner, ed., *The Wolf-Man, with the Case of the Wolf-Man by Sigmund Freud* (New York: Basic Books, 1972).

38 See also Achille Mbembe, "Necropolitics," *Public Culture* 15, no. 1 (2003): 40. In this important paper, Mbembe explores the presence of bare life in earlier periods, especially as constituted by slavery and colonialism. "Moreover, I have put forward the notion of necropolitics and necropower to account for the various ways in which, in our contemporary world, weapons are deployed in the interest of maximum destruction of persons and the creation of death-worlds, new and unique forms of social existence in which vast populations are subjected to conditions of life conferring upon them the status of living dead. The essay has also outlined some of the repressed topographies of cruelty (the plantation and the colony in particular) and has suggested that under conditions of necropower, the lines between resistance and suicide, sacrifice and redemption, martyrdom and freedom are blurred."

39 Giorgio Agamben, *Homo Sacer: Sovereign Power and Bare Life*, trans. Daniel Heller-Roazen (Stanford, CA: Stanford University Press, 1998), 188. "There is no return from the camps to classical politics. In the camps, city and house became indistinguishable, and the possibility of differentiating between our biological body and our political body—between what is incommunicable and mute and what is communicable and sayable—was taken from us forever. . . . It will be necessary to examine how it was possible for something like a bare life to be conceived [within the disciplines of politics, philosophy, science, and law], and how the historical development of these very disciplines has brought them to a limit beyond which they cannot venture without risking an unprecedented biopolitical catastrophe."

40 Agamben, *Remnants of Auschwitz*, 44. "The living dead . . . were termed 'donkeys'; in Dachau they were 'cretins,' in Stutthof 'cripples,' in Mauthausen 'swimmers . . .'" the list of rhymes continues. The term *drowned* is famously used in Primo Levi's *The Drowned and the Saved*. Agamben: "They are those who 'touched bottom': the Muslims, the drowned. The survivors speak in their stead, by proxy, as pseudo-witnesses; they bear witness to a missing testimony. And yet to speak here of a proxy makes no sense; the drowned have nothing to say," 34.

41 Jacques Rancière, "The Saint and the Heiress: A Propos of Godard's *Histoire(s) du Cinema*," trans. T. S. Murphy, *Discourse* 24, no. 1 (2002): 115.

42 Michael Witt, *Jean-Luc Godard, Cinema Historian* (Bloomington: Indiana

University Press, 2013), 127. Witt then quotes Godard: "Cinema 'stammered' history, and then at a given moment it no longer did it. The concentration camps weren't filmed; people didn't want to show them or see them. And that was the end: cinema stopped there."

43 Libby Saxton, "Anamnesis and Bearing Witness: Godard/Lanzmann," in *For Ever Godard*, ed. Michael Temple, James S. Williams, and Michael Witt (London: Black Dog Publishing, 2004), 369.

44 Saxton, "Anamnesis and Bearing Witness," 369.

45 Saxton, 369.

46 We can note here, again, the many intersections between Godard's way of thinking cinematically and Abraham and Torok's psychoanalytic theories, as the analysts, too, define reality as that which cannot be given symbolic form: "Reality can then be defined as what is rejected, masked, denied precisely as 'reality'; it is that which *is*, all the more so since it must not be known; in short, Reality is defined as a *secret*." Abraham and Torok, "Topography of Reality," 157. Italics in original.

47 Morgan, *Late Godard*, 7. The Godard quotation is from Jean Narboni and Tom Milne, eds., *Godard on Godard* (London: Secker and Warburg, 1972), 171–96, 192.

48 Witt and Godard, "Godard Interview." Godard responds: "It's true that it's rather cheerful compared to others; those who have called it pessimistic are wrong. On the contrary, it's rather childlike and optimistic—but we've lived for a year on that optimism and now it's exhausted."

49 Judith Butler, *Precarious Life: The Powers of Mourning and Violence* (London: Verso, 2004), 37. Butler describes her own version of the living-dead condition of the incorporated lost object: "If violence is done against those who are unreal, then, from the perspective of violence, it fails to injure or negate those lives since those lives are already negated. But they have a strange way of remaining animated and so must be negated again (and again). They cannot be mourned because they are always already lost or, rather, never 'were,' and they must be killed, since they seem to live on, stubbornly, in this state of deadness," 53.

50 Abraham, "The Shell and the Kernel," 85. "Thus, psychoanalytic theory speaks in an anasemic discourse. What justifies such a discourse? At first nothing except its sheer existence. . . . The very fact that, running counter to the known laws of discursive ratiocination, such a discourse actually occurs . . . amply confirms that its allusion meets a resonance in us capable of founding the discourse and allowing it to reveal, by its advance toward this nonpresence in us, the place from which all meaning ultimately springs," 85.

51 Susan Forde, "The Bridge on the Neretva: Stari Most as a Stage of Memory in

Post-Conflict Mostar, Bosnia–Herzegovina," *Cooperation and Conflict* 51, no. 4 (2016): 471.

52 Maha Armaly, Carlo Blasi, and Lawrence Hannah, "Stari Most: Rebuilding More Than a Historic Bridge in Mostar," *Museum International* 56, no. 4 (2004): 9.

53 A detailed discussion of the political and social conflicts surrounding the reconstruction project is given in Forde, "The Bridge on the Neretva." The details are beyond the scope of this chapter, though Forde's discussion of the reconstructed site as a tourist attraction are instructive: "The narrative of the reconstruction of Stari Most is intentionally sanitized and romanticized in its symbolism and purpose. Through the space of performance and consumption which surrounds the bridge, the staging of the bridge can be regarded as a 'Disneyization.' . . . The exoticization of the staging of the space . . . allows the performed narrative to be internationally consumed," 477.

54 Philip Rosen, *Change Mummified: Cinema, Historicity, Theory* (Minneapolis: University of Minnesota Press, 2001), 50. The idea of preservation was a foundation of the project from the start: "the ultimate choice of rebuilding a new bridge 'as it was' by using the same technology and materials as in the original bridge was decided by the people of Mostar." Armaly, Blasi, and Hannah, "Stari Most," 13.

55 Within the framework of Abraham and Torok's work, this is the function of psychic objectivation. Whereas demetaphorization refers to the cryptophore's process of taking literally what is meant figuratively, objectivation involves "pretending that the suffering is not an injury to the subject but instead a loss sustained by the love object." This displacement of loss from subject to object is what allows the subject to be magically "healed" through the preservation of the object within a crypt in the Self. Abraham and Torok, "Mourning or Melancholia," 126–27.

56 Witt and Godard, "Godard Interview."

57 Burlin Barr, "Shot and Counter-Shot: Presence, Obscurity, and the Breakdown of Discourse in Godard's *Notre musique*," *Journal of French and Francophone Philosophy* 18, no. 2 (2010): 79.

58 Witt and Godard, "Godard Interview."

59 Louis Marin, *Utopics: The Semiological Play of Textual Spaces*, trans. Robert A. Vollrath (Amherst, MA: Humanity Books, 1984), xiii. Frederic Jameson expands on Marin's ideas by theorizing utopias as negative experiences born out of the present contradictions: utopias arise from the critical inversion of the limits of the present. In this case, utopias are not simply the incorporation of nonplaces within the topography of the present. See Fredric Jameson, *Valences of the Dialectic* (London: Verso, 2010). For the topographic nature of utopia, see Louis

Marin, "Frontiers of Utopia: Past and Present," *Critical Inquiry* 19, no. 3 (1993): 397–420.

60 Abraham and Torok, "Mourning or Melancholia," 134. Elsewhere they expand on this connection between incorporation and an imaginary utopia: "The ego needs to keep alive at all costs that which causes its greatest suffering. Why this obligation? It is understandable if we consider the following. The imago, along with its external embodiment in the object, was set up as the repository of hope; the desires it forbade would be realized one day. Meanwhile, the imago retains the valuable thing whose lack cripples the ego. . . . The imagoic and objectal fixation is cemented precisely by the contradictory and therefore utopian hope that the imago, the warden of repression, would authorize the removal." Maria Torok, "The Illness of Mourning and the Fantasy of the Exquisite Corpse," in *The Shell and the Kernel*, vol. 1, *Renewals of Psychoanalysis*, ed. and trans. Nicholas Rand (Chicago: University of Chicago Press, 1994), 116.

61 See Erin Schlumpf, "Notre Musique," in *A Companion to Jean-Luc Godard*, ed. Tom Conley and T. Jefferson Kline (Hoboken, NJ: John Wiley and Sons, 2014), 514–26.

Notes to Chapter 4

1 "Naomi Uman: The Ukrainian Time Machine, Fragments from a Diary (Program Notes for Redcat Screening at CalArts)," December 12, 2011, http://www.redcat.org/sites/redcat.org/files/event/linked-files/2012-07/12.12.11_Uman.pdf.

2 Saskia Sassen, *The Global City: New York, London, Tokyo* (Princeton, NJ: Princeton University Press, 2001).

3 Walter Benjamin, "Surrealism: The Last Snapshot of the European Intelligentsia," in *Critical Theory and Society: A Reader*, ed. Stephen Eric Bonner and Douglas MacKay Kellner (New York: Routledge, 89), 172–83.

4 Jacques Derrida, *Specters of Marx: The State of the Debt, the Work of Mourning, and the New International*, trans. Peggy Kamuf (New York: Routledge, 94), 99.

5 Quoted in "Naomi Uman: The Ukrainian Time Machine," Creative Capital—Investing in Artists Who Shape the Future, accessed October 15, 2014, http://creative-capital.org/project_contexts/view/54/project:92.

6 Abraham and Torok give the formula of cryptic incorporation as: "*Wo Ich war soll Es warden*: Where there was Ego, there should be Id." As such, incorporation functions as the parodic reversal of Freud's own formulation of the goal of psychoanalytic technique, which states that "where id was, there ego shall be." If the Freudian cure aimed to enlarge the field of the subject by gaining mastery

over the unruled primary processes, incorporation creates a cyst within the ego that mimics the therapeutic process by enclosing an Id (in the guise of the lost object) within the Self.

7 Jean-Louis Baudry, "Ideological Effects of the Basic Cinematographic Apparatus," in *Narrative, Apparatus, Ideology: A Film Theory Reader*, ed. Philip Rosen, trans. Alan Williams (New York: Columbia University Press, 86), 289. "In focusing it, the optical construct appears to be truly the projection-reflection of a 'virtual image' whose hallucinatory reality it creates. It lays out the space of an ideal vision and in this way assures the necessity of a transcendence—metaphorically (by the unknown to which it appeals—here we must recall the structural place occupied by the vanishing point) and metonymically (by the displacement that it seems to carry out: a subject is both 'in place of' and 'a part for the whole')."

8 Abraham and Torok, *Wolf Man's Magic Word*, 5.

9 For example, Danni Zuvela, "A Little Light Teasing: Some Special Affects in Avant-Garde Cinema," *Continuum: Journal of Media Cultural Studies* 26, no. 4 (2012): 594–95. "The chemicals literally remove the image detail of the female actors from the image area of the film emulsion . . . the distinct image in *Removed* is image of an absence."

10 Akira Mizuta Lippit, *Ex-Cinema: From a Theory of Experimental Film and Video* (Berkeley: University of California Press, 112), 123.

11 Soledad Santiago, "Milking the Subject: Experiments in Film," *Santa Fe New Mexican*, January 27, 106.

12 Derrida defines the supplement as simultaneous addition and substitution. Following from Rousseau, the supplement is the mark of culture, the inscription of writing, that substitutes itself for an origin (nature, speech) by adding to this original the very element that is lacking in it. It replaces by adding.

13 Denis Hollier, *Against Architecture: The Writings of Georges Bataille* (Cambridge, MA: MIT Press, 1989), 69.

14 Claire Johnston, *Notes on Women's Cinema* (London: Society for Education in Film and Television, 1973), 31.

15 Kaja Silverman, *The Acoustic Mirror: The Female Voice in Psychoanalysis and Cinema* (Bloomington: Indiana University Press, 1988), 23.

16 Linda Williams, "When the Woman Looks," in *The Dread of Difference: Gender and the Horror Film*, ed. Barry Keith Grant (Austin: University of Texas Press, 1996), 21. "The audience's belated adoption of the woman's point of view undermines the usual audience identification and sympathy with the look of the cinematic character. But it may also permit a different form of identification and sympathy to take place, not between the audience and the character who looks, but between the two objects of the cinematic spectacle who encounter one

another in this look—the woman and the monster."

17　The classic study considering pornography in (some of) its complex textuality is Linda Williams, *Hard Core: Power, Pleasure, and the "Frenzy of the Visible,"* expanded 1999 ed. (Berkeley: University of California Press, 1999). The point, as I hope is clear, is not that *Removed* is an antipornography film, but that it is a film that works to rediscover the eroticism of the pornographic image.

18　Jean Laplanche and Jean-Bertrand Pontalis, *The Language of Psychoanalysis*, trans. Donald Nicholson-Smith (New York: W. W. Norton, 1973), 455. "For psycho-analysis, [transference is] a process of actualization of unconscious wishes. Transference uses specific objects and operates in the framework of a specific relationship established with these objects. Its context *par excellence* is the analytic situation." I am playing on the notion of *Removed* as a contact sheet from which a past image is *transferred* into Uman's film, actualizing the wish of the original (the women's absence) using the specific objects of the body and the chemical erasure.

19　Laplanche and Pontalis, *Language of Psychoanalysis*, 455. "Classically, the transference is acknowledged to be the terrain on which all the basic problems of a given analysis play themselves out: the establishment, modalities, interpretation and resolution of the transference are in fact what define the cure."

20　Williams expands Clover's initial conception of the body genre to include not only the "low" genres of pornography and horror but also the more respectable melodrama. She identifies their shared features: the spectacle of the body caught in the grips of intense sensation, their focus on ecstatic moments of excess, and the use of women's bodies for the embodiment of pleasure, fear, and pain. Clover goes on to emphasize that what differentiates body genres from other displays of embodied sensation and emotion is their intended effect on the audience: "What may especially mark these body genres as low is the perception that the body of the spectator is caught up in an almost involuntary mimicry of the emotion or sensation of the body on the screen along with the fact that the body displayed is female." See Linda Williams, "Film Bodies: Gender, Genre, and Excess," *Film Quarterly* 44, no. 4 (1991): 4.

21　Lippit, *Ex-Cinema*, 41.

22　Abraham and Torok, "Mourning or Melancholia," 126–27.

23　Walter Benjamin, "Surrealism: The Last Snapshot of the European Intelligentsia," *New Left Review*, no. 108 (1978): 56.

24　Santiago, "Milking the Subject."

25　Catherine Russell, *Experimental Ethnography: The Work of Film in the Age of Video* (Durham, NC: Duke University Press, 1999), 2–22.

26　Hal Foster, "The Artist as Ethnographer?" in *The Return of the Real: The*

Avant-Garde at the End of the Century (Cambridge, MA: MIT Press, 1996), 306.

27 "Redcat Program Notes."
28 Henri Lefebvre, *Rhythmanalysis: Space, Time, and Everyday Life*, trans. Stuart Elden and Gerald Moore, Bloomsbury Revelations (London: Bloomsbury, 2014), 41.
29 "Redcat Program Notes."
30 Russell, *Experimental Ethnography*, 241.
31 Lippit, *Ex-Cinema*, 158.
32 "Redcat Program Notes."
33 Henri Lefebvre, *The Production of Space*, trans. Donald Nicholson-Smith (Malden, MA: Blackwell Publishing, 1991), 207.
34 Abraham and Torok made an initial and decisive breakthrough in the Wolf Man case when they discovered the importance of his nanny's English, which they call his "childhood language," within his cryptic speech. Each of his cryptonyms, they showed, was composed of fragments taken from Russian, his mother tongue, from the paternal German of his Freudian analysis, and—most cryptically—from his boyhood nanny's English words. It was through these translinguistic homophones, or homophonic word fragments, that the Wolf Man was able to hide his magic word behind a screen of unintelligibility while letting each of his incorporated guests have their say. The act of decipherment involved a checking and cross-checking of dictionaries in multiple languages, often in complete disregard to the words' semantic field. "We do not know Russian," admit the analysts at a critical junction in *The Magic Word*. "We can barely sound out the words in the dictionary, but this difficulty is also our good fortune. It permits us to avoid the blinders of language to follow better the avenues of our own listening." In Abraham and Torok, *Wolf Man's Magic Word*, 34.
35 Paul Virilio, *The Lost Dimension*, trans. Daniel Moshenberg (New York: Semiotext(e), 1991), 120–21. "With the notion of homelands, the secular oppositions of town and country ceases, and at the same time that the geomorphological unity of the State dissolves. Gone is all autonomy understood as the conditional independence accorded to different local sub-sections. *We now have instead an internal extraterritorial entity* which, as it abolishes the niceties distinguishing metropolitan inhabitation from colonial population, does away with the rule of the city, the very necessity of political citizenship for the administered populations."
36 To avoid confusion, I emphasize: it is these particular cinematic practices that turn off-screen space into a metaphorical space. The off-screen is the first and most *concrete* space of the cinematic image. It signifies the world whose allegory the visible image is. Uman returns the off-screen to this initial power by passing

it through an informational practice of revision.

37 The same oscillation was present in Franju and his exploration of the taboo image, which appeared as either a textual and critical aporia or as the completed set of substitutions by which the film itself "interpreted" its own figural matrix.

38 Sigmund Freud, "Splitting of the Ego in the Process of Defence," in *The Standard Edition of the Complete Psychological Works of Sigmund Freud*, trans. James Strachey, vol. 23: *Moses and Monotheism, An Outline of Psycho-Analysis and Other Works* (London: Hogarth Press, 1964), 271–78. "Now we come across fetishists who have developed the same fear of castration as non-fetishists and react in the same way to it. Their behaviour is therefore simultaneously expressing two contrary premises. On the one hand they are disavowing the fact of their perception—the fact that they saw no penis in the female genitals; and on the other hand they are recognizing the fact that females have no penis and are drawing the correct conclusions from it. The two attitudes persist side by side throughout their lives without influencing each other. Here is what may rightly be called a splitting of the ego."

39 Abraham and Torok, *Wolf Man's Magic Word*, 79.

40 Michel Foucault uses this expression in *The Order of Things* to refer to the rhetorical dimension of words that lost their sequential order and are instead spatialized. "This is because words have their *locus*, not in *time*, but in a *space* in which they are able to find their original site, change their positions, turn back upon themselves, and slowly unfold a whole developing curve: a *tropological* space." See Michel Foucault, *The Order of Things: An Archaeology of the Human Sciences* (New York: Vintage Books, 1994), 114. Derrida makes use of this term to describe the path he will follow in opening the cryptic words of Abraham and Torok: "Neither a metaphor nor a literal meaning, the displacement I am going to *follow* here obeys a different *tropography*. That displacement takes the form of everything a crypt implies: *topoi, death, cipher*." In Derrida, "Fors: The Anglish Words of Nicolas Abraham and Maria Torok," 1979, xiii.

41 See Fredric Jameson, "Cognitive Mapping," in *Marxism and the Interpretation of Culture*, ed. Cary Nelson and Lawrence Grossberg (Urbana: University of Illinois Press, 1987), 347–60.

42 Timothy J. Dunn, *The Militarization of the U.S.-Mexico Border, 1978–1992* (Austin: University of Texas Press, 1996), 159.

43 California Dairies' corporate website emphasizes its global reach: "California Dairies, Inc. produces 43 percent of California's milk or 9 percent of the milk produced in the United States on 500 dairies. A manufacturer of quality fluid milk products, butter and milk powders, California Dairies, Inc. has sales of more than $3 billion across all 50 states and in more than 50 foreign countries."

California Dairies, "About California Dairies, Inc.," accessed February 22, 2015, http://www.californiadairies.com/about.

44 See Abraham and Torok, "Mourning or Melancholia."
45 Marc Augé, *Non-places: An Introduction to Supermodernity*, 2nd ed. (London: Verso, 2008), 28. "The installations needed for the accelerated circulation of passengers and goods (high-speed roads and railways, interchanges, airports) are just as much non-places as the means of transport themselves, or the great commercial centers, or the extended transit camps where the planet's refugees are parked." While Sassen argues that a number of cities have become global cities, centers of economic and communicational power, Marc Augé again follows Virilio in arguing that the interconnectedness of these global (and thus external) centers has created a single virtual metacity whose power spans the globe. Augé further speaks of the dominant aesthetic fact of supermodernity as the "long shot" imposing a sense of global distance that makes us overlook local conditions of rupture.
46 Augé, *Non-places*, 77.
47 Augé, 90.
48 Augé, xi.
49 Derrida, "Fors: The Anglish Words of Nicolas Abraham and Maria Torok," xvii.
50 Derrida, xii.
51 Abraham and Torok, *Wolf Man's Magic Word*, 76.
52 Derrida, "Fors: The Anglish Words of Nicolas Abraham and Maria Torok," xxxix.

Notes to Conclusion

1 Francesco Casetti, "Theory, Post-Theory, Neo-Theories: Changes in Discourses, Changes in Objects," *Cinemas* 17, no. 2/3 (2007): 35.
2 Gilles Deleuze, *Cinema 2*, 189. "The body is no longer the obstacle that separates thought from itself, that which it has to overcome to reach thinking. It is on the contrary that which it plunges into or must plunge into, in order to reach the unthought, that is life. Not that the body thinks, but, obstinate and stubborn, it forces us to think, and forces us to think what is concealed from thought, Life."
3 In this book, the body under erasure took form across two intersecting vectors: the white and black screen and the depth and surface of the image. Thus, in Franju's films, the body under erasure appeared as the white luminosity of Christiane's mask and its rhyme with the white horse being led to slaughter. For Godard, the body under erasure was figured in the black interval of closed eyes across which incommensurate images were brought into relation in *Notre*

musique. For Bava in his early horror films, however, what embodied the body under erasure was the abyssal depth of a point-of-view shot that doubled a look across the gap left by the looker's absent body. And, for Uman, it was the surface of the image transformed into figural and linguistic lines of inscription that gave shape to the body under erasure.

4   Catherine Malabou, *The New Wounded: From Neurosis to Brain Damage*, trans. Steven Miller (New York: Fordham University Press, 2012), 201.
5   Baucom, *Specters of the Atlantic*, 132.
6   Malabou, *New Wounded*, 189. "The limit of psychoanalysis is its failure to admit the existence of a beyond of the pleasure principle. This beyond, which would also be the beyond of all healing, of all possible therapy, never appears in Freud's text. It does appear in contemporary neurology—but without ever being *thought*."
7   Catherine Malabou, *Ontology of the Accident: An Essay on Destructive Plasticity*, trans. Carolyn Shread (Cambridge: Polity, 2012), 18.
8   Abraham, "The Shell and the Kernel," 80.
9   Nicolas Abraham, "Psychoanalytic Aesthetics: Time, Rhythm, and the Unconscious," in *Rhythms: On the Work, Translation, and Psychoanalysis*, ed. Nicholas Rand and Maria Torok, trans. Benjamin Thigpen and Nicholas Rand (Stanford, CA: Stanford University Press, 1995), 118.
10 Abraham, "Psychoanalytic Aesthetics," 113.
11 Abraham and Torok, *Wolf Man's Magic Word*, 16.

BIBLIOGRAPHY

Abraham, Nicolas. "Notes on the Phantom: A Complement to Freud's Metapsychology." In *The Shell and the Kernel*, edited and translated by Nicholas Rand, 1:171–76. Renewals of Psychoanalysis. Chicago: University of Chicago Press, 1994.

———. "The Phantom of Hamlet or the Sixth Act, Preceded by The Intermission of 'Truth.'" In *The Shell and the Kernel*, edited and translated by Nicholas Rand, 1:187–205. Renewals of Psychoanalysis. Chicago: University of Chicago Press, 1994.

———. "Psychoanalytic Aesthetics: Time, Rhythm, and the Unconscious." In *Rhythms: On the Work, Translation, and Psychoanalysis*, edited by Nicholas Rand and Maria Torok, translated by Benjamin Thigpen and Nicholas Rand, 107–30. Stanford, CA: Stanford University Press, 1995.

———. *Rhythms: On the Work, Translation, and Psychoanalysis*. Translated by Nicholas Rand and Benjamin Thigpen. Meridian: Crossing Aesthetics. Stanford, CA: Stanford University Press, 1995.

———. "The Shell and the Kernel: The Scope and Originality of Freudian Psychoanalysis." In *The Shell and the Kernel*, edited and translated by Nicholas Rand, 1:79–98. Renewals of Psychoanalysis. Chicago: University of Chicago Press, 1994.

Abraham, Nicolas, and Maria Torok. "'The Lost Object—Me': Notes on Endocryptic Identification." In *The Shell and the Kernel*, edited and translated by Nicholas Rand, 1:139–56. Renewals of Psychoanalysis. Chicago: University of Chicago Press, 1994.

———. "Mourning or Melancholia: Introjection versus Incorporation." In *The Shell and the Kernel*, edited and translated by Nicholas Rand, 1:125–38. Renewals of Psychoanalysis. Chicago: University of Chicago Press, 1994.

———. *The Shell and the Kernel: Renewals of Psychoanalysis*. Edited and translated by Nicholas Rand. Vol. 1. Chicago: University of Chicago Press, 1994.

———. "The Topography of Reality: Sketching a Metapsychology of Secrets." In *The Shell and the Kernel*, edited and translated by Nicholas Rand, 1:157–61. Renewals of Psychoanalysis. Chicago: University of Chicago Press, 1994.

———. *The Wolf Man's Magic Word: A Cryptonymy*. Translated by Nicholas Rand. Theory and History of Literature. Minneapolis: University of Minnesota Press, 1986.

Agamben, Giorgio. *Homo Sacer: Sovereign Power and Bare Life*. Translated by Daniel Heller-Roazen. Stanford, CA: Stanford University Press, 1998.

———. *Remnants of Auschwitz: The Witness and the Archive*. Translated by Daniel Heller-Roazen. New York: Zone Books, 2002.

Alter, Nora. "Mourning, Sound, and Vision: Jean-Luc Godard's *JLG/JLG*." *Camera Obscura* 15, no. 2 (2000): 75–103.

Armaly, Maha, Carlo Blasi, and Lawrence Hannah. "Stari Most: Rebuilding More Than a Historic Bridge in Mostar." *Museum International* 56, no. 4 (2004): 6–17.

Augé, Marc. *Non-places: An Introduction to Supermodernity*. 2nd ed. London: Verso, 2008.

Bakhtin, M. M. *The Dialogic Imagination*. Edited by Michael Holquist. Translated by Caryl Emerson and Michael Holquist. University of Texas Press Slavic Series 1. Austin: University of Texas Press, 1981.

Barr, Burlin. "Shot and Counter-Shot: Presence, Obscurity, and the Breakdown of Discourse in Godard's *Notre musique*." *Journal of French and Francophone Philosophy* 18, no. 2 (2010): 65–85.

Baucom, Ian. *Specters of the Atlantic: Finance Capital, Slavery, and the Philosophy of History*. Durham, NC: Duke University Press, 2005.

Baudry, Jean-Louis. "Ideological Effects of the Basic Cinematographic Apparatus." In *Narrative, Apparatus, Ideology: A Film Theory Reader*, edited by Philip Rosen, translated by Alan Williams, 286–98. New York: Columbia University Press, 1986.

Bava, Mario. *L'Espresso*. Interview by Dante Matelli. Translated by Roberto Curti. May 1979.

———. Terror Fantastic #3. Interview by Ornella Volta. Print. Translated by Alwin Dewaele and Troy Howarth. December 1971.

Bazin, André. "Marginal Notes on Eroticism in the Cinema." In *What Is Cinema*, edited and translated by Hugh Gray, 2:169–75. Berkeley: University of California Press, 1971.

Benjamin, Walter. "Surrealism: The Last Snapshot of the European Intelligentsia." *New Left Review*, no. 108 (1978): 47.

———. "Surrealism: The Last Snapshot of the European Intelligentsia." In *Critical Theory and Society: A Reader*, edited by Stephen Eric Bonner and Douglas MacKay Kellner, 172–83. New York: Routledge, 1989.

Bini, Andrea. "Horror Cinema: The Emancipation of Women and Urban Anxiety." In *Popular Italian Cinema: Culture and Politics in a Postwar Society*, edited by Flavia Brizio-Skov, 53–82. London: I. B. Tauris, 2011.

Boyer, M. Christine. *The City of Collective Memory: Its Historical Imagery and Architectural Entertainments*. Cambridge, MA: MIT Press, 1996.

Browne, Nick. "The Spectator-in-the-Text: The Rhetoric of Stagecoach." *Film Quarterly* 29, no. 2 (1975): 26–38.

Burch, Nöel. *Theory of Film Practice*. Translated by Helen R. Lane. Princeton, NJ: Princeton University Press, 1981.

Butler, Judith. *Precarious Life: The Powers of Mourning and Violence*. London: Verso, 2004.

Cahill, James Leo. "Anacinema: Peter Tscherkassky's Cinematic Breakdowns." *Spectator—The University of Southern California Journal of Film and Television* 28, no. 2 (2008): 90–101.

Caldwell, Lesley. "What Do Mothers Want? Takes on Motherhood in *Bellisima*, *Il Grido*, and *Mamma Roma*." In *Women in Italy, 1945–1960: An Interdisciplinary Study*, edited by Penelope Morris, 225–37. New York: Palgrave Macmillan, 2006.

California Dairies. "About California Dairies, Inc." Accessed February 22, 2015. http://www.californiadairies.com/about.

Casetti, Francesco. "Theory, Post-Theory, Neo-Theories: Changes in Discourses, Changes in Objects." *Cinemas* 17, no. 2/3 (2007): 33–45.

Clover, Joshua. "Communist Realism." In *Reading Capitalist Realism*, edited by Alison Shonkwiler and Leigh Claire La Berge, 242–47. Iowa City: University of Iowa Press, 2014.

Conterio, Martyn. *Black Sunday*. Devil's Advocates. Leighton Buzzard, UK: Auteur Publishing, 2015.

Cook, David. *A History of Narrative Film*. 3rd ed. New York: W. W. Norton, 1996.

Cramer, Michael. *Utopian Television: Rossellini, Watkins, and Godard beyond Cinema*. Minneapolis: University of Minnesota Press, 2017.

Dalle Vacche, Angela. *The Body in the Mirror: Shapes of History in Italian Cinema*. Princeton, NJ: Princeton University Press, 1992.

Debord, Guy. *The Society of the Spectacle*. Translated by Donald Nicholson-Smith. Rev. ed. New York: Zone Books, 1995.

Deleuze, Gilles. *Cinema 1: The Movement-Image*. Translated by Hugh Tomlinson and Barbara Habberjam. Minneapolis: University of Minnesota Press, 1986.

———. *Cinema 2: The Time-Image*. Translated by Hugh Tomlinson and Robert Galeta. Minneapolis: University of Minnesota Press, 1985.

Derrida, Jacques. "Fors: The Anglish Words of Nicolas Abraham and Maria Torok." In *The Wolf Man's Magic Word: A Cryptonymy*, translated by Barbara Johnson, xi–xlviii. Minneapolis: University of Minnesota Press, 1979.

———. *Specters of Marx: The State of the Debt, the Work of Mourning, and the New International*. Translated by Peggy Kamuf. New York: Routledge, 1994.

Dunn, Timothy J. *The Militarization of the U.S.-Mexico Border, 1978–1992*. Austin: University of Texas Press, 1996.

Durgnat, Raymond. *Franju*. Berkeley: University of California Press, 1968.

Dyer, Rebecca, and Francois Mulot. "Mahmoud Darwish in Film: Politics, Representation, and Translation in Jean-Luc Godard's *Ici et ailleurs* and *Notre musique*." *Cultural Politics* 10, no. 1 (2014): 70–91.

Emmelhainz, Irmgard. "From Third Worldism to Empire: Jean-Luc Godard and the Palestine Question." *Third Text* 23, no. 5 (2009): 649–56.

Federici, Silvia. *Caliban and the Witch: Women, The Body, and Primitive Accumulation*. New York: Autonomedia, 2004.

Fisher, Mark. *Capitalist Realism: Is There No Alternative?* Ropley, UK: John Hunt Publishing, 2009.

Foot, John. *Italy's Divided Memory*. New York: Palgrave Macmillan, 2009.

Forde, Susan. "The Bridge on the Neretva: Stari Most as a Stage of Memory in Post-conflict Mostar, Bosnia-Herzegovina." *Cooperation and Conflict* 51, no. 4 (2016): 467–83.

Foster, Hal. "The Artist as Ethnographer?" In *The Return of the Real: The Avant-Garde at the End of the Century*, 170–203. Cambridge, MA: MIT Press, 1996.

Foucault, Michel. *The Order of Things: An Archaeology of the Human Sciences*. New York: Vintage Books, 1994.

Freud, Sigmund. "Analysis Terminable and Interminable." In *The Standard Edition of the Complete Psychological Works of Sigmund Freud*, edited and translated by James Strachey. Vol. 23. London: Hogarth Press, 1964.

———. *Beyond the Pleasure Principle*. Translated by James Strachey. Vol. 18. *The Standard Edition of the Complete Psychological Works of Sigmund Freud*. London: Hogarth Press, 1920.

———. "Mourning and Melancholia." In *The Standard Edition of the Complete Psychological Works of Sigmund Freud*, edited and translated by James Strachey, 14:237–60. London: Hogarth Press, 1957.

———. "Splitting of the Ego in the Process of Defence." In *The Standard Edition of the Complete Psychological Works of Sigmund Freud*, translated by James Strachey, 23: *Moses and Monotheism, An Outline of Psycho-Analysis and Other Works*, 271–78. London: Hogarth Press, 1964.

———. "'Wild' Psycho-Analysis." In *The Standard Edition of the Complete Psychological Works of Sigmund Freud*, edited and translated by James Strachey, 11:221–27. London: Hogarth Press, 1957.

Gardiner, Muriel, ed. *The Wolf-Man, with the Case of the Wolf-Man by Sigmund Freud*. New York: Basic Books, 1972.

Gelder, Ken. *Reading the Vampire*. London: Routledge, 1994.

Geroulanos, Stefanos. "Postwar Facial Reconstruction: Georges Franju's *Eyes without a Face*." *French Politics, Culture, and Society* 31, no. 2 (2013): 15–33.

Ginsborg, Paul. *A History of Contemporary Italy: Society and Politics, 1943–1988*. London: Penguin Books, 1990.

Ginsburg, Shai. "Between Documentary and Agit-Prop: Jean-Luc Godard's *Ici et ailleurs*." *Tikkun* 22, no. 1 (2007): 76.

Godard, Jean-Luc. *Introduction to a True History of Cinema and Television*. Translated by Timothy Barnard. Montreal: Caboose, 2012.

Greene, Naomi. *Landscapes of Loss: The National Past in Postwar French Cinema*. Princeton, NJ: Princeton University Press, 1999.

Guattari, Félix. *The Three Ecologies*. Translated by Ian Pindar and Paul Sutton. 1989. Reprint, London: Bloomsbury Academic, 2008.

Günsberg, Maggie. *Italian Cinema: Gender and Genre*. New York: Palgrave Macmillan, 2004.

Hawkins, Joan. *Cutting Edge: Art-Horror and the Horrific Avant-Garde*. Minneapolis: University of Minnesota Press, 2000.

Hollier, Denis. *Against Architecture: The Writings of Georges Bataille*. Cambridge, MA: MIT Press, 1989.

Howarth, Troy. *The Haunted World of Mario Bava*. Rev. and expanded ed. Baltimore: Midnight Marquee Press, 2014.

Ince, Kate. *Georges Franju*. French Film Directors. Manchester: Manchester University Press, 2005.

Jameson, Fredric. "Cognitive Mapping." In *Marxism and the Interpretation of Culture*, edited by Cary Nelson and Lawrence Grossberg, 347–60. Urbana: University of Illinois Press, 1987.

———. *Valences of the Dialectic*. London: Verso, 2010.

Jenks, Carol. "The Other Face of Death: Barbara Steele and *La maschera del demonio*." In *Popular European Cinema*, edited by Richard Dyer and Ginette Vincendeau, 149–62. London: Routledge, 1992.

Johnston, Claire. *Notes on Women's Cinema*. London: Society for Education in Film and Television, 1973.

Kracauer, Siegfried. *Theory of Film: The Redemption of Physical Reality*. New York: Oxford University Press, 1960.

Laplanche, Jean, and J. B. Pontalis. *The Language of Psychoanalysis*. Translated by Donald Nicholson-Smith. London: Hogarth Press, 1973.

Lefebvre, Henri. *The Production of Space*. Translated by Donald Nicholson-Smith. Malden, MA: Blackwell Publishing, 1991.

———. *Rhythmanalysis: Space, Time, and Everyday Life*. Translated by Stuart Elden and Gerald Moore. Bloomsbury Revelations. London: Bloomsbury, 2014.

Lippit, Akira Mizuta. *Ex-cinema: From a Theory of Experimental Film and Video*. Berkeley: University of California Press, 2012.

Lowenstein, Adam. "Films without a Face: Shock Horror in the Cinema of Georges Franju." *Cinema Journal* 37, no. 4 (1998): 37–58.

———. *Shocking Representation: Historical Trauma, National Cinema, and the Modern Horror Film*. New York: Columbia University Press, 2005.

Lucas, Tim. *Mario Bava: All the Colors of the Dark*. Cincinnati: Video Watchdog, 2007.

MacCormack, Patricia. "Barbara Steele's Ephemeral Skin: Feminism, Fetishism, and Film." *Senses of Cinema*, no. 22 (October 2002). http://sensesofcinema.com/2002/feature-articles/steele/.

Malabou, Catherine. *The New Wounded: From Neurosis to Brain Damage*. Translated by Steven Miller. New York: Fordham University Press, 2012.

———. *Ontology of the Accident: An Essay on Destructive Plasticity*. Translated by Carolyn Shread. Cambridge: Polity, 2012.

Marin, Louis. "Frontiers of Utopia: Past and Present." *Critical Inquiry* 19, no. 3 (1993): 397–420.

———. *Utopics: The Semiological Play of Textual Spaces*. Translated by Robert A. Vollrath. Amherst, MA: Humanity Books, 1984.

Mbembe, Achille. "Necropolitics." *Public Culture* 15, no. 1 (2003): 11–40.

Metz, Christian. "The Imaginary Signifier." Translated by Ben Brewster. *Screen* 16, no. 2 (1975): 14–76.

Mitchell, Allan. "The Paris Morgue as a Social Institution in the Nineteenth Century." *Francia* 4 (1976): 581–96.

Morgan, Daniel. *Late Godard and the Possibilities of Cinema*. Berkeley: University of California Press, 2013.

Morrey, Douglas. *Jean-Luc Godard*. French Film Directors. Manchester: Manchester University Press, 2005.

"Naomi Uman The Ukrainian Time Machine." *Creative Capital—Investing in Artists Who Shape the Future*. Accessed October 15, 2014. http://creative-capital.org/project_contexts/view/54/project:92.

"Naomi Uman: The Ukrainian Time Machine, Fragments from a Diary (Program Notes for Redcat Screening at CalArts)." December 12, 2011. http://www.redcat.org/sites/redcat.org/files/event/linked-files/2012-07/12.12.11_Uman.pdf.

Nash, Mark. "Vampyr and the Fantastic." *Screen* 17, no. 3 (1976): 29–67.

Neer, Richard. "Godard Counts." *Critical Inquiry* 34, no. 1 (2007): 135–73.

Partyka, Ewa. "The Influence of the Grand-Guignol on the Chiaroscuro and Giallo Horror Movies of Mario Bava." In *Redefining Kitsch and Camp in Literature and Culture*, edited by Justyna Stepien, 53–68. Newcastle upon Tyne: Cambridge Scholars, 2014.

Pasolini, Pier Paolo. "The 'Cinema of Poetry.'" In *Heretical Empiricism*, edited by Louise K. Barnett, translated by Ben Lawton and Louise K. Barnett, 167–86. Bloomington: Indiana University Press, 1988.

Pavsek, Christopher. "What Has Come to Pass for Cinema in Late Godard." *Discourse* 28, no. 1 (2006): 166–95.

Rancière, Jacques. "The Saint and the Heiress: A Propos of Godard's *Histoire(s) du Cinema*." Translated by T. S. Murphy. *Discourse* 24, no. 1 (2002): 113–19.

Rapaport, Herman. *Between the Sign and the Gaze*. Ithaca, NY: Cornell University Press, 1994.

Rashkin, Esther. *Family Secrets and the Psychoanalysis of Narrative*. Princeton, NJ: Princeton University Press, 1992.

Restivo, Angelo. *The Cinema of Economic Miracles: Visuality and Modernization in the Italian Art Film*. Durham, NC: Duke University Press Books, 2002.

Rosen, Philip. *Change Mummified: Cinema, Historicity, Theory*. Minneapolis: University of Minnesota Press, 2001.

Ross, Kristin. *Fast Cars, Clean Bodies: Decolonization and the Reordering of French Culture*. Cambridge, MA: MIT Press, 1996.

Roudinesco, Elisabeth. *Jacques Lacan & Co.: A History of Psychoanalysis in France, 1925–1985*. Translated by Jeffrey Mehlman. Chicago: University of Chicago Press, 1990.

Rousso, Henry. *The Vichy Syndrome: History and Memory in France since 1944*. Translated by Arthur Goldhammer. Cambridge, MA: Harvard University Press, 1991.

Russell, Catherine. *Experimental Ethnography: The Work of Film in the Age of Video*. Durham, NC: Duke University Press, 1999.

Santiago, Soledad. "Milking the Subject: Experiments in Film." *Santa Fe New Mexican*, January 27, 2006.

Sassen, Saskia. *The Global City: New York, London, Tokyo*. Princeton, NJ: Princeton University Press, 2001.

Saxton, Libby. "Anamnesis and Bearing Witness: Godard/Lanzmann." In *For Ever Godard*, edited by Michael Temple, James S. Williams, and Michael Witt, 364–79. London: Black Dog Publishing, 2004.

Schlockoff, Alain. "The Poetic Universe of Georges Franju." *Video Watchdog*, no. 108 (2004): 20–33.

Schlumpf, Erin. "Notre musique." In *A Companion to Jean-Luc Godard*, edited by Tom Conley and T. Jefferson Kline, 514–26. Hoboken, NJ: John Wiley and Sons, 2014.

Schwab, Gabriele. *Haunting Legacies: Violent Histories and Transgenerational Trauma*. New York: Columbia University Press, 2010.

Schwartz, Louis-Georges. "Typewriter: Free Indirect Discourse in Deleuze's Cinema." *SubStance* 34, no. 3 (2005): 107–35.

Shonkwiler, Alison, and Leigh Claire La Berge. "Introduction: A Theory of Capitalist Realism." In *Reading Capitalist Realism*, edited by Alison Shonkwiler and Leigh Claire La Berge, 1–25. Iowa City: University of Iowa Press, 2014.

Silverman, Kaja. *The Acoustic Mirror: The Female Voice in Psychoanalysis and Cinema.* Bloomington: Indiana University Press, 1988.

Sloniowski, Jeannette. "'It Was an Atrocious Film': Georges Franju's Blood of the Beasts." In *Documenting the Documentary: Close Readings of Documentary Film and Video*, edited by Barry Keith Grant and Jeannette Sloniowski, 171–87. Detroit: Wayne State University Press, 1998.

Testa, Carlo. *Italian Cinema and Modern European Literatures, 1945–2000.* Westport, CT: Praeger, 2002.

Torok, Maria. "Fantasy: An Attempt to Define Its Structure and Operation." In *The Shell and the Kernel*, translated by Nicholas Rand, 1:27–36. Renewals of Psychoanalysis. Chicago: University of Chicago Press, 1994.

———. "The Illness of Mourning and the Fantasy of the Exquisite Corpse." In *The Shell and the Kernel*, 1:107–24. Renewals of Psychoanalysis. Chicago: University of Chicago Press, 1994.

Torok, Maria, and Nicholas Rand. *Questions for Freud: The Secret History of Psychoanalysis.* Cambridge, MA: Harvard University Press, 1997.

Virilio, Paul. *The Lost Dimension.* Translated by Daniel Moshenberg. New York: Semiotext(e), 1991.

Williams, Linda. "Film Bodies: Gender, Genre, and Excess." *Film Quarterly* 44, no. 4 (1991): 2–13.

———. *Hard Core: Power, Pleasure, and the "Frenzy of the Visible."* Expanded 1999 ed. Berkeley: University of California Press, 1999.

———. "When the Woman Looks." In *The Dread of Difference: Gender and the Horror Film*, edited by Barry Keith Grant, 15–34. Austin: University of Texas Press, 1996.

Willis, Deborah. "Reading the Early Modern Witch: Horror Films of the 1960s and 1970s." In *The English Renaissance in Popular Culture*, 103–14. New York: Palgrave Macmillan, 2010.

Witt, Michael. "The Death(s) of Cinema According to Godard." *Screen* 40, no. 3 (1999): 331–46.

———. "Going through the Motions: Unconscious Optics and Corporal Resistance in Miéville and Godard's *France/tour/détour/deux/enfants*." In *Gender and French Cinema*, edited by Alex Hughes and James S. Williams, 171–94. Oxford: Berg, 2001.

———. *Jean-Luc Godard: Cinema Historian.* Bloomington: Indiana University Press, 2013.

Witt, Michael, and Jean-Luc Godard. "The Godard Interview: I, a Man of the Image." *Sight and Sound* 15, no. 6 (2005): 28–30.

Wood, Robin. "Franju, Georges." In *The St. James Film Directors Encyclopedia*, edited by Andrew Sarris, 181–83. Detroit: Visible Ink Press, 1998.

Worland, Rick. "The Gothic Revival (1967–1974)." In *A Companion to the Horror Film*, edited by Harry M. Benshoff, 273–91. Oxford: John Wiley and Sons, 2014.

Zuvela, Danni. "A Little Light Teasing: Some Special Affects in Avant-Garde Cinema." *Continuum: Journal of Media Cultural Studies* 26, no. 4 (2012): 589–602.

Index

Abraham, Nicolas. *See also* Abraham, Nicolas and Maria Torok
    on anasemia, 100, 196n13
    on phantom effect in *Hamlet*, 61, 77
    on psychoanalysis, 201n50
    on rhythm, 152
    on rhythmizing consciousness, 185–86n14
    on translation, 9–10
    on wild analysis, 178
Abraham, Nicolas and Maria Torok
    on anasemia, 17
    on body, 177
    on broken symbol, 106
    on crypt, 29, 39, 43
    on cryptonyms, 13, 30, 182n12
    on cryptophore, 129–30
    on detecting crypt in patient's words, 48
    and development of cryptonymy, 5–6, 10–11
    on evidence of Wolf Man's incorporations, 141
    and film studies, 21–22
    on Holocaust survivors, 115–16
    on incorporation, 19, 137–38, 146–47, 155, 164, 182n7, 188–89n36, 203–4nn60, 6
    on internal hysteria, 186n17
    on introjection, 182n7, 188–89n36
    on language, 191n7
    on opening crypt, 171
    on psychoanalysis, 7, 47, 176, 183n23
    on reality, 47, 117, 201n46
    on refusal to mourn, 52
    on reincarnation of "shadow of the object," 27
    on rereading and reconstruction of gaps across documents, 26
    on rhyme in cryptonymy, 88
    on silence, 40
    on symbol, 189–90n43
    on transgenerational phantom, 15–16, 63–64
    on translation, 20
    on unmarked enigma in Freud's Wolf Man case history, 48
    on wild analysis, 197n16
    on witness status of Wolf Man, 175
    on Wolf Man's cryptic speech, 95, 98, 206n34
    on word-objects, 180
Adler, Sara, 111
Agamben, Giorgio, 114–15, 116, 199n36, 200nn39, 40
airplane, in *Eyes without a Face*, 37
Algerian revolution, 33–34, 185nn9, 11
Alter, Nora, 95, 98, 196n7
anacinema, 197–98n21
anasemia, 100, 105, 116–17, 196n13, 201n50
anasemic montage
    affective powers of, 122–23
    in Godard's works, 17–18, 99–110, 118
    as historical construct, 127
    relationship between fiction and reality within, 120–22
Armes, Roy, 53

art cinema, 73, 75, 86–87, 89
Augé, Marc, 163, 164, 208n45
autobiography, intersection of ethnography and, 149, 150
automobile, 36, 42, 185n13

Bakhtin, M. M., 183n18
Barr, Burlin, 127
Baucom, Ian, 12, 177
Baudry, Jean-Louis, 204n7
Bava, Eugenio, 64, 191n9
Bava, Mario. See also *Black Sunday*
   body under erasure in, 4, 209n3
   and burned letter, 61–64, 190n2
   films of, between *Black Sunday* and *Kill, Baby . . . Kill!*, 194n39
   Kill, Baby . . . Kill!, 81–94
   overview of, 14–16
   phantom-image in works of, 64–65
   and rejection of neorealism, 90, 195n53
   Scorsese on, 78, 193n32
   trauma from Eugenio's past transferred to, 191n9
Benjamin, Walter, 138, 147, 153
Bini, Andrea, 69
black screen, 109, 128, 133, 148, 161, 198n28
Black Sunday
   female looks in, 192n16
   narrative enigmas and absent body in, 75–81
   phantom-image in, 65–72, 73–74, 194n37
   symbolism of witch in, 193n30
Blood of the Beasts, 47–56, 189n41
body genres, 146, 205n20
body under erasure, 3, 9, 136, 150, 176–80, 208–9n3

borders and border zones, 135–37, 159–60, 164–66
Boyer, M. Christine, 41–42
Breton, André, 138
broken symbol
   in Godard's works, 106–10, 123–30
   in *Leche*, 156–57
burned letter, of Mario Bava, 61–64, 190n2
Butler, Judith, 123, 201n49

Cahill, James Leo, 197–98n21
Caldwell, Lesley, 92
California Dairies, 162–63, 207n43
capitalism, transition to, in Italy, 76–77, 193n30
capitalist realism, 3, 181n3
Casetti, Francesco, 175
censorship, 49–50, 181n4
cinefantastique, 72–74
cinematic crypt-machine, 8–19
city, as topography of internal exclusion in *Hôtel des Invalides*, 41–47
clichés, 108–10
Clover, Joshua, 181n3, 205n20
cognitive mapping, 159–60
Conterio, Martyn, 78
Cook, David, 89
corporeal double vision, 143
corporium, 102, 197n16
countershot, 106–10, 112, 113, 115, 117, 118, 120, 123, 127–28
cow carcasses, in *Mala Leche*, 160–61
coyote, 159
crypt
   Derrida on, 164–65, 187–88n26
   detecting, in patient's words, 48
   function of, 6, 29–30, 135
   historical, 15, 47–56, 102

as institutional force of silence, 43
intrapsychic, 6, 25, 29–30, 164, 171
opening, 171–72
psychic, 164–65, 179
and transgenerational phantom, 63
visual, 8–9
crypt-city, 41–47
crypt-image
   defined, 8
   Deleuze on, 187n22
   Eyes without a Face and unique properties of, 33–41
   in Franju's films, 13–14, 27–33
   of Godard, 96–97
   Hôtel des Invalides as, 44–45
   in *Mala Leche*, 165
   in *Removed*, 145, 150–51
crypt-machine, cinema as, 8–19
cryptonyms (taboo words), 6, 8, 13, 30, 40, 166, 182n12, 183–84n24
cryptonymy
   and challenges to film studies, 19–26
   development of, 5–6, 10–11
   function of, 176–78
   history and trauma in, 11–12
   rhyme in, 88, 89
   textual, 6–7
crypt-screen, 52

Dalle Vacche, Angela, 85, 194–95n46
dead, living identification with, 38–39
death drive, 7, 50, 69, 111, 176, 177, 192n17
Debord, Guy, 2
debt, 165–66
Deleuze, Gilles
   on cinema of bodies, 176, 208n2
   on cinematic representation following WWII, 1
   on Godard's refusal of cinematic cliché, 108
   on Godard's use of irrational cuts, 198n28
   on incompossible worlds, 187n22
   on societies of control, 32
demetaphorization, 146–47, 162, 177, 179, 202n55
Derrida, Jacques
   on anasemia, 100, 105
   on artificiality of crypt, 187–88n26
   on condition of haunting, 139
   on cryptic discourse, 84–85
   on link between cryptonymy, personal history, and historical trauma, 11
   on perception, 172
   on psychic crypt as foreign body, 164–65
   on supplement, 204n12
   on tropography of undocumented bodies, 207n40
Dieu, Nade, 111
disavowal, 62, 162, 190n3
disfigurations, 33, 35, 38, 40, 48, 53
divided memory, 14
documentary, versus history, 117
domestic violence, 166–70
Dracula films, 69
Dunn, Timothy, 160
Durgant, Raymond, 53
Dziga Vertov Group, 103, 112, 121

Emmelhainz, Irmgard, 196–97n14
erasure, in *Removed*, 141–48. *See also* body under erasure
ethnography
   experimental, 136–37, 149–50, 153, 154
   intersection of autobiography and, 149, 150

Eyes without a Face (*Les yeux sans visage*), 33–41, 48, 53, 144, 185n11, 189n40

failed mourning, in Godard's works, 99–106
family crypt, 37, 38, 83, 90, 91
fantasy, 47, 50
Fascism, 86, 87
Federici, Silvia, 76, 80, 193n30
female monster, 69. See also witches
feminism, 76–79, 149
Ferenczi, Sándor, 138
fetish image, 73, 97
fiction
  Godard on, 121
  and reality within anasemic montage, 120–22
figural taboo, 31–32, 47, 48, 151
film studies and theory, 19–26, 175–76
Fisher, Mark, 3
Foot, John, 14
Forde, Susan, 124, 202n53
foreign taboo, 31–32, 48–51
Foster, Hal, 149–50
Foucault, Michel, 207n40
found footage, 136–37, 139, 153–55
France/tour/détour/deux/enfants, 110, 198–99n29
Franju, Georges
  Blood of the Beasts, 47–56, 189n41
  body under erasure in, 4, 208–9n3
  contrasted with Bava, 65
  crisis of interiorities in, 56–57
  crypt-image and taboo body in works of, 27–33
  Eyes without a Face (*Les yeux sans visage*), 33–41, 48, 53, 144, 185n11, 189n40
  Hôtel des Invalides, 41–47
  Le Grand Méliès, 57–59
  as marginal and displaced in French film history, 27–28, 190n45
  Mon chien, 30–31
  overview of, 12–14
  spatial incongruities and subject matter of, 43–44
  taboo image in films of, 30, 31–32, 207n37
  white images in films of, 59
Freda, Riccardo, 85–86, 90, 195n53
free indirect discourse, 74, 193n24
free indirect POV shot, 72, 74–75
Freud, Sigmund
  and case history of Wolf Man, 48, 54–55, 98, 118, 196n6
  and cryptic incorporation, 203–4n6
  crypt in psychic topography of, 43
  on death drive, 192n17
  on disavowal, 190n3
  dream interpretation theory of, 182n6
  on melancholia, 38, 39, 186n15
  seduction theory of, 188n32
  on splitting of ego, 207n38
  on wild analysis, 21
Fuses, 146

Le gai savoir, 109
Gelder, Ken, 194n35
genre films, 85–86, 89
Germany Year 90 Nine Zero, 99
Germany Year Zero, 87–90
Geroulanos, Stefanos, 53, 189n40
Ginsburg, Shai, 101
globalization, 164, 208n45
Godard, Jean-Luc
  anasemic montage and elsewhere of failed mourning in works of, 99–106

broken symbol and countershot in
   works of, 106–10
on filming of concentration camps,
   200n42
France/tour/détour/deux/enfants, 110
Le gai savoir, 109
on Hawks movie, 95
in history of cinematic cryptonymy,
   95–99
missing bodies in works of, 4
on need for musical literacy, 199n32
Notre music, 16–18, 100, 104, 110–23,
   201n48
overview of, 16–18
Le petit soldat, 33
talks of, given at Concordia University,
   195–96n4
on truthful image, 197n18
Gorgon, 199n36
Gorin, Pierre, 101, 107, 108
Le Grand Méliès, 57–59
Guattari, Félix, 92
guilt
   communal, 83, 93
   generational, 90
   in *Germany Year Zero*, 88
Günsberg, Maggie, 93

Hamlet (Shakespeare), 77
Hand Eye Coordination, 139–41, 161
Hawkins, Joan, 185n11
Hawks, Howard, 113
Heisenberg, Werner, 199n32
Hill, Leslie, 185n9
His Girl Friday, 113
historical crypt, 15, 47–56, 102
historical interval, 110–23
historical montage, 16
historical reconstruction, 42, 123–30

historical taboo, 49–50
history, versus documentary, 117
Hollier, Denis, 143
Holocaust, 34, 36, 41, 52, 114–20,
   189n40, 200nn39, 40, 201n42
homelands, 206n35
Horror Chamber of Dr. Faustus, The,
   34–35
Hôtel des Invalides, 41–47
Howarth, Troy, 81, 91

Ici et ailleurs, 100–108, 197n15
Ince, Kate, 30
incest, 39, 40, 68, 78
incompossible narration, 187n22
incorporated object, 135, 162, 201n49
incorporation
   Abraham and Torok on, 19
   and erasure of bodies defined by
      global exteriority, 164
   formula of cryptic, 203–4n6
   introjection and, 138, 155, 182n7,
      188–89n36
   of old forms in Uman's films, 137–39,
      140, 141, 145–47
   and preservative repression in
      Leche, 155
   as utopian gesture, 129–30, 203n60
internal hysteria, 186n17
internal off-screen
   as act of deframing, 146
   defined, 5, 19
   in Uman's films, 136–39, 147, 148–50,
      157–59, 172–73
interval, 4, 18, 98–100, 105, 106, 108,
   110–23, 127–29
intrapsychic crypt, 6, 25, 29–30, 164, 171
introjection, 10, 29–30, 130, 137–38,
   182n7, 184n5, 188–89n36

irrational cut, 52, 198n28
Israel-Palestine conflict. See *Ici et ailleurs*; *Notre music*

Jameson, Frederic, 159, 202n59
Jenks, Carol, 67–68, 70, 191n11, 192n16
Johnson, Barbara, 196n13
Johnston, Claire, 144

Kill, Baby . . . Kill!, 81–94
Kracauer, Siegfried, 51, 52, 53–55, 188n36

La Berge, Leigh Claire, 181n3
labor power, regulation of, 160
language, 165–66, 191n7
Lanzmann, Claude, 119
Laplanche, Jean, 193n26, 205nn18, 19
Leche
  absence in, 151
  crossing of image boundaries in, 171–72
  found image in, 154–55
  fragmentary images and sounds in, 151–52
  internal off-screen in, 157–58, 172–73
  overview of, 18–19
  portraiture in, 163
  and preservative repression, 155–56
  themes in, 148–50
  Uman's embodied presence in, 156–57, 158
  visual imperfections in, 152–53
  writing in, 161, 162
Lefebvre, Henri, 152
letter, burned, of Mario Bava, 61–64, 190n2
Lippit, Akira Mizuta, 143, 146, 153–54
lost dimension, 157

Lowenstein, Adam, 35, 49, 50, 52, 189n40
Lucas, Tim, 68, 79, 81, 91, 191n9, 193n32

MacCormack, Patricia, 66
Malabou, Catherine, 177, 209n6
Mala Leche
  absence in, 151
  crossing of image boundaries in, 171–72
  gaze of dead in, 160–61
  internal off-screen in, 158–59, 172–73
  intertitles in, 161–62
  monetary, linguistic, and visual debt in, 165–66
  nondocumentation of domestic violence in, 166–70
  nonplaces in, 162–65
  overview of, 18–19
  themes in, 148–50
  US-Mexico border in, 159–60
Marin, Louis, 129, 202n59
masks
  in *Black Sunday*, 65, 66, 70
  in *Eyes without a Face*, 33–34, 36, 38–39, 40, 48
Mbembe, Achille, 200n38
melancholia, 38–39, 95–99, 186n15
Méliès, 57–59
metonymy of words, 13, 25–26
Metz, Christian, 21, 183n21
Miéville, Anne-Marie, 100–105, 108, 110
mirror effect of horror, 51
Mitchell, Allan, 186–87n19
Mon chien, 30–31
montage. See anasemic montage; historical montage
monuments, preserving and reconstructing past, 125–26

Morgan, Daniel, 95, 112
morgue, 186–87n19
Morrey, Douglas, 107, 187n24
Mostar bridge, 123–30, 202nn53, 54
mourning, 38–39, 52, 123, 184n5
muselmann, 114–15, 116
Mussolini, Benito, 191n9

Nash, Mark, 72–73
Native Americans, 127–28, 130, 131
Nazi extermination camps, 34, 36, 41, 52, 114–20, 200nn39, 40, 201n42
necropolitics, 200n38
necropower, 200n38
Neer, Richard, 197n18
neorealism, 85, 86–87, 89–90, 195n53
New Wave / nouvelle vague, 121, 122
nonknowledge, 22, 63, 90–91
nonplaces, 145, 163–65, 208n45
Notre music
   anasemic montage in, 100, 104
   called book by Godard, 199n32
   graveyard of stone and lost utopian object in, 123–33
   and historic interval, 110–23
   optimism of, 201n48
   overview of, 16–18
nouvelle vague / New Wave, 121, 122
Numéro deux, 122

objectivation, 146–47, 151, 158, 202n55
obscurity, of clear image, 112
occupation, perpetual, 132–33
off-screen space, 5, 33, 82, 157–58, 161, 172, 206–7n36. *See also* internal off-screen

Palestinian struggle. See *Ici et ailleurs*; *Notre music*

Pankejeff, Sergei, 199–200n37. *See also* Wolf Man
paradise, 132–33
Paris
   in *Hôtel des Invalides*, 44, 45
   housing and treatment of dead in, 186–87n19
   postwar period in, 41–42
Partyka, Ewa, 84
Pasolini, Pier Paolo, 72, 74–75, 192n23, 193n24
Pavsek, Christopher, 97, 99
peplum, 85
Péqueux, Gilles, 125, 126, 129
perception, 99, 172
Le petit soldat, 33, 185n9
phantom-image / phantom-POV
   in *Black Sunday*, 65–72, 73–74
   of *cinefantastique* and Pasolini, 72–75
   defined, 15, 64–65
   in *Kill, Baby . . . Kill!*, 81–94
   in *Notre music*, 131
pleasure principle, 177, 186n14, 209n6
politics of revision, 153–54
Pontalis, Jean-Bertrand, 193n26, 205nn18, 19
pornographic fetish, and phantom body in *Removed*, 142–46, 158, 205n17
Positif, 28
postwar France. *See also* Paris
   return of Nazi victims and redevelopment in, 41–42
   spatial order of, in Franju's films, 28–29
pretextual scene
   in Bava's films, 64–65, 76, 78, 82, 85
   defined, 9
   in Franju's films, 39, 57
psychic crypt, 164–65, 179
psychic objectivation, 202n55

psychoanalysis, 7, 10–11, 47, 175–76, 177, 201n50, 209n6
psychoanalytic listening, 111, 118, 183n23

Rancière, Jacques, 119
Rand, Nicholas, 182n6
Rapaport, Herman, 184n24
Rashkin, Esther, 16, 186n18
realism, 85
reality
    Abraham and Torok on, 117, 201n46
    and fiction within anasemic montage, 120–22
    Franju's destabilization of boundaries of, 47
    in Franju's elaboration of taboo image, 47
    Godard on, 121
    as image of avoidance in *Blood of the Beasts*, 47–56
reality principle, 186n14
recycled cinema, 153–54
Removed, 141–48, 150–51, 158, 172, 173, 205n17
Restivo, Angelo, 86
restoration, 125
return to zero, 108–9
revision, politics of, 153–54
rhyme
    in cryptonymy, 88, 89
    visual, 112–13
rhythm and rhythmizing consciousness, 152, 185–86n14
Rosen, Philip, 125
Ross, Kristin, 36, 42, 102
Rossellini, Roberto, 87–90
Rousso, Henry, 27, 29, 41
Russell, Catherine, 149, 153, 154

Sassen, Saskia, 137, 208n45
Saxton, Libby, 119–20
Schlumpf, Erin, 132
Schneeman, Carolee, 146
Schwab, Gabriele, 13, 93
Schwartz, Louis-Georges, 74, 192–93n24
Scorsese, Martin, 61, 78, 193n32
secrets, 63, 82–85, 92
seduction theory, 188n32
Shoah, 119
Shonkwiler, Alison, 181n3
shot/countershot structure, 112, 113, 117, 123, 127–28
silence(s)
    about World War II, 29
    crypt as institutional force of, 43
    in *Kill, Baby . . . Kill!*, 82–83, 90, 92
    as object for analysis, 40
silent witness, 116, 165
Silver, Alain, 62
Silverman, Kaja, 144
Sloniowski, Jeannette, 53, 189n41
soundtrack, in Bava's films, 82
space / spatial decryption / spatial incongruities, 43–44, 84–85, 135–36
Steele, Barbara, 66–67, 73–74, 76
superimposition, 44, 84, 92, 158, 198n21
surrealism, 138, 147
sword-and-sandal film, 85

taboo body, 8, 23, 27–33, 48, 56–57
taboo image
    defined, 24
    facets of, 31–32
    in Franju's films, 30, 31–32, 207n37
    function of, 56
    in *Notre music*, 131–32
    reality in Franju's elaboration of, 47
    and unfathomable image, 54–56

taboo-POV, in *Eyes without a Face*, 35–36
taboo words. *See* cryptonyms (taboo words)
temporality, in *Leche*, 152
Testa, Carlo, 85, 195n53
testimony, as textuality, 114–15
time travel, experimental ethnography as, 153, 154
Torok, Maria. *See also* Abraham, Nicolas and Maria Torok
   on Freudian theory of dream interpretation, 182n6
   on incorporated object, 135
   verbarium of crypt-words in Wolf Man analysis of, 197n16
train, in *Eyes without a Face*, 36
transference, 77, 205nn18, 19
transgenerational phantom, 15–16, 63–72, 93
translation, 9–10, 20
Transylvania, 194n35
truthful image, 44, 102, 197n18
Tscherkassky, Peter, 197–98n21
Two or Three Things I Know about Her, 42, 187n24

Uman, Naomi. *See also Leche*; *Mala Leche*
   absent figure incorporated within image in films of, 137–41
   body under erasure in films of, 209n3
   and border zones, 135–37
   Hand Eye Coordination, 139–41, 161
   missing bodies in works of, 4
   overview of, 18–19
   Removed, 141–48, 150–51, 158, 172, 173, 205n17
undocumented bodies, 158–59

unfathomable image, 53–56
unseeable image, 14, 65, 118–19
Until Victory, 101–2
unwatchable taboo, 31–32, 41
Ursini, James, 62
US–Mexico border, 159–60
utopia(s), 123, 128–33, 163, 202–3nn59, 60

vampires, 79–80, 194n35
Vampyr, 72–73, 74
Virilio, Paul, 157, 206n35
visual crypt, 8–9
visual reproduction, in *Black Sunday*, 67–68
visual rhymes, 112–13

Whip and the Body, The, 82
white images, in Franju's films, 33–34, 36, 38–39, 40, 48, 59
white screen, 198n28
wild analysis, 21, 178, 182n6
Williams, Linda, 69, 145, 204–5nn16, 20
Willis, Deborah, 77
witchcraft, 76–77
witches, 79–80, 193n30. *See also* female monster
witness
   silent, 116, 165
   as textuality, 114–15
   Uman as partial, 166
Witt, Michael, 16, 96, 98, 111, 119, 122, 198–99n29
Wolf Man
   analysis of, 171
   buried cryptic life of, 190–91n5
   cryptic speech of, 95, 98, 206n34
   evidence of incorporations of, 141
   failed analysis of, 196n6

Wolf Man (*continued*)
    life of, 199–200n37
    silences in analytic case histories of, 24, 26, 48, 54–55
    as silent witness, 165, 175
Wood, Robin, 44
word thing, 161–62, 166
Worland, Rick, 86

World War II. *See also* Holocaust
    communal guilt regarding, 93
    crisis of representation following, 1–8
    and prominence of gothic films in Italy, 86
    and women's roles in postwar Italy, 92–93

zero, return to, 108–9

www.ingramcontent.com/pod-product-compliance
Lightning Source LLC
Chambersburg PA
CBHW071817230426
43670CB00013B/2486